THE POLICE AND THE HOMELESS

THE POLICE AND THE HOMELESS

Creating a Partnership Between Law Enforcement and Social Service Agencies in the Development of Effective Policies and Programs

Edited by

MARTIN L. FORST

Doctor of Criminology
The URSA Institute
San Francisco, California

CHARLES C THOMAS • PUBLISHER, LTD.
Springfield • Illinois • U.S.A.

Published and Distributed Throughout the World by

CHARLES C THOMAS • PUBLISHER, LTD.
2600 South First Street
Springfield, Illinois 62794-9265

© *1997 by* CHARLES C THOMAS • PUBLISHER, LTD.
ISBN 0-398-06689-2 (cloth)
ISBN 0-398-06690-6 (paper)
Library of Congress Catalog Card Number: 96-43226

With **THOMAS BOOKS** *careful attention is given to all details of manufacturing
and design. It is the Publisher's desire to present books that are satisfactory as to
their physical qualities and artistic possibilities and appropriate for their particular
use.* **THOMAS BOOKS** *will be true to those laws of quality that assure a good
name and good will.*

Printed in the United States of America
SC-R-3

Library of Congress Cataloging-in-Publication Data

The police and the homeless : creating a partnership between law
enforcement and social service agencies in the development of
effective policies and programs / edited by Martin L. Forst.
    p.   cm.
Includes bibliographical references and index.
ISBN 0-398-06689-2 (cloth). — ISBN 0-398-06690-6 (paper)
1. Police services for the homeless—United States. 2. Police
social work—United States. 3. Homeless persons—Services for—
United States. 4. Homelessness—United States. I. Forst, Martin
Lyle.
HV8079.23.P65   1997
363.2'33—dc20
                                                                96-43226
                                                                CIP

CONTRIBUTORS

Sue Beattie is a licensed clinical psychologist and the director of Adult Treatment Services at Mental Health Services West, the downtown community mental health center in Portland, Oregon. Dr. Beattie has worked at Mental Health Services West since 1985 and has a particular interest in the delivery of emergency mental health services and the development of effective treatment models for diverse clinical populations. She also works as a forensic mental health examiner and maintains a small private practice. Dr. Beattie received her Ph.D. from the University of Montana in 1984.

Gordon Scott Bonham directs the Center for Suburban and Regional Studies at Towson State University. He was principal evaluator on the Homeless Outreach Team project in the Baltimore transit center, upon which his contribution to this book is based. Dr. Bonham earlier evaluated Louisville's Project Connect for homeless substance abusing men when he was conducting applied research at the University of Louisville. Although his research has covered many different topics, it has focused on the social health and well-being of the individual in society. Of particular interest has been the interaction of organizational structures with individual decisions in fostering change. He received his Ph.D. in sociology from the University of Michigan (Ann Arbor) and began his research career with the National Center for Health Statistics.

Daschel E. Butler has been with the Berkeley, California, police department for twenty-five years—the last six as chief of police. He was recently a member of the Measure "O" municipal ordinance committee regarding homeless persons in Berkeley. Chief Butler earned a bachelor of arts degree in criminology from the University of California at Berkeley. He is a member of numerous professional and social organizations.

Robert A. DeGraff is Association for Portland Progress (APP) vice-president for policy and, as such, is responsible for the development of the association's positions on a wide variety of public

v

policy issues, including business development, public safety and human services. For nearly seven years he was the public safety director for the Association for Portland Progress and was responsible for APP's crime prevention program and was its principle liaison to the Portland Police Bureau. He was also a staff member to the Human Services and Nightlife District Task Forces. He has a bachelor of arts degree in sociology from the University of Oregon and a J.D. from Northwestern School of Law and Lewis and Clark College.

J. Howard Finck is president/CEO of Friends of Youth, a treatment, prevention, and housing agency for youth and families in high-risk situations. He has been with Friends of Youth, located in Redmond, Washington, since 1979. Prior to his current position, he was director of field services (probation) and other positions in Ventura County, California. He is on the Children and Family Task Force of King County (Seattle) and the Youth Shelter Task Force for the state of Washington. Mr. Finck has worked with children at risk for thirty years.

Martin Forst is a criminologist specializing in social science research at the URSA Institute in San Francisco, California. He received his bachelor's degree in psychology at the University of California, Berkeley. He earned a master's and doctorate in criminology also at the University of California, Berkeley. He has worked on numerous research projects in the fields of criminal and juvenile justice. More recently, he served as evaluator for three years for the San Francisco Transbay Terminal Homeless Outreach Project and served on the San Francisco Mayor's Task Force on Homelessness. He is the author or editor of numerous articles or books, including *Missing Children: The Law Enforcement Response,* published by Charles C Thomas, Publisher.

Maria Foscarinis is executive director of the National Law Center on Homelessness and Poverty, which she founded in 1989. She is a 1981 graduate of Columbia Law School, where she was editor of the *Law Review.* She also holds a master's degree in philosophy from Columbia University. Ms. Foscarinis has been active in legal issues affecting homeless people since 1983, when she took a *pro bono* case representing homeless families while practicing corporate litigation. In 1985, she moved to Washington to establish the office of the National Coalition for the Homeless, then based in New York. She has litigated many cases to enforce federal legal rights of homeless people.

Anthony Gardner is staff attorney at HomeBase, a public policy law firm in San Francisco devoted to ending homelessness. He holds a bachelor of arts degree from The American University, a J.D. degree from Hastings College of Law (in San Francisco), and has done graduate work at Columbia University. At HomeBase, Mr. Gardner focuses on homeless civil rights issues, continuum of care planning for the homeless, regional homelessness initiative planning, and state and federal policy development.

Roma Guy, MSW, is the Director of the Bay Area Homelessness Program and a lecturer in the Department of Health Education and Social Work at San Francisco State University. She has been a community activist for women's rights, sexuality rights and an advocate for grassroots organizing and politics. She has been a leader in building women's institutions such as the Women's Building, La Casa de las Madres (battered women's shelter) and The Women's Foundation.

Rick Herz is the civil rights monitor at the National Law Center on Homelessness and Poverty. Mr. Herz is a 1993 graduate of the University of Virginia Law School. After graduating from law school, Mr. Herz clerked for the Honorable Raymond A. Jackson, of the United States District Court for the Eastern District of Virginia. Mr. Herz has primary responsibility for civil rights issues at the National Law Center.

Della M. Hughes, executive director of the National Network of Runaway and Youth Services, received her M. Div. from Vanderbilt University Divinity School and her M.S.S.W. from the University of Tennessee School of Social Work. She has over twenty years of experience in working with youth and with youth programs, including serving as an advocate with and for youth families. Currently, in addition to her other responsibilities, Ms. Hughes convenes a national consortium guiding the planning for and implementation of Community Youth Development with the National Network, as well as in other organizations.

Julie Larson earned her bachelor's degree from The Evergreen State College in Olympia, Washington. She has worked as a mental health professional with the homeless mentally ill for eleven years. She helped develop and is currently the project director for Project Respond, a mobile crisis response and outreach program of Mental Health Services West in Portland, Oregon. She also works as a consultant and provides training to police, paraprofessionals and lay persons in working effectively with persons who suffer from mental illness.

Peter Lindstrom is a law intern at HomeBase, a public policy law firm in San Francisco devoted to ending homelessness. He holds a B.A. degree from California State University at Hayward and is currently a J.D. degree candidate at Golden Gate University School of Law. At HomeBase, Mr. Lindstrom focuses on homeless civil rights and homeless veterans issues.

Terry McDonald has been with the Phoenix Police Department for 24 years, the last 16 as lieutenant. He is the unit commander of the Neighborhood Response Unit (NRU), a multipurpose unit providing service to the Central Arizona Shelter Services (CASS) shelter and surrounding neighborhoods, as well as to the public housing sites and downtown Phoenix. Officers for the NRU are chosen after a competitive interview process and work closely with neighborhood groups and organizations utilizing community-based policing concepts. They are also trained in tactical response methods for demonstrations and civil disturbance situations.

Tony Narr is a senior research associate with the Police Executive Research Forum (PERF) located in Washington, D.C. He is responsible for management services programs, management studies of police departments, research, and special projects. Tony also serves as director of the Senior Management Institute for Police. He has worked on a variety of projects with PERF over the past ten years, including PERF's program on police response to homeless people and development of model police and the investigative protocol for the investigation of domestic elder abuse. Tony holds an undergraduate degree in technology and management from Maryland University and a master's degree in personnel administration from Central Michigan University.

Mary Orton has served as the executive director of Arizona's largest homeless shelter since 1985. The organization, Central Arizona Shelter Services (CASS), is a community-based nonprofit agency that serves more than 6,000 homeless children and adults each year—more than 60,000 people since its founding. Prior to becoming the director of CASS, Ms. Orton served as a congressional aide to U.S. Representative Morris K. Udall. Earlier, she served as a VISTA volunteer in poor communities in Texas.

Michele Ostrander has been involved in the battered women's movement for the last four years. She has worked with the Houston

Area Women's Center as the information and referral coordinator since April 1994. She has also volunteered for the last two years as a group facilitator for PIVOT—a batters intervention and prevention program. She has a master of arts degree in experimental psychology from St. Bonaventure University located in southwestern New York State.

Bev Ovrebo, DrPh, MPH, is a professor of health education at San Francisco State University. A longtime homelessness activist and researcher, she is the founder of the Bay Area Homelessness Program. Currently she is principle investigator of the Robert F. Kennedy Fellows Program at San Francisco State University.

Martha Plotkin is an associate director with the Police Executive Research Forum in Washington, D.C., an organization of police professionals dedicated to advancing progressive policing. She directs the organization's publications, legislative and communications programs. In addition, she has directed and worked on such research projects as the police response to domestic elder abuse victims and the homeless. She holds a B.A. degree in psychology from Brandeis University. She received her J.D. from George Washington University Law School.

Kathleen M. Quinn graduated *magna cum laude* from Westfield State College, Westfield, Massachusetts, in 1976, with a bachelor of science degree in criminal justice. She holds a certificate of special studies in administration and management (C.S.S.) from Harvard University, conferred in 1989. She received her juris doctorate from Boston College Law School, *cum laude,* in 1993, where she served as executive editor of the *Boston College Third World Law Journal* and interned as a staff attorney at the Massachusetts Supreme Judicial Court. She was admitted to the New Jersey State and Federal District Court bars in 1993 and to the Commonwealth of Massachusetts bar in 1995.

Rita Schwartz is director of development and policy for the Partnership for the Homeless, a nationwide leader in services for the homeless. She is responsible for planning, development and policy. Ms. Schwartz spent many years in New York City government, working in legislative affairs, government relations and policy development for the Health and Hospital Corporation, the City Department of the Aging, and the New York City Department of Parks, Recreation and Cultural Affairs. Immediately before joining The Partnership for the Homeless, she worked as the supervisor of Government and Community Affairs for the Port Authority of New

York and New Jersey. She was senior advisor on the homeless, developing social welfare policies for the port authority to deal compassionately with the homeless in transportation facilities and the World Trade Center. She received her B.S. in music from the State University of New York at Potsdam and an M.A. in public administration from New York University.

PREFACE

Homelessness in America is reaching epidemic proportions and it will not disappear in the near future. Various estimates put the number of homeless persons in the United States from 600,000 to three million, many of whom are women and children. Because of shrinking budgets at the federal, state, and local levels of government, traditional social service agencies have failed to adequately address this pressing social problem. And as in many instances when social service agencies cannot respond, law enforcement agencies are asked to step in and solve social problems. Many cities across the country have begun to enact ordinances to restrict or control homeless persons in various ways. So-called "quality of life" laws, for example, prohibit persons from sleeping in parks, panhandling, and sitting in specified areas of town. Yet this *law enforcement* approach to the problem of homelessness is not effective. At best, it moves homeless persons from one part of town to another. Current policies to *criminalize* homelessness will prove frustrating and futile for all parties concerned.

Partnership is one of the watchwords for the 1990s. And to address social problems, one of the most effective partnerships is between law enforcement agencies and social service agencies as well as the private sector. This book is comprised of original articles written by experts in the field of homelessness. The articles are written by people from a variety of fields—law enforcement personnel, lawyers, social service providers, researchers, policy analysts, and a business representative. The articles provide an overview of the problem of homelessness, a review of current legal issues, a description of successful partnerships with social service programs, and a model public-private partnership. In combination, the articles give law enforcement management and staff guidance in developing effective policies and programs in their communities to meet the challenge of homelessness in the future.

M.L.F.

xi

CONTENTS

		Page
Preface		v
Chapter		
1.	THE POLICE AND THE HOMELESS: AN INTRODUCTION	3
	Martin L. Forst	
2.	HISTORICAL PERSPECTIVES ON HOMELESSNESS	21
	Roma Guy and Bev Ovrebo	
3.	NEW MUNICIPAL ORDINANCES REGULATING HOMELESS PEOPLE	29
	Maria Foscarinis and Rick Herz	
4.	THE DOUBLE-EDGED SWORD OF ADVOCACY FOR THE HOMELESS	42
	Kathleen Marie Quinn	
5.	POLICE: THE FORGOTTEN SERVICE PROVIDER	58
	Martha Plotkin and Tony Narr	
6.	HOMELESSNESS: COMPASSIONATE ENFORCEMENT	87
	Dash Butler	
7.	POLICE ON THE HOMELESSNESS FRONT LINE: A POSTMORTEN OF SAN FRANCISCO'S MATRIX PROGRAM	98
	Anthony Gardner and Peter Lindstrom	
8.	DOMESTIC VIOLENCE AND HOMELESSNESS	118
	Michele Ostrander	
9.	PROJECT RESPOND: EFFECTIVE RESPONSE TO THE HOMELESS MENTALLY ILL	131
	Julie Larson and Sue Beattie	
10.	RE-RUNNING A FAILED PROGRAM: THE USE OF SANCTIONS TO SOLVE FAMILY PROBLEMS	150
	J. Howard Finck and Della M. Hughes	

11. HOMELESS IN TRANSIT FACILITIES:
    "WHERE DO WE GO FROM NOWHERE"?   168
    Rita Schwartz

12. HOMELESSNESS AND THE POLICE
    IN PHOENIX, ARIZONA   181
    Mary Orton and Terry McDonald

13. BALTIMORE'S PROJECT CONNECT   197
    Gordon Scott Bonham

14. DEALING WITH HOMELESS POPULATIONS:
    THE PORTLAND MODEL OF PUBLIC—
    PRIVATE PARTNERSHIPS   216
    Robert A. DeGraff

Index   229

THE POLICE AND THE HOMELESS

Chapter 1

THE POLICE AND THE HOMELESS: AN INTRODUCTION

MARTIN L. FORST

When the Washington, D.C. police shot a homeless man, Marcelino Corniel, in front of the White House on December 20, 1994, it dramatized the tensions between homeless populations and law enforcement agencies throughout the United States. This incident underscored the need for greater understanding between the police and the homeless community.

Homelessness has varied in its scope and intensity during different historical periods in America. Hundreds of thousands of people across the country found themselves homeless during the Great Depression. Homeless encampments mushroomed and food lines swelled. Law enforcement agencies were called upon to regulate the dispossessed and quell civil unrest. America is again facing an epidemic of homelessness in all sections of the country, in rural as well as urban areas. Among the homeless are people of all races, single adults and families, the aged and the young.

The increase in homelessness over the past decade has created what many consider to be a significant "social problem." And as is typically the case, society asks lawmakers to "do something" about perceived social problems. In this instance, lawmakers often responded by "criminalizing" homelessness. Hundreds of cities have enacted so-called "quality of life" ordinances, making it illegal to panhandle and sleep in public places.

For better or worse when other agencies or programs fail, the police are called upon to confront social ills. To the extent that police are summoned to address criminal activities in society and to the extent that society criminalizes homelessness, law enforcement will become increasingly embroiled in this complex social situation.

It is often assumed, at least by the general public, that the police concentrate on high-publicity crimes, such as murder, rape, and kid-

3

napping. In reality, law enforcement officers spend an inordinate amount of time attending to "social problem" behaviors—family conflicts, runaway teens, substance abuse, mental illness, and the like. Law enforcement agencies must interact with marginalized members of society, including those people without a home. How police departments deal with homeless persons is a function of local public policy and program planning, as well as police management and training.

Because law enforcement agencies must regulate homeless persons, it is essential to learn more about this growing segment of the American public. It is imperative that law enforcement officers be fully informed about the homeless population, including the problems they face, as well as the varied social programs that are most successful in alleviating their plight. Finally, it may be necessary to redefine the police role. It is suggested here (and several articles in this book will illustrate the point) that the police need to work collaboratively with other social service agencies. After all, homelessness is not simply a law enforcement "problem." It is an interwoven set of social, economic, public and mental health issues that require a coordinated response. A collaborative approach—one that includes law enforcement in the planning and implementation process—will be most cost effective.

THE ISSUE OF NUMBERS

Nobody knows how many homeless people there are in the United States. Estimates vary, in part because there is no uniform definition of homelessness, either in law or in social science research. Even conceptions of homelessness—or "residential instability" as some people call it—vary. Some researchers consider only those people living on the streets or in public places, while others include those who are still in a residence but are at "high risk" of eviction.

Securing precise numbers of the homeless population is also problematic because of obvious methodological and logistic issues. Many homeless people are transient, moving from one jurisdiction to another in short time intervals. Some are hard to find, living under freeway overpasses, in cars, or in squats. Some "double up" with friends or relatives. Some hide from any governmental officials, including census takers. People may want to become invisible for several reasons: some have pending arrest warrants, some fear enforced psychiatric treatment, and some homeless women fear that their children will be taken away.

Nevertheless, there have been several attempts at enumeration. The official 1990 U.S. Census claimed that there were 228,372 homeless persons in the United States (178,638 in shelters and 49,734 on the streets).[1] This figure was frequently criticized, particularly by homeless advocates, because of the inadequacies in methodology. Critics claimed, for example, that census takers did not sufficiently look under all bridges and freeway overpasses to find the hidden homeless.

The Clinton administration in 1994 set the number of homeless people at closer to 600,000 nationally.[2] Another influential point-in-time study by the Urban Institute also estimated the number of homeless at about 600,000.[3] Homeless advocacy groups often put the figure somewhat higher—from 700,000 up to three million.[4]

Some recent studies have used broader definitions of homelessness and therefore calculate a larger number of homeless persons. A Columbia University study published in 1994, for instance, indicates that homelessness is much more prevalent than previously assumed.[5] In terms of absolute numbers, according to the Columbia study, roughly 26 million adult Americans have experienced some form of homelessness, including being forced to live on the streets or with someone else. Approximately 13.5 million Americans have been without any place to stay for at least a few days at some time in their lives. An additional 12.5 million have avoided landing on the streets (being literally homeless) by moving in with family members or friends from a few days to a year. In an accompanying editorial in the *American Journal of Public Health* (where the Columbia University study was published), Yale University's Dr. Robert Rosenheck states that these figures contradict the belief that "homelessness is an aberration affecting Americans who have distinct personal histories or who are situated on the fringes of society."[6]

Efforts to secure accurate counts of the homeless will undoubtedly continue. The federal Department of Housing and Urban Development requires a careful and scientific count of homeless persons in its grant applications from municipalities. It is clear that law enforcement agencies can and should play a role in determining the nature and extent of their local homeless populations. Many law enforcement agencies throughout the country already assist in this process.

The hard fact is that it will be a long time, if ever, before consistent and reliable figures are available. Nevertheless, as the recent federal plan to combat homelessness states, "The clear point is that recent studies confirm that the number of persons who have experienced homelessness is very large and greater than previously known or acknowledged."[7]

WHO ARE THE HOMELESS?

Attempting to make generalizations about homeless people is fraught with danger, possibly leading to gross misconceptions and inappropriate stereotyping. This in turn can generate bad policymaking as well as poor police-community relations.

Homeless people are not a monolithic group; they are almost as diverse as the general population. The single adult male alcoholic is very different from the domestically abused woman kicked out of her residence onto the streets. The hallucinating bag lady walking in the park is different from the family recently evicted because the father lost his job. The Vietnam veteran with post-traumatic stress disorder is different from the teenage girl on her own because she had been sexually abused by her stepfather.

Some people view the homeless population in rather narrow terms, a vision that includes only those people who are seen on the streets or in public places. These homeless people are frequently labeled as "bums," "vagrants," or "transients." The president's recent report uses the term "street homelessness" to signify this group.[8]

Henry Cisneros, secretary of the federal Department of Housing and Urban Development (HUD), divides the homeless into two broad groups.[9] One consists of those persons with long-term and disabling conditions. These are the people law enforcement personnel are most likely to encounter on the streets. And the second is made up of those people in "crisis poverty," that is, people who are functional but so poor that a sudden emergency, such as loss of a job, pushes them onto the streets.

Some authorities use a broader conception of homelessness, including those people who are "marginally housed" or at risk of losing their lodging. The federal government, in the Stewart B. McKinney Homeless Assistance Act of 1987, defines homeless as:

(1) An individual who lacks a fixed, regular, and adequate nighttime residence, and;
(2) An individual who has a primary nighttime residence that is:
    (i) A supervised publicly or privately operated shelter designed to provide temporary living accommodations (including welfare hotels, congregate shelters, and transitional housing for the mentally ill);

    (ii) An institution that provides a temporary residence for individuals intended to be institutionalized; or

    (iii) A public or private place not designated for, or ordinarily used as, a regular sleeping accommodation for human beings.

(3) This term does not include any individual imprisoned or otherwise detained under an Act of Congress or a state law.[10]

Although there is a broad array of homeless persons, some generalizations can be made about their demographic characteristics. Among the best and most recent data come from the tenth annual survey by the U.S. Conference of Mayors entitled, "Hunger and Homelessness in America's Cities."[11] This 1994 study summarized data on homelessness from 30 cities throughout the United States. On average, single men account for 48 percent of the homeless population, while single women account for 11 percent. Ethnic minorities are disproportionately represented among homeless people, especially homeless families.

Veterans, particularly Vietnam veterans, appear to be overrepresented among the homeless population. About 23 percent of the homeless are veterans, according to the mayors' conference study. The President's study indicates that about 30 to 45 percent of the entire male homeless population have served in the armed forces. As the president's report states, "Indeed, the number of homeless Vietnam veterans today is greater than the total number of military personnel who died in Vietnam."[12] About 40 percent of all homeless veterans are African American or Hispanic. Homeless vets tend to be somewhat older and better educated than other single homeless men, but otherwise they have similar characteristics and problems.

The United States has a long history of homeless families. "Automobile families," that is, those living out of their cars, date back to the 1920s. As vividly and humanely described by Jonathan Kozol in *Rachael and Her Children*,[13] families are now the fastest-growing segment of the homeless population. According to the U.S. Conference of Mayors' report, families make up 39 percent of all homeless persons. However, the proportion varies from place to place. In many cities families make up the majority of the homeless population, and a few cities report that up to 90 percent of their homeless are comprised of families.[14] Although some parents have substance abuse problems, it is crisis economic situations that are most likely to drive families onto the streets.

Tragically, children constitute a significant proportion of the homeless population. Although unaccompanied youths (i.e., not under the supervision of a parent or guardian) make up only three percent of the homeless population, all homeless children (including those under the care of their parent) comprise about 25 percent of the homeless. The National Academy of Sciences estimates that upwards of 100,000 children are without a place to stay on any given night.[15] These unfortunate youths suffer many hardships. As many as one-third of homeless children do not attend school on a regular basis, and they face serious medical, psychological and social problems that can persist throughout life.

Homeless persons often suffer from a multiplicity of personal problems. About three-fourths of the homeless population have a history of some form of institutional stay, whether in a juvenile correctional facility, mental hospital, jail, prison, or inpatient chemical dependency treatment program.

Most studies indicate that there are inordinately high levels of substance abuse among the homeless population, particularly single men and women who live on the streets. The president's report concludes that at least half of the adult homeless population has a current or past alcohol or drug use problem. The 1994 report by the U.S. Conference of Mayors, mentioned above, states that 43 percent of the homeless are drug or alcohol abusers. Some estimates are even higher. The authors of *A Nation in Denial,* for example, claim that substance abuse along with mental illness runs as high as 85 percent in the homeless population.[16]

Many homeless persons have mental health or emotional problems. The president's report claims that up to one-third of the adult homeless population suffers severe mental illness. The 1994 report by the U.S. Conference of Mayors contends that 26 percent of homeless people are mentally ill. Some estimates of mental illness run as high as 90 percent,[17] although such figures may be derived from selected (and therefore biased) samples.

Experts disagree about the relationship between homelessness and mental illness. The prevailing assumption is that persons who have serious psychiatric problems cannot function properly in society—keep a job or a residence—and are therefore thrust out onto the streets to survive. But there are also those who believe that mental health symptoms develop as a *result* of being homeless. In one study of single men, Dr. Marilyn Winkleby, an epidemiologist at Stanford University, contends that "addictive and mental disorders appeared to play little or no role in causing homelessness in more than one-half of these single adults," but "both of these problems increased significantly after the people lost their residences."[18]

Debate also surrounds the role that deinstitutionalizing mental hospitals played in creating the high proportion of homeless persons with psychiatric symptoms. Some researchers believe that the deinstitutionalization in the 1970s led to many mental patients being cast into the streets. In 1984 the Lamb American Psychiatric Association Task Force estimated that about 35 percent of the homeless population had become homeless as a result of deinstitutionalization.[19] And a study based in Boston found that 27 percent of all discharged mental patients experience homelessness within six months of release.[20]

Other authorities disagree. They point out that many homeless people on the streets, specifically those with mental health problems, are too young to have been released from mental hospitals. After all, a quarter or more of all homeless persons are children. The high proportion of mentally ill homeless adults results from related factors. With stricter civil commitment laws and with reduced state and local budgets for mental health treatment, it is simply more difficult to have a person committed to a secure psychiatric facility. As a consequence, more and more people with psychiatric problems must fend for themselves.

PUBLIC HEALTH CONCERNS

Much has been made recently in the scholarly and scientific literature about traditional crime, particularly violent crime, becoming a public health issue. Public health experts are expanding their horizons and are now focusing, for example, on the epidemeology and health consequences of gun violence. Crime is a public health problem.

The reverse logic also holds. Some public health issues are of importance to law enforcement personnel. A dramatic example comes from San Francisco. A homeless enclave had emerged in Golden Gate Park in 1993 and early 1994. Reports from park personnel indicated that the site was strewn with "piles of suitcases, feces, broken shopping carts and other objects littered on the ground."[21] Police and other city officials determined that the area was a health hazard and was "too dangerous to clean up by hand."[22] Instead, the city brought in a bulldozer to scoop up the materials and carry them away. This incident provoked searing criticism, and it was decided that if a similar situation arose in the future, the homeless people would receive sufficient warning about the police action. Nevertheless, the incident underscores the concern among law enforcement officials about health issues when dealing with at least some segments of the homeless community.

Examples abound of public health issues of interest to law enforcement personnel. How the HIV/AIDS epidemic affected police practices is but one. There are no definitive figures on HIV/AIDS among the homeless for many reasons, including confidentiality laws. But some estimates have surfaced. The U.S. Conference of Mayors' study suggests that about eight percent of the homeless population has AIDS. Another recent study specifically examined the level of HIV positivity in a sample of psychiatric patients in a New York City shelter for homeless men. The study, which collected data on the HIV serostatus of men discharged from the shelter over a two-year period, discovered that almost 20 percent of the men were HIV positive.[23] In terms of absolute numbers, the figures can be staggering. In New York City, for example, there are roughly 10,000 homeless people afflicted with AIDS.

Tuberculosis is another pressing public health concern, since the United States is witnessing a rising number of multidrug-resistant (MDR) cases of TB. A recent study published in the *Journal of the American Medical Association* painted a distressing picture of the medical aspects of homeless populations in San Francisco.[24] The researchers gathered data from men and women standing in four food lines and from others staying in shelters. They also interviewed hundreds of persons living on the streets, under freeway overpasses, in parks, and other public places. The study found that, in general, about one-third of the homeless sample had tuberculosis. By ethnicity, 23 percent of the whites, 37 percent of blacks, and 57 percent of Hispanics were infected with TB.

Another research strategy is to determine what percentage of the persons with a specified disease are homeless. The president's report suggests that in large metropolitan areas, between 25 and 40 percent of the persons with active TB are homeless (or are in imminent danger of homelessness). Moreover, some persons infected with HIV may face increased risk of TB infection as a result of unhealthy living conditions. Up to 50 percent of new TB patients are also HIV infected.

Even street kids have health problems of concern to law enforcement officers. Many homeless teens engage in "survival sex" (i.e., they exchange sex for food, lodging or money) or in other high-risk behaviors. As a result they suffer serious health consequences. One study of homeless youth, for example, found that 6 percent had hepatitis B and 37 percent had had a sexually transmitted disease at some point in their lives.[25] A related study found that slightly over 16 percent of the homeless youths had injected drugs.[26]

Death is at the extreme end of public health problems. Hundreds of homeless persons die each year in public places; municipal and county coroners all too frequently log-in street deaths due to exposure. San Francisco provides some specific information, since its Department of Public Health keeps detailed coroner's data. In 1995, 142 homeless persons died in streets, alleys, and shelters.[27] In San Francisco, 1995 was the eighth straight year in which more than 100 homeless people died in the streets. About 25 percent of those deaths were attributed to drug overdose—particularly from heroin, cocaine, and amphetamines. Another leading cause of death was suicide, especially among those people with a history of psychiatric illness.

The fact is that homeless people are at higher risk of many health problems—malnutrition, infectious diseases, and respiratory illnesses. A 1994 editorial in the *American Journal of Public Health* states: "Homelessness is a serious public health issue in its own right.... [H]omeless people suffer from associated conditions such as mental illness, alcoholism, tuberculosis, and a substantial excess of deaths."[28] It is therefore important for law enforcement agencies, and public policy planners in general, to view homelessness in its larger context. Law enforcement, social service, and public health officials should work in concert to provide appropriate and humane services.

EMERGING LEGAL ISSUES

A 1993 opinion poll in San Francisco inquired about citizens' perceptions of local social problems. One question asked, "What is the biggest problem facing the city today"? The number one concern among the respondents was homelessness. This issue was rated almost twice as serious as the next biggest problem—crime.[29]

When citizens perceive a social problem and that problem seems to affect them adversely, they look to their legislative bodies for solutions. This is true at the federal, state, and local levels. Following this logic, there has been a push at the various levels of government to enact laws to control the homeless, particularly the visibly homeless, such as those who loiter around commercial areas.

The federal and state governments have taken some steps to address the "homeless problem." Most of their actions, however, relate to providing funds for emergency housing—or other types of low-income housing. The federal and state responses generally do not have a direct effect on law enforcement agencies. Most of the homelessness legislation that affects the police emerges from the local level—county boards of supervisors and city councils.

The main strategy at the local level has been to enact so-called "quality of life" ordinances, prohibiting such activities as sleeping in parks, panhandling, and the like. In November 1994, the National Law Center on Homelessness and Poverty released its survey of 49 cities in the United States about approaches those municipalities have taken to control homelessness.[30] The survey found that 42 of the 49 cities had either passed punitive ordinances or selectively enforced laws aimed at criminalizing homelessness. That survey also found that 62 percent of the 49 cities in the survey enacted or enforced anti-panhandling laws in 1994. The authors of the report state, "For many cities, doing something about homelessness has increasingly meant doing something to homeless people instead of doing something to address their plight."[31]

One example (of hundreds) of local action comes from Orange County in southern California. Civic Center Plaza in the city of Santa Ana, the county seat, had become filled with homeless persons and the often associated side effects—litter, shopping carts, sleeping bags, and blankets hung to make tents. Many of the state, county, and city workers were dismayed about coming to work in such an environment.

The city council of Santa Ana decided to take drastic action—to deal with what it considered to be a deplorable situation. In one of a series of official memoranda in 1988, the city council decided to "move all vagrants and their paraphernalia out of Santa Ana."[32] Among other steps, the council decided to make it a crime for persons to "camp" on public land. This ordinance allowed the police to order the homeless to "move on" or face arrest. The law did have a noticeable effect on the front of the plaza area. Most of the one to three thousand homeless who congregated there left, but they did not go far. They did not travel to neighboring cities, because those city councils have passed similar ordinances. They have simply made themselves less visible. In Santa Ana, as in many cities throughout the country, the homeless travelled to other neighborhoods.

But the situation did not end there. The homeless, with the help of their advocates, filed suit, claiming that the new ordinance was unconstitutional. This case, a test case, is making its way to the United States

Supreme Court. The U.S. Department of Justice filed on the side of the homeless, claiming it is unconstitutional to "criminalize" the "simple existence" of the homeless. Homeless advocates point out that there may be as many as three thousand homeless persons in Santa Ana, and yet there are only 332 shelter beds. The advocates ask, Where else are homeless people supposed to go? On the other side, more than 90 California communities have filed briefs in support of Santa Ana's new ordinance.

Homeless advocates as well as city officials around the country await the outcome of this and similar cases. If the appellate courts allow such laws, it will mean greater use of law enforcement agencies to aggressively deal with the homeless. If the laws are stricken down or restricted, different strategies will then be developed. In the meantime, the police are still called upon to do society's dirty work.

STRAIN ON LOCAL RESOURCES

At a December 1994 news conference, Detroit Mayor Dennis Archer told reporters, "We are on the front lines" when it comes to combating homelessness.[33] He was referring to the mayors and other local officials throughout the United States.

According to the 1994 report by the U.S. Conference of Mayors, in 27 cities (out of the 30 surveyed), families and individuals relied on food aid not only in emergency situations but also as a regular source of nourishment. There was a 12 percent increase in the requests for emergency food among the homeless in the 30 cities. On average, however, 15 percent of the requests for emergency food aid went unmet in 1994. The resources available for emergency food centers decreased by four percent, and about half of the 30 cities surveyed said their agencies were unable to provide enough food.

Emergency shelter resources are also in short supply. According to the mayor's survey, requests for emergency shelter increased by 13 percent during 1994, but the number of emergency shelter beds increased by an average of only 6 percent. The mayors' study found that shelters in 72 percent of the cities surveyed turned away requests for assistance because of lack of resources. Twenty-one percent of the requests by homeless individuals and 25 percent of the requests by homeless families appear to have gone unfulfilled. Demand frequently far outstrips supply.

San Francisco exemplifies the shortage of shelter beds. San Francisco has 20 emergency shelters designed to serve all segments of the homeless population—adult males, females, families, and teens. The capacity of these 20 shelters is 1,395 beds. But all of the shelters are filled to capacity every night. Shelter managers are forced to turn away hundreds of people each night—thousands on a yearly basis. Many shelters have instituted a lottery system to make admission more equitable. A recent report recommended that San Francisco boost spending on homeless services by at least $18 million to help solve this dreadful shortage.[34]

One of the implications of this situation is that in the future, there will be fierce competition for scarce resources at the federal, state, and local levels. Among those in the battle will be local agencies in the same jurisdiction fighting over the same few dollars. For instance, Departments of Public Health, Social Services and law enforcement agencies will be competing for limited budgetary resources. It is imperative that all local agencies work together—not against each other.

THE CHANGING ROLE OF LAW ENFORCEMENT

Collaboration is the name of the game in the 1990s. This is a time of scarce budgetary resources at the federal, state, and local levels. It is also a time when different types of agencies must work together to solve increasingly complex problems with less money. This is the age when there must be partnerships among agencies or organizations—both public-private partnerships as well as partnerships among governmental agencies.

Public-private partnerships are emerging throughout the country, and they are increasingly involving law enforcement agencies. For example, the Business Alliance program was started in 1992 to help disadvantaged communities improve economic self-sufficiency and stimulate entrepreneurship. A business alliance is a voluntary organization of individuals and businesses that band together to promote the commercial, financial, economic, and civic interests of a community. The original Business Alliance pilot programs were developed as part of Operation Weed and Seed, under grants from the U.S. Department of Justice. The goal of Weed and Seed is to "weed out" crime and antisocial behavior and to prevent crime from returning by "seeding in" a variety of public and private efforts to strengthen the community. This can and should include law enforcement agencies. As a recent federal monograph states:

Any community involved in planning for revitalization can benefit from the Business Alliance concept without implementing the full Weed and Seed strategy; however, such planning must ensure that neighborhoods provide safe environments in which businesses can be reestablished. Community policing is essential for attracting economic enterprises through which the community, law enforcement, and business can support revitalization efforts.[35]

Another example of the partnership approach at the federal level is the Center for Substance Abuse Prevention's (CSAP) Community Partnership initiative. The thrust of the Community Partnership program is to encourage a variety of local agencies to work together to address drug and alcohol problems in their areas. CSAP has made 252 Community Partnership awards nationwide; California alone received 26 such grants. The basic idea is to have law enforcement, drug treatment and drug prevention agencies work together. These partnership programs have coaxed law enforcement and community-based organizations to sit down and talk—to plan community strategies to combat alcohol, tobacco and other drugs. Many communities are for the first time developing comprehensive and coordinated alcohol and drug policies, involving the participation of all of these agencies.

This approach has been extended to crime issues in general. In a recent federal report, summarizing some of the emerging partnerships, it appears that law enforcement agencies work well with a variety of other community agencies. "Law enforcement officers are showing that working in partnership with community members is an effective and productive way to address a community's problems and needs. This effectiveness can translate into less crime, less fear of crime, and a greater sense of community power and cohesion."[36]

This same partnership approach should also be undertaken in the area of homeless services. Interestingly, one example of this approach comes from the transportation industry through a consortium of federal agencies. In 1991, New York City, Baltimore, and San Francisco were awarded three-year federal grants from, jointly, the U.S. Departments of Transportation, Health and Human Services, Housing and Urban Development, and Agriculture (which administers the food stamp program). These federal departments were seeking evidence of improved coordination of local services as a result of this demonstration grant. The goal of the projects was to get homeless people out of transit facilities. To accomplish this goal, police, transit staff, social service workers, and the private sector worked together. The programs conducted outreach and found appropriate services (e.g., shelter, mental health) and provided transportation to relevant agencies.

The collaborative approach at the local level should always include law enforcement in the planning and implementation process. The police should work with social service and health care providers as well as the private sector. This should be done for social policy planning as well as for actual line work with people on the streets. The collaborative approach will be the most cost effective. Simply arresting persons and throwing them in jail, only to have them return to the streets again, is not effective. Collaboration helps end the revolving-door phenomenon.

As part of the collaborative effort, the police may have to alter their traditional roles. Part of this change is taking place on the streets. Police are the ultimate community outreach workers. Street outreach has been most often used by community health workers or substance abuse specialists to reach substance abusers, but it is also being used to help homeless persons. Outreach will increasingly be used by the police, often as part of a team of professionals to interact with homeless persons.

There are many examples of police outreach. In San Francisco, the California state police have jurisdiction over the Transbay Terminal, the large transit terminal owned and operated by CalTrans, the state transportation agency. The specified officers who patrol the facility call themselves "night shepherds," because they keep track of the homeless population at night. That is, they did until CalTrans closed the terminal at night in order to force the homeless to go elsewhere.

New York City also uses a team approach. In 1994, New York Mayor Rudolph Giuliani proposed assigning a new team of police officers to encourage the homeless to get off the streets and move to shelters. Under the plan, the Police Department trained about 36 plainclothes officers and their supervisors to work the streets from vans. According to Deputy Mayor Peter J. Powers, the intent of the program is to help the homeless, not to make the streets inhospitable to them.

A recent editorial regarding homelessness in the *American Journal of Public Health* states: "Effective action is urgently needed in the areas of housing, health care, employment, and education. The alternative of continued social disintegration will have grave consequences for the national health and welfare. . . ."[37] I would advocate for the inclusion of law enforcement in any action plan to address homelessness. As one recent government report on collaboration states, "Partnerships work best if participants are willing to focus on the shared objective rather than on their own agendas, and if leadership is shared."[38]

ORGANIZATION OF THE BOOK

The chapters in this book address some of the issues outlined above and show that law enforcement agencies are playing, and will continue to play, an increasing role in society's quest to deal with homeless persons in their communities. The articles that follow are arranged from the general to the specific. That is, the articles begin with an overview of the homelessness in the United States, including a historical perspective, and proceed to specific examples of local programs or strategies designed to address the law enforcement role in helping homeless persons. A brief outline of the articles follows:

- Roma Guy and Beverly Ovrebo provide a historical perspective on homelessness in America, including social strategies to address homelessness.
- Maria Foscarinis and Rick Herz outline some of the ways municipalities (and counties) have drafted legislation to control homeless persons in their communities. These new laws or ordinances, naturally, have direct implications for law enforcement agencies.
- Kathleen Quinn provides a more specific analysis of legal issues regarding homeless persons, specifically search and seizure appellate case law.
- Anthony Gardner Peter Lindstrom describe some of the legal and ethical issues in the application of San Francisco's Matrix program.
- Martha Plotkin and Tony Narr summarize the Police Executive's Research Forum's recent study of law enforcement responses to homelessness.
- Daschel Butler describes from the perspective of the police chief the changing role of law enforcement, especially regarding their interactions with homeless persons. He discusses the policies and procedures of the Berkeley, California police department.
- Rita Schwartz provides an analysis of a specialized type of law enforcement issue, that is, homeless people in transit facilities such as bus and train stations.
- Julie Larson and Sue Beattie discuss the issue of mental health among homeless persons and how law enforcement agencies can

cooperate with mental health professionals to help mentally ill homeless street persons.

- Mary Orton and Terry McDonald discuss the collaborative approach between law enforcement and the Central Arizona Shelter Services in Phoenix.
- J. Howard Finck and Della Hughes provide a greater understanding of teens, both runaway and homeless, who inhabit many street corners in both large and small cities throughout the country.
- Michele Ostrander discusses the issue of domestic violence and how it relates to homeless women. This type of social situation presents unique problems for law enforcement officers.
- Gordon Scott Bonham discusses his research on homeless persons in Baltimore and how in the future there should be greater cooperation between law enforcement and social service agencies to serve homeless populations.
- Robert DeGraff discusses the private-public partnership in working with homeless persons in downtown Portland, Oregon. The business community worked with the public sector to alleviate homelessness in Portland's commercial area.

ENDNOTES

1. See: Irene Glasser, *Homelessness in Global Perspective.* New York: G. K. Hall and Company, 1994, p. 114.
2. *Priority Home: The Federal Plan to Break the Cycle of Homelessness.* Washington, D.C.: Interagency Council on Homelessness, 1994, p. 2.
3. Martha Burt and B. Cohen, "America's Homeless: Numbers, Characteristics and the Programs that Serve Them." Washington, D.C.: The Urban Institute, 1989.
4. See: Irene Glasser, *Homelessness in Global Perspective.* New York: G. K. Hall and Company, 1994; and, Joel Blau, *The Visible Poor: Homelessness in the United States.* New York: Oxford University Press, 1992.
5. Bruce Link, Ezra Susser, Ann Stueve, Jo Phelan, Robert E. Moore, and Elmer Struening, "Lifetime and Five-Year Prevalence of Homelessness in the United States." *American Journal of Public Health, 84(12):* 1907–1912, 1994.
6. Robert Rosenheck, "Editorial: Homelessness in America." *American Journal of Public Health, 84(12):* 1885–1886, 1994.
7. *Priority Home,* op. cit., p. 21.
8. *Priority Home,* ibid., p. 48.
9. *Priority Home,* ibid., p. 3.

10. *Priority Home,* ibid., pp. 22–23.
11. U.S. Conference of Mayors, "A Status Report on Hunger and Homelessness in America's Cities: 1994," Washington, D.C., 1994.
12. *Priority Home,* op. cit., p. 50.
13. Jonathan Kozol, *Rachael and Her Children: Homeless Families in America.* New York: Fawcett Columbine, 1988.
14. Ibid., p. 5.
15. Joel Blau, op. cit., p. 26.
16. Alice S. Baum and Donald W. Burnes, *A Nation in Denial: The Truth About Homelessness.* Boulder, CO: Westview Press, 1993.
17. Edmund V. Ludwig, "The Mentally Ill Homeless: Evolving Involuntary Commitment Issues." *Villanova Law Review, 36:* 1087, 1991.
18. San Francisco *Chronicle,* Dec. 21, 1994, p. A16.
19. Edmund V. Ludwig, op. cit., p. 1087.
20. E. Fuller Torey, "Who Goes Homeless? We Can't Begin to Solve the Problem of Homelessness Until We Realize that It Isn't About Homes." *National Review,* Aug. 26, 1991, p. 34.
21. San Francisco *Chronicle,* March 9, 1994, p. A11.
22. San Francisco *Chronicle,* ibid.
23. Ezra Susser, Eliecer Valencia, and Sarah Conover, "Prevalence of HIV Infection Among Psychiatric Patients in a New York City Men's Shelter." *American Journal of Public Health, 83(4):* 568–570, 1993.
24. San Francisco *Chronicle,* Aug. 12, 1994, p. A20.
25. Martin L. Forst, "Sexual Risk Profiles of Delinquent and Homeless Youths." *Journal of Community Health, 19(2):* 101–114, 1994.
26. Martin L. Forst, "A Substance Use Profile of Delinquent and Homeless Youths." *Journal of Drug Education, 24(3):* 219–231, 1994.
27. San Francisco *Chronicle,* Jan. 2, 1996, p. A11.
28. Robert Rosenheck: op. cit., p. 1886.
29. San Francisco *Chronicle,* Dec. 27, 1993, p. A9.
30. "No Homeless People Allowed: A Report on Anti-Homeless Laws, Litigation and Alternatives in 49 United States Cities." Washington, D.C.: National Law Center on Homelessness and Poverty, December 1994.
31. Ibid., p. 1.
32. *The Sacramento Bee,* Jan. 1, 1995, p. A1.
33. San Francisco *Chronicle,* Dec. 20, 1994, p. A2.
34. "Survey of Emergency Shelters for Homeless Persons in San Francisco." San Francisco, CA: Polaris Research and Development, March 1992.
35. U.S. Bureau of Justice Assistance, "Business Alliance: Planning for Business and Community Partnerships." Washington, D.C.: Bureau of Justice Assistance, August 1994, p. 2.
36. National Crime Prevention Council, "Working as Partners with Community Groups," Washington, D.C.: U.S. Bureau of Justice Assistance, BJA Community Partnership Bulletin, September 1994, p. 1.

37. Rosenheck, op. cit., 1994, p. 1886.
38. National Crime Prevention Council, "Partnerships to Prevent Youth Violence," Washington, D.C.: U.S. Bureau of Justice Assistance, BJA Community Partnership Bulletin, August 1994, p. 6.

Chapter 2

HISTORICAL PERSPECTIVES ON HOMELESSNESS

ROMA GUY AND BEVERLY OVREBO

Everything old is new again.

Homelessness is not new. Neither is the current trend to criminalize homelessness. Since 1980, homelessness has grown at epidemic proportions. Currently numbering in the millions, the exact count of homeless people in the U.S. is unknown. One of the most reliable estimates is by Link et al. who, in a nationwide telephone survey, found that 5.7 million people were homeless between 1985 and 1990. This is an astounding number, especially when one considers that in 1980 the number of homeless was well less than 100,000.[1]

Blau[2] categorizes homelessness in the United States into five periods:

1. The Colonial Era: Many English colonists were poor and homeless, Native Americans were displaced from their homelands, and Africans were brought to the colonies as slaves;
2. The Post-Civil War Era: Massive homelessness resulted from reconstruction, the displacement of veterans of both armies, mushrooming immigration, the dislocation of Native Americans to reservations, and the urban migration of former slaves;
3. The "Gilded Age": Homelessness corresponded with an economic "bust," unregulated capitalism, and exploding immigration;
4. The Great Depression: An estimated one percent of the U.S. population was homeless[3]; and
5. The current era of homelessness.

What these five eras have in common is that all were periods of social and economic dislocation. In each of these eras, the rich got richer and the poor got homeless. Some hold the view that homelessness is a social aberration that tends to correct itself. In fact, in each of the first four eras homelessness abated due to macro socioeconomic and demographic shifts. Colonies and the "frontier" provided a safety valve for the relocation of

poor people. The underclass provided a cheap, surplus labor force for
the millions of unskilled jobs which were part of the pre-industrial and
industrial eras; the underclass were also the front-line troops for all of
the major wars. The third and fourth periods of homelessness were
followed by eras of progressive reform, focusing on labor, housing and
civil rights.

The beginning of the current era was met with denial that homelessness
existed in the United States. Now that homelessness has become part of
everyday live in this country, the dominant view seems to be that
homelessness is part of the natural order. However, homelessness is not
innate to human society—rather, it is a manifestation of social organization.
Otherwise stated, over the past decades, the United States has created
homelessness.

Homelessness is symptomatic of deep structural changes in the United
States, a consequences of systematic disinvestment in workers and the
poor. Since the early 1970s, U.S. policy has focused on investment in
international trade and disinvestment in social welfare. Since the end of
the Second World War, the lowest quintile of Americans have experienced a 13 percent reduction in wealth while the highest quintile has
experienced an 8 percent increase.[4] Reaganomics was a devastating
policy, effectively reducing social services, entitlement programs and the
nation's stock of affordable housing. Combined with chronic unemployment and a shrinkage in real wages, the numbers of poor and near poor
swelled during the 1980s. In the 1981–82 recession alone, 2.2 million
Americans lost their jobs. Many of them became homeless and remain
homeless to this day.[5]

The current period is distinct from the previous four eras in that
homelessness has proliferated simultaneous with regressive reform. The
current disinvestment in the poor and the social infrastructure, the loss
of low-skilled jobs, and the absence of a frontier or other safety valve for
excess poor, have created a situation where underlying social processes
are fueling the increase in homelessness. Furthermore, the existence of
the very progressive housing and labor reforms that once served to curtail
the exploitation of the poor now impede poor people from employing
and housing themselves. Poor people are dependent upon social policies
and social infrastructures to survive; at the same time these policies and
infrastructures are abandoning them.

Homelessness has grown too large to be either denied or ignored. It is
a national problem with local manifestations. It is at the local level that

homelessness is most visible and where the majority of efforts to address it occur. A major trend is to criminalize homelessness—to attempt to control homelessness by controlling homeless people. This is an old strategy, one which is as old as human society itself. It is naive, inhumane and ineffective.

POLICE AND THE HOMELESS

The law in all its majesty forbids both rich and poor from sleeping under bridges.

—Anatole France

A national problem with local manifestations, homelessness has evoked the most vigorous control efforts at the municipal level where police are charged with the front-line response. The criminalization of homelessness, which has its roots in British Common Law, has risen sharply again in recent years. The National Law Center, which monitors the passage and enforcement of anti-homeless legal actions, reports a sharp increase in anti-homeless legal actions over the past five years. Its 1995 survey of 49 cities found consistency across jurisdictions of ordinances which both criminalized homelessness and targeted homelessness as a status offense. Sixty-two percent of the cities had laws against panhandling; more than 25 percent had laws which restricted access to public places. Almost the same percentages had conducted police sweeps. All of these laws define homelessness as a status offense and, once passed, require that police enforce them.[6]

Laws against homelessness have their roots in British Common Law. The first vagrancy law, the Statute of Laborers, was passed in 1349, in response to the decimation of the labor force from the Black Death. By this statute, "every able-bodied person without other means of support was required to work for wages fixed at the level preceding the Black Death; it was unlawful to accept more, or to refuse an offer to work, or to flee from one county to another to avoid offers of work or to seek higher wages, or to give alms to able-bodied beggars who refused to work."[7]

The punishment for acts against this statute was fifteen days imprisonment. By the sixteenth century, vagrancy laws were amended to include anyone considered idle or unwilling to work, and legal actions were stiffened to include whipping, burning, cutting off of ears, branding, and death. For the first time, vagrancy laws made distinctions between different types of poor people: worthy paupers (usually able-bodied men) deemed unwilling to work; and unworthy paupers (usually women, old people, children and the disabled) deemed unable to work. Criminal penalties were generally reserved for the former group (labeled loafers and beggars), while the undeserving poor were relegated to almshouses and private and public benevolence.[8]

During this era of British colonialism, many paupers were sent to the colonies (including the thirteen colonies which became the United States) either as punishment or, in lieu of incarceration, as indentured servants. In the colonies, British vagrancy laws were generally adopted. Paupers and beggars roamed populated areas and were accorded the same treatment as in England. However, there was an important social use for paupers in the colonial era. Poor people were encouraged to wander into unsettled areas (i.e., homelands of native peoples) to claim the land for themselves, and thus for England. This continued well into the twentieth century in the United States, where poor people could gain autonomy, dignity, and redefinition as settlers and pioneers by colonizing land.

By the turn of the twentieth century, the frontier began to close, and the place for, and the social uses of, the vagrant poor again became problematic. The urban home for poor, migratory men became known as "skid row," and "the term homeless, once generally used to describe the vagrant classes as a whole, became specifically applied to the single unattached worker who lived on skid row between jobs."[9]

Social tolerance of homelessness lessened, and laws against vagrancy were once again strictly enforced. As homelessness has increased over the past 15 years, vagrancy laws, although ruled unconstitutional by the Supreme Court, are being again invoked in laws aimed against the homeless.

SOCIAL USES OF THE HOMELESSNESS

In many respects, a society has the deviance it deserves.
— Edwin Schur[10]

Homeless people are an archetypal deviant class—serving as a negative social example, giving a clear message of where the norms of society are placed, elevating the status of society's "normals." As Schur[11] writes, " . . . placing some persons in these devalued categories necessarily implies valued status for others, the so-called conformists. It is their rules that are applied, their standards that are legitimized, their 'respectability' and power that are sustained and reinforced."

As deviants, homeless people are convenient scapegoats, blamed for increasing social costs, social disruption and criminal activity, and the failure of the economy to function fairly, efficiently and effectively for its supporters and adherents. The existence of deviants also gives evidence of the need for state intervention, legitimizing the existence of actions of welfare, therapeutic and legal systems.

Spitzer[12] outlines six mechanisms for the control of deviance, all of which are currently being applied towards homeless people:

1. *Containment:* Homeless people are relegated to certain neighborhoods and areas of the city.
2. *Commodification:* Efforts are made to create industries and profitable activities out of managing homeless people; as Spitzer writes: " . . . societies may more profitably manage populations by viewing them as human capital than as human waste."[13]
3. *Normalization:* Homeless people are accommodated by society by being rendered invisible and kept from view.
4. *Conversion:* Homeless people are converted to supporters of the social system, recruited as garbage collectors, street sweepers, and recruiting voters.
5. *Support of Criminal Enterprise:* Certain criminal activities associated with deviance are pushed into areas where homeless people are contained and are allowed to proliferate (e.g., drug sales and prostitution).
6. *Social Processing:* Social workers, health care professionals and the police are assigned the role of tracking, processing and treating the homeless.

According to Spitzer,[14] deviants tend to be placed into two categories: as "social trash" (which tends to be white, female and old) and "social dynamite" (which tends to be young men of color). One can see this classification in the views and treatments of homeless people who tend to be labeled as harmless and worthless (Spitzer's "social trash") or "dangerous" (Spitzer's "social dynamite"). Gender, race and age are the bases for this social typing. Young men of color, especially African American men, tend to be perceived as the most dangerous, and elderly white women are viewed as both the most worthless and harmless.[15] The "worthless" homeless tend to be invisible and are the province of the health and social welfare systems. "Shopping bag ladies" are archetypal worthless homeless.[16] The "dangerous" homeless are often the targets of public controversy and police action and are more likely to be processed by the criminal justice system. For example, in San Francisco, African American men account for over 30 percent of all homeless arrests in the Matrix program while comprising only 10 percent of the population.

YOU CAN'T SOLVE HOMELESSNESS BY SOLVING HOMELESSNESS

I sit on a man's back choking him, doing everything I can to let him know how sorry I am for his condition, doing everything I can to help him, except get off his back.
— Leo Tolstoy

The current trend to criminalize homelessness is emblematic of public policy which attempts to solve major social problems by treating their symptoms. The vain attempt to solve homelessness by controlling and correcting homeless people directly is not only unjust and inhumane but it has the effect, as history instructs, of actually exacerbating the problem. Homelessness is, in public policy parlance, an intractable, or "wicked," problem. It is the kind of problem which, if not addressed at the level of root causes, tends to fight back. Wicked problems are complex in nature and, according to Beauchamp,[17] have the following characteristics:

1. They are connected to all the problems of society. In homelessness, one finds many of the most complex social problems of our day: the lack of affordable housing, poverty and hunger, disability, drug and alcohol use, violence, racism, sexism, ageism, AIDS and other disease.
2. They occur to a relative minority of the population and benefit the majority or a powerful minority. Although the number of homeless Americans is now in the millions, this is a very small portion of the total population. Even when homelessness was at its peak in this society (during the Great Depression), only 1 percent of the total U.S. population was homeless at any given time.
3. When "solved" at the level of their symptoms, wicked problems tend to get worse. Homelessness has been treated as an emergency (e.g., providing temporary shelter and food to support basic survival) rather than as a symptom of deep structural change in our society. Homelessness policy has neither eliminated entrances into, nor exits from, homelessness. As a result, municipalities throughout the country have spawned homelessness industries and have

redirected police energy and resources to moving homeless people around.

4. They are political in nature, looking different to different stake-holders. Homelessness looks different to the store owner than to the homeless man who sleeps in the store's doorway; homelessness has different stakes for the tourist industry than it does for shelter providers.

5. Their existence promotes the status quo. As costly as it is, home-lessness exists because economic and social benefits accrue: home-lessness contributes to the depression of wages and is a by-product of the lucrative real estate industry. Homelessness is directly tied to the size of police budgets and the growth of the private security companies and is a major justification for the boom in jail and prison construction.

CONCLUSION

History reveals that homelessness is a consequence of major social and economic change. Controlling homeless people has *never* controlled homelessness itself. The criminalization of homelessness is a classic example of victim blaming, locating the problem of homelessness within individuals, assigning blame and responsibility to the least powerful members of our society for a major social problem. Police and service providers are assigned responsibility for solving homelessness, yet are limited to treating its symptoms. As in the past, macro solutions are required. There are no more frontiers or colonies; a major world war is not survivable. Homelessness will only be solved by a new kind of macro solution. It is time, as Tolstoy suggests, to get off the backs of the poor. Homelessness calls out for a shift to reinvest in people and in social infrastructures. Until that occurs, police will continue to be assigned the futile task of controlling an uncontrollable problem, and homelessness will continue, tragically, to grow.

ENDNOTES

1. Link, B., Susser, E., Stueve, A., Phelan, J., Moore, R.E., and Struening, E. "Lifetime and Five-Year Prevalence of Homeless in the United States." *American Journal of Public Health, 84(12),* 1907–1912, 1994.

2. Blau, J. *The Visible Poor: Homelessness in the United States.* New York: Oxford University Press, 1992.

3. Burt, M. R. *Over the Edge: The Growth of Homelessness in the 1980s.* New York: Russell Sage Foundation, 1992.

4. Ibid.

5. Hopper, K. and Hamburg, J. "The Making of America's Homeless From Skid Row to New Poor, 1945–1984." In Bratt, R. et al. (Eds.), *Critical Perspectives on Housing.* Philadelphia, PA: Temple University Press, 1986.

6. Janofsky, M. "Many Cities in Crackdown on Homeless." *New York Times,* Friday, December 16, 1994, p. A34.

7. Chambliss, W. "The Law of Vagrancy." Andover, MA: Warner Module Publications, Module 4, p. 3.

8. Ibid.

9. Wallace, S.E. *Skid Row as a Way of Life.* Totowa, NJ: Bedminster Press, 1965, p. 18.

10. Schur, E. *The Politics of Deviance: Stigma Contests and the Uses of Power.* Englewood Cliffs, NJ: Prentice-Hall, 1980. p. 10.

11. Ibid., p. 8.

12. Spitzer, S. "Toward a Marxian Theory of Deviance." In Pontell, H. N. (Ed.), *Social Deviance: Readings in Theory and Research.* Englewood Cliffs, NJ: Prentice-Hall, 1993.

13. Ibid.

14. Ibid.

15. Ibid.

16. Golden, S. *The Women Outside: The Meanings and Myths of Homelessness.* Berkeley, CA: University of California Press, 1992.

17. Beauchamp, D.E. "Public Health as Social Justice." *Inquiry,* XII, March 1976.

Chapter 3

NEW MUNICIPAL ORDINANCES REGULATING HOMELESS PEOPLE

MARIA FOSCARINIS AND RICK HERZ

INTRODUCTION

The problem of homelessness in America is large and growing.[1] The latest data indicate that at least 700,000 people live in the streets and shelters of America at any one time.[2] As many as 1.3 million may live in the streets and shelters at least part of the time.[3] An estimated two to three million people experience homelessness during the course of any given year,[4] and at least 12 million, 6.5 percent of the American adult population, have been homeless at some point in their lives.[5] Members of families with children comprise 39 percent of the homeless population.[6]

Although many cities seek constructive solutions to homelessness, other cities act in a hostile manner toward homeless people. In recent years, a growing number of cities have responded to the problem by passing or enforcing "anti-homeless" laws or policies.[7] Regrettably, this is a quite common contemporary response to the problem of homelessness rather than an isolated phenomenon. For many cities, doing something about the problem of homelessness has increasingly involved a punitive law enforcement response. Actions frequently taken against homeless people include restrictions on begging and homeless persons' use of public places, police "sweeps" designed to remove homeless people from specific areas, selective enforcement of generally applicable laws, and restrictions on those who provide services to homeless people.

Many cities engage in these actions despite resources to help homeless people that are woefully inadequate. In the absence of sufficient shelter space, homelessness has forced large numbers of people to seek shelter or simply to remain in public places that were not designed to serve as living space. While public spaces are properly for the use of all citizens, homeless or housed, homeless people literally have nowhere else to eat, sleep or simply be than the streets and other public places. Moreover, in the absence of sufficient jobs or income, homeless people may literally have no means to meet basic survival needs other than begging for change. In this context, penalizing such activities amounts to criminalizing homelessness. To the extent that they make it impossible for homeless people to remain in a given jurisdiction without violating its laws, such laws suggest a new, extreme response to homelessness: the banishment of homeless people.

BACKGROUND

Cities' specific targeting of homeless people is actually the latest manifestation of an official hostility toward displaced poor people which has a long history in Anglo American law. Beginning at least as far back as the fourteenth century, English law responded to various social dislocations which encouraged or forced poor people to move from their dwelling places with a series of laws which criminalized wandering or vagrancy and which allowed communities to refuse to accept the in-migration of individuals who could not prove that they would not require public assistance.[8] These laws were originally enacted in the wake of the Plague's devastation of the English workforce in order to protect the feudal order by preventing movement in search of higher wages.[9] Later these laws were designed to protect communities from the threats to the public safety and morality and to the public fisc which were perceived to accompany the influx of poor people.[10]

Similar laws were adopted for similar reasons in the American colonies, and they remained firmly entrenched in the legal landscape until well into the twentieth century.[11] For example, as late as 1960, the law of every state in the country punished as vagrants individuals without visible means of support who did not work although able.[12]

Eventually, however, the American judiciary began to reject some of the traditional means for excluding and criminalizing poor people, as well as their underlying rationales. In 1941, the Supreme Court invalidated a California ordinance which made it a misdemeanor to bring a non-resident indigent into the state. The Court rejected both traditional justifications for these types of laws (protection of the public purse and public safety), holding that states have a duty to share the burden of providing assistance to the needy, and that "we do not think it will now be seriously contended that because a person is without employment and without funds he constitutes a 'moral pestilence.' Poverty and immorality are not synonymous."[13] In 1969 the Court struck down statutes denying welfare assistance to people who had not resided in their jurisdictions for at least one year before applying for aid. The Court held that the "purpose of inhibiting migration by needy persons into the State is constitutionally impermissible" because all citizens have the right to travel interstate without unreasonable burdens.[14]

In 1972, the Court unanimously struck down a city vagrancy statute which was "derived from early English law."[15] The Court held the law to be impermissibly vague because it did not give fair notice of what was forbidden and because it encouraged arbitrary enforcement.[16] In fact, the Court noted that in enacting vagrancy laws, "[d]efiniteness is designedly avoided so as to allow the net to be cast at large, to enable men to be caught who are vaguely undesirable in the eyes of police and prosecution, although not chargeable with any particular offense."[17] The Court concluded that the implicit presumption in generalized vagrancy standards that those who can be arrested under them will become future criminals is "too precarious for a rule of law."[18]

Similarly, the Supreme Court in 1983 invalidated a law which made it a crime to loiter or wander without apparent reason if one failed to provide credible identification and account for his or her presence when requested to do so by a police officer.[19] The Court held that the law was impermissibly vague and that it implicated the constitutional right to freedom of movement.[20]

RECENT DEVELOPMENTS

The above-cited cases have limited the ability of states and localities to prevent the in-migration of poor people and of law enforcement to arrest "vaguely undesirable" people on the suspicion that they are likely to become criminals. Nevertheless, although the cases have also discredited the rationales underlying such laws, many cities have relied on similar rationales to adopt new, narrower laws focused specifically on homeless people. Thus, the recent trend toward enacting or enforcing anti-homeless laws and policies suggests an incorporation of the discredited rationales of the traditional laws into current law or official policy. For example, the City of Dallas justified its law banning sleeping anywhere in a public place by baldly asserting that it could properly conclude that "limiting persons' presence in public places would make less likely the incidence of crime."[21]

Banishment

Actions commonly taken against homeless people take a variety of forms. Some cities have adopted comprehensive policies with the clear intent of driving homeless people out of town or parts of town. Such actions are direct descendants of the traditional English laws, and they have similar effects on the targeted population. The Dallas law, for example, makes it physically impossible for a homeless person to remain in Dallas for longer than that person can remain awake if that person is to avoid violating the law. This is essentially banishment. Other cities have also effectively criminalized homeless people's mere living within a jurisdiction by enacting similar laws and policies. For example, since 1988 the official policy of the city of Santa Ana, California has been to attempt to rid itself of its homeless residents.[22] Since then, the city has at various times utilized a number of different means to harass homeless people, including throwing out their belongings[23] and discriminatorily arresting them for minor infractions.[24] In August of 1992, the city attempted to make it illegal for homeless people to live in the city by criminalizing camping or storing personal property in any outdoor area of the city.[25] Miami and San Francisco have also adopted pervasive campaigns of arrest for such "crimes" as sleeping and eating in public, as well as other "nuisance" crimes. In each case, these policies were adopted despite the fact that there was not enough shelter space in those cities—and so no place other than public spaces for homeless people to perform necessary activities.

Given these laws' purposes and effects, it should come as no surprise that they have been challenged in court in a variety of different cities. A federal district court in Miami[26] held that homeless people have no choice but to be in public places, and that, as a result, their performance of harmless, life-sustaining behaviors in public is inseparable from their involuntary homeless status. The court held that in these circumstances, criminalizing such conduct is tantamount to criminalizing involuntary status and therefore violates the Eighth Amendment.[27] A federal district court in Dallas agreed with this reasoning, but the decision was vacated by the Fifth Circuit, which found that the plaintiffs did not have standing since they had not been convicted under the law.[28] In contrast, federal district courts in Baltimore[29] and San Francisco[30] rejected similar claims because they were unwilling to conclude that homelessness is a status and because the policies targeted behavior. These courts focused on the distinction between status and conduct, whereas the Dallas and Miami courts were persuaded by the involuntariness of the conduct in light of the absence of alternatives.

Plaintiffs in these cases have also argued that the cities' practices violate the right to travel. This argument asserts that arresting homeless people for public sleeping or performing other necessary acts in public has the primary purpose and actual effect of penalizing and deterring homeless people's migration to or remaining in a city since they cannot do either without facing arrest. The court in Miami accepted this argument,[31] but the court in San Francisco rejected it.[32]

Sweeps

Not all cities' actions are as comprehensive as the policies described above. Some cities focus their law enforcement response on certain neighborhoods and engage in sweeps, i.e., attempts to "sweep" homeless people from a given area of the city, usually upscale neighborhoods, downtown areas or shopping districts. Sweeps are frequently used to "spruce up" a city before a big event which draws a large number of out-of-town visitors. They have been accomplished in a variety of ways. Some cities have evicted homeless people from makeshift shelters and frequently have destroyed or seized their property in the process. Other cities have simply instituted a general crackdown on the homeless people in a given area in order to dissuade them from staying. This has involved discriminatory enforcement of generally applicable rules as well as enforcement of laws specifically aimed at homeless people, such as aggressive panhandling or anti-sleeping ordinances. In a particularly egregious example, local groups report that the city of Cleveland engaged in an official policy of actively discouraging homeless people from visiting two areas of the city and of driving those who return to outlying industrial areas and leaving them there.[33]

Sitting Ordinances

A few cities have attempted to rid their downtowns of "undesirables" by prohibiting sitting or lying down on a sidewalk in a commercial area during certain times of the day. Permitting homeless people to remain in a downtown area only so long as they are able to remain standing obviously places an extremely difficult burden on all homeless people in that area, and especially on disabled and elderly homeless people and homeless children. For them it may be impossible to stand or walk without pausing to rest. Because homeless people are typically destitute, they will not be able to afford to rest in any commercial establishments. Therefore, such ordinances may effectively ban homeless people from the given area during daylight hours, forcing them into outlying residential areas which are far from the service providers homeless people depend on to survive.

Two federal district courts have ruled on the constitutionality of such laws. A Seattle court upheld that city's sidewalk ordinance against a First Amendment challenge, holding that there was no violation because sitting or lying is not expressive conduct and people can still exercise free speech rights without sitting or lying down in violation of the ordinance.[34] A court in Berkeley, however, preliminarily enjoined that city's prohibition on sitting. The court held that sitting itself can be expressive conduct and that some plaintiffs' ability to engage in speech depends on being able to sit.[35]

Amtrak

Amtrak has engaged in similar attempts to force homeless people to leave Penn Station in New York City. Amtrak's police enforced a policy of arresting or ejecting people who appeared homeless from Penn Station. Some of those ejected also alleged that the Amtrak police used excessive force. A federal district court, however, enjoined Amtrak from continuing its policy in the absence of evidence that a person had committed any crime. The court found that Amtrak's rules of conduct vested too much discretion in Amtrak police and implicated plaintiffs' freedom of movement and therefore violated due process protections. The court also found that the defendants acted arbitrarily and that homeless people have the right to be in Penn Station without being confronted by the police.[36]

Other Laws

Even when not enforced as part of a general strategy to rid an area or entire city of homeless people, laws aimed at criminalizing behaviors necessarily attendant to homelessness are particularly burdensome. These laws are not only susceptible to discriminatory enforcement, they are, like the older vagrancy laws, essentially enacted for that purpose, since the prohibited behavior is only seen as problematic when it is engaged in by "undesirables." For example, laws like Santa Ana's[37] which prohibit storing property in public places are not intended to be enforced against middle class residents who happen to leave property unattended in public, despite the fact that the law's terms prohibit such behavior.

Panhandling Ordinances

Enactment and/or enforcement of anti-panhandling ordinances has also been quite common in recent times. Begging is one of the most visible and poignant reminders of the prevalence of poverty in American society. Therefore, the fact that many cities have sought to limit or eradicate it should come as no surprise.

Blanket bans on panhandling, however, have been struck down as violating the First Amendment.[38] Some cities, however, such as Milwaukee, Wisconsin, do persist in enforcing such blanket bans.[39] Most of the cities which are currently adopting new anti-panhandling ordinances typically have limited the scope of those ordinances to aggressive panhandling or panhandling in certain places. This increased narrowness is most likely a response to court rulings invalidating broader bans. Nevertheless, such laws frequently suffer from another defect: they fail to cover anything which is not already illegal under traditional criminal laws.

While overlapping definitions of offenses is not necessarily a problem in and of itself, these laws, like public place restrictions, may allow or even encourage law enforcement officers to harass homeless people engaged in innocent and even constitutionally protected behavior. For example, panhandlers in Washington, D.C. have told one of the authors that police officers have interpreted the city's anti-aggressive panhandling ordinance to prohibit holding cups while soliciting and have arrested panhandlers who have done so. Anti-panhandling laws frequently also prohibit people from soliciting in certain places, such as in the immediate vicinity of an ATM. These provisions similarly provide law enforcement with an excuse to move homeless people out of areas where they are unwelcome.

A number of courts have ruled on such laws. In Seattle, a federal district court held that although begging is protected speech, the ordinance was not unconstitutionally vague or overbroad when given the limiting construction that it only applies to threats.[40] In Baltimore,

another federal district court noted that although panhandling is chari-
table solicitation fully protected by the First Amendment, the city's law
did not violate that amendment because it was narrowly tailored to serve
compelling state interests in protecting citizens and promoting tourism.
That court further held, however, that since the city could not demon-
strate a compelling state interest in making the content-based distinction
between prohibiting only aggressive panhandling and prohibiting all
aggressive solicitation for money, the law was unconstitutional under the
Equal Protection Clause.[41]

To avoid the Equal Protection Clause problem, many of the most
recent laws regulate all aggressive solicitation as opposed to just aggressive panhandling. Two federal district courts in California have recently
held that such anti-solicitation ordinances were unconstitutional under
the California Constitution because they impermissibly regulated speech
based on its content in that they distinguished between those speakers
who ask for money and those who do not.[42]

Law enforcement efforts have not been limited to actions taken against
homeless people themselves. Cities have also shut down service providers or limited their operations and prevented the opening of new
facilities. For example, San Francisco has arrested over 350 people for
distributing food to homeless people at Civic Center Plaza,[43] and Collier
County, Florida sharply limited a church's efforts to shelter homeless
people on its property.[44] Given the nearly universal inability of cities to
adequately provide for the homeless people in their communities, cities'
efforts to discourage or preclude private provision of needed services is
especially disturbing.

A law enforcement response to the problem of homelessness is extremely
counterproductive. Homeless men, women and children must struggle
to acquire the basic necessities of life. Law enforcement actions directed
against them not only make their daily life harsher, they also further
burden their ability to escape their already difficult plight, particularly
since they frequently result in fines, jail time and a criminal record.
Neo-vagrancy laws and policies, like their English and American antece-
dents, do not purport to address the problem of homelessness or its
underlying causes. Rather they seek to regulate homeless people and, if
possible, to move the problem. These laws also distract attention and
resources from proactive responses to homelessness and polarize the
very parties who need to cooperate in order to find viable solutions.

PROACTIVE ALTERNATIVES

Clearly, cities could have a significantly more constructive impact on the problem of homelessness if they were to reject such policies. While some commentators have attributed the profusion of anti-homeless policies to a decrease in public "sympathy" for homeless people,[45] a recent poll found that there is no such compassion fatigue. Roughly 65 percent of Americans would be willing to pay higher taxes specifically to increase government spending on homeless people, a number that has changed little over the past ten years.[46] This suggests that proactive responses to homelessness would not only be smart and humane policy, they would also be popular.

In fact, a number of cities have enacted programs which provide examples of proactive alternatives to neo-vagrancy laws and policies. For example, in Nashville, a local judge helped to persuade the Downtown Merchants' Association to withdraw a proposed aggressive begging law by explaining that existing laws already cover essentially the same conduct and by noting that homelessness is a social issue that should be dealt with in ways other than anti-begging legislation. The merchants' association and local advocates then worked together on alternative approaches to dealing with downtown Nashville's homeless. Outreach workers began working with downtown merchants to teach them to better recognize behaviors which require social services as opposed to law enforcement responses. Moreover, the chamber of commerce and the chief of police began working with the advocates and homeless individuals to develop a plan to address the inordinate amount of street violence homeless people face.

Another example of a proactive approach which can easily be copied in other places is the "Miami meal tax." Dade County, prompted at least in part by the successful suit against its neo-vagrancy arrest policies, adopted a 1 percent tax on restaurant meals at restaurants grossing over $400,000 per year in order to fund facilities and services for homeless people. The tax went into effect in October of 1993. The meal tax plan contemplates building emergency shelters and transitional and permanent housing in order to create a system with a "continuum of care" approach. Although the allocation of funding has been controversial, the tax provides an excellent example of how a local government can raise a large amount of money for needed services in a relatively painless way.

Some police departments have enacted programs which train officers to deal with homeless people in a constructive way or through which officers actually provide outreach to homeless people.[47] Cities have provided services and alternative accommodations for homeless people residing in public places.[48] Voucher programs have been established whereby people give vouchers instead of cash to panhandlers.[49] While not all of these programs are perfect, they are certainly preferable to law enforcement responses.

A common thread which runs through many of these alternatives is cooperation between cities and businesses on the one hand and homeless people and their advocates on the other. These are exactly the groups that are usually polarized by criminalization campaigns. Some of the relationships underlying this cooperation were actually forged in the context of attempts to enact anti-homeless legislation. However, such attempts are far more likely to destroy or preclude the formation of these relationships than to foster them. Cities interested in responding proactively to the problem of homelessness ought to be looking for ways to build these bridges instead of burning them.

CONCLUSION

The recent increase in anti-homeless laws and ordinances presents a major threat to homeless people. Like everyone else, homeless people should be expected to obey the law. Governments, however, act inhumanely, and frequently unconstitutionally, when they specifically target homeless people through unequal enforcement of existing laws or through the criminalization of innocent conduct which is unavoidable for homeless people. Moreover, in enacting, enforcing, and defending such measures in court, cities not only waste scarce resources, foster divisiveness and divert attention from proactive responses, they also make it more difficult for homeless people to break the cycle of homelessness. Cities, homeless people, businesses, advocates, and law enforcement agencies should make every effort to work together to promote proactive solutions to the problem, rather than battling over anachronistic, counterproductive reactions.

ENDNOTES

1. This chapter is in large part based on information contained in and research conducted for the National Law Center on Homelessness and Poverty's three

reports on the subject of anti-homelessness laws and policies: *No Homeless People Allowed* (1994), *The Right to Remain Nowhere* (1993), and *Go Directly to Jail* (1991). A shorter version of this chapter will appear in *The Journal of Intergroup Relations.*

2. Wright, J. and Devine, J., "Housing Dynamics of the Homeless: Implications for a Count," *American Journal of Orthopsychiatry, 65(3),* 320, 328 July, 1995; Burt, M., "Critical Factors in Counting the Homeless," *American Journal of Orthopsychiatry, 65(3),* 334, 335 July 1995.

3. Wright and Devine at 327.

4. Burt at 336.

5. Link, B. et al., "Lifetime and Five-Year Prevalence of Homelessness in the United States: New Evidence on an Old Debate." *American Journal of Orthopsychiatry, 65(3),* 347, 353 July 1995.

6. United States Conference of Mayors, "A Status Report on Hunger and Homelessness in America's Cities: 1994" 2, 1994.

7. For a detailed discussion of this trend, see: National Law Center on Homelessness and Poverty, *No Homeless People Allowed,* December 1994.

8. Simon, Harry, "Towns Without Pity: A Constitutional and Historical Analysis of Official Efforts to Drive Homeless Persons from American Cities," 66 *Tulane L. Rev.,* 631, 635–638, March 1992.

9. *Id.* at 635, 637; *Papachristou v. Jacksonville,* 405 U.S. 156, 161 (1972).

10. Simon at 637–38.

11. *Id.* at 638–640.

12. *Id.* 639–40, n. 55.

13. *Edwards v. California,* 314 U.S. 160, 177 (1941).

14. *Shapiro v. Thompson,* 394 U.S. 618, 629–30 (1969). Similarly, the Court in *Maricopa Hospital v. Maricopa County,* 415 U.S. 250 (1974) struck down a county durational residency requirement for the provision of medical care to indigents. The Court held that medical care was "as much a 'basic necessity of life' to an indigent as welfare assistance" and that therefore its denial, like the denial in *Shapiro,* was an impermissible penalty on interstate travel. *Id.* at 259.

15. *Papachristou v. Jacksonville,* 405 U.S. 156, 161 (1972).

16. *Id.* at 162.

17. *Id.* at 166, quoting *Winters v. New York,* 333 U.S. 507, 540, (1948) (Frankfurter, J., dissenting).

18. *Id.* at 171.

19. *Kolender v. Lawson,* 461 U.S. 352 (1983).

20. *Id.*

21. *Johnson v. City of Dallas,* Brief of Appellants, 5th Cir. No. 94-10875, 22 (December 19, 1994).

22. *Tobe v. City of Santa Ana,* 94 Daily Journal D.A.R. 1449, 1450 (1994), (quoting *Vagrants,* Municipal Memorandum, June 16, 1988), rev'd 95 Daily Journal D.A.R. 5239.

23. Di Rado, Alicia, "City Takes New Tack to Roust Homeless," *Los Angeles Times,* July 1, 1993, at B7, quoting Harry Simon (Legal Aid Attorney); Witter, Jere,

"No Place in Their Hearts for the Homeless," *Los Angeles Times,* April 22, 1993, at B11. Eng. Lily, "Santa Ana Homeless Suit Settled," *Los Angeles Times* (Orange County edition), February 6, 1990.

24. *Hinsley v. City of Santa Ana,* No. 636360 (California Superior Court Orange County 1990).

25. Santa Ana Ordinance NS-2160.

26. *Pottinger v. City of Miami,* 810 F. Supp. 1551, 1561-5 (S.D. Fla. 1992).

27. The Supreme Court held in *Robinson v. California,* 370 U.S. 660 (1962), that the Eighth Amendment forbids the criminalization of involuntary status.

28. *Johnson v. City of Dallas,* No. 94-10875, slip. op. (5th Circuit August 23, 1995).

29. *Patton v. Baltimore City,* Civil No. S 93-2389, Memorandum Opinion at 52–53, (D.Md. August 19, 1994).

30. *Joyce v. City of San Francisco,* 846 F. Supp 843 (N.D. Ca. 1994); *Joyce,* Order, No. C-93-4149 DLJ, (N.D. Ca. August 18, 1995) (granting summary judgment).

31. 810 F. Supp. at 1578–1583.

32. *Joyce,* 846 F. Supp. at 860; *Joyce,* Order at 15 (noting that the Supreme Court has only applied strict scrutiny under a right to travel analysis where the law in question facially discriminates between residents and nonresidents).

33. *No Homeless People Allowed* at 77.

34. *Roulette v. City of Seattle,* 850 F. Supp. 1442 (W.D. Washington 1994). The Court also rejected a substantive due process claim (holding that the ordinance is rationally related to the city's legitimate interests in ensuring pedestrian safety and protecting the economic vitality of commercial areas), a vagueness claim (holding that the prohibition and the enumerated exceptions are sufficiently specific), and an equal protection claim (finding no facial discrimination and no evidence that the city council was targeting homeless people).

35. *Berkeley Community Health Project v. City of Berkeley,* No. C 95-0665 CW (N.D. Ca. 1995).

36. *Streetwatch v. AMTRAK,* 94 CIV 4254 (CBM) (S.N.Y. 1995).

37. Santa Ana Ordinance NS-2160.

38. *Loper v. New York City Police Department,* 999 F.2d 699 (2nd Cir. 1993); *Heathcott v. Las Vegas Metro. Police Officers,* CV-S-93-045-LDG (D. Nev. 1994), *Blair v. Shanahan,* 775 F. Supp. 1315 (N.D. Cal 1991). *Blair* also held that a blanket ban on panhandling violated the Equal Protection Clause because the law's distinction between beggars and those who initiate conversations not involving requests for money was content-based discrimination that was not narrowly tailored to serve substantial state interests in prohibiting threats. *Blair* at 1325.

39. City of Milwaukee Ordinances, 106-1.1.

40. *Routlette v. City of Seattle,* 850 F. Supp. 1442 (W.D. Washington 1994). The Court did strike down the "circumstances" section of the ordinance, which had listed various circumstances to consider in determining whether there was an intent to intimidate. Since the Court had limited construction of the ordinance to only prohibit "threats" and since the section described some speech which was clearly protected, the Court found that the section rendered the law both vague and overbroad and had to be struck down. *Id.* at 1453–4.

41. *Patton* at 55–69.

42. *Berkeley Community Health Project v. City of Berkeley,* No. C 95-0665 CW (N.D. Ca. 1995); *Church of the Soldiers of the Cross of Christ v. City of Riverside,* No CV 94-8047 LGB (C.D. Ca. 1995).

43. *No Homeless People Allowed* at 32–33.

44. *Id.* at 43–44.

45. See: e.g., Smolowe, Jill, "Giving the Cold Shoulder," *Time,* 28–31, December 6, 1993; Ferguson, Sarah, "Us vs. them: America's growing frustration with the homeless," *Utne Reader,* 50–55, Sept./Oct. 1990; Ifill, Gwen, "Sympathy Wanes for Homeless," *Washington Post,* A6, May 21, 1990.

46. Toro, Paul and Manrique, Manuel, National Public Opinion Poll, Wayne State University (data from Spring 1994). Interestingly, this percentage varies very little between Republicans and Democrats. *Id.* Another poll has placed this percentage as high as 81%. *Business Week/* Harris Poll, *Business Week,* November 1, 1994, p. 35.

47. *No Homeless People Allowed* at 103–106.

48. *Id.* at 112–113.

49. *Id.* at 97–103.

Chapter 4

THE DOUBLE-EDGED SWORD OF ADVOCACY FOR THE HOMELESS[1]

Kathleen Marie Quinn, Esq.

Have we reached that point in society's evolution where, in order to extend Fourth Amendment protection to the homeless to be free from unreasonable searches and seizures, we must also accept the existence and conditions of homelessness? In granting an expectation of privacy to a homeless man, the Connecticut Supreme Court, in *Connecticut v. Mooney,*[2] broke new ground in defining the constitutional rights of the homeless. Ironically, the court has pushed the homeless into an even further precarious position by finding that society has accepted homelessness as a cultural norm. *Connecticut v. Mooney* sought to clarify a fine point of constitutional law in that it further defines Fourth Amendment protections, though establishing a theoretical right for the homeless to be free from unreasonable search and seizure does little for the day-to-day plight of the homeless. Although courts have interpreted the Fourth Amendment[3] to protect people and privacy, and not simply property, from unreasonable search and seizure, the Connecticut ruling was the first in which the highest court of a state ruled that such rights pertain to the personal belongings left at "home" by the homeless.

I. *CONNECTICUT V. MOONEY,* A CASE DESCRIPTION

David Mooney, a homeless man, was tried for felony murder and robbery in the first degree. During his trial, Mooney filed a motion to suppress evidence that the police had obtained from a search of his personal property, specifically from a duffel bag and a cardboard box that he had kept in his "home," an area under a bridge. The trial court denied Mooney's motion, allowing in evidence obtained from this search that linked Mooney to the murder and robbery. Mooney was convicted and subsequently brought an appeal. The Connecticut Supreme Court held that the trial court should have granted the motion to suppress the evidence. Consequently, the supreme court reversed the lower court's judgment and remanded the case for a new trial.

A. Facts of the Case

David Mooney, an unemployed carpenter, had been living under a bridge abutment beneath a highway overpass by the State Street entrance ramp to route I-91 in New Haven, Connecticut, a piece of property owned by the state, for about a month prior to his arrest. A steep, crushed stone embankment and heavy underbrush separated the area in which Mooney lived from the I-91 entrance ramp. For about two weeks before setting up his home under the bridge, Mooney had lived beside a fence near the Trumbull Street entrance to I-91. When another homeless man moved in close by, Mooney left that location, presumably for reasons of privacy, and moved to the bridge abutment at the State Street area.

The jury could reasonably have found the following facts. On July 30, 1987, David Mooney took Mark Allen, to whom Mooney owed money for drugs, to the Branford, Connecticut condominium of Theodore Genovese, with whom Mooney claimed to have had a sexual relationship. The reason for the visit was for Mooney to pay the debt to Allen by stealing items of personal property from Genovese. Mooney told Allen to play along with the homosexual angle as a cover for Allen's gaining entry into Genovese's home. When Mooney and Allen arrived at the condominium, Genovese invited them in and offered them drinks. Mooney and the victim took a shower together, but after a certain amount of sexual contact, Mooney began beating Genovese. Allen pulled Mooney off the victim, but then left the bedroom to search the condominium for items to steal. Mooney then killed Genovese by strangling him with a cord. Allen fled the condominium, taking with him coins, a VCR, and the victim's car. Genovese's body was discovered on the floor of the bedroom the next day, July 31, 1987.

The police arrested Allen in connection with Genovese's murder on August 5, 1987. Allen admitted being in the condominium the day of the murder and stealing the various items, but denied involvement in the murder. In statements to the police, Allen implicated Mooney in Genovese's murder, and the police subsequently obtained an arrest warrant for Mooney and arrested him on the night of August 5, 1987.

At the hearing on Mooney's motion to suppress, the parties disclosed the following facts. While Mooney was in custody following his arrest, Detective Anthony Morro of the Branford Police Department met Mooney's girlfriend shortly after midnight on August sixth. Morro asked her to take him to the place where Mooney had been living at the time of the murder. After scrambling up the embankment, Morro searched the area and found a blanket that Mooney used as a mattress, a sleeping bag, a closed cardboard box, a suitcase, a closed duffel bag, and some trash. To shield them from public sight, Mooney had placed all of the items up on the metal and cement beams of the highway support structure, using the beams as shelves, with the exception of the blanket, duffel bag, and trash, which were lying on the ground. Detective Morro opened the duffel bag on the ground and found a paper bag inside that contained around $700 in coins.

Rather than searching any of the other items at that time, Morro contacted the Branford police evidence officer and requested that he come to the scene, tag the various items and bring them to the police department where they were then opened and searched. The state subsequently admitted into evidence at the trial the cardboard box that contained a size 38 belt, the coins, a pair of bloodstained white pants, and pieces of jewelry that were all in the duffel bag. Aside from the belt, which Mooney asserted belonged to a drinking companion who had left it on a park bench, Mooney claimed ownership of all of these items.

At the trial, the state succeeded in connecting Mooney to Genovese's murder by introducing items that the police had seized from Mooney's closed containers—including the white, bloodstained pants and the size 38 belt (the same size as worn by the victim). Mark Allen identified the pants as those worn by Mooney on the day of the murder.

During the month that Mooney lived under the bridge abutment, he was the sole occupant of that area. Mooney slept at the site in the evenings and would leave the area daily, but not before securing his belongings in the same manner in which the police had found them up on the girders, so that people at the bottom of the embankment could not see the items. Though hiding the items in this manner afforded a degree of privacy, Mooney acknowledged that not only had a highway worker clearing brush stumbled upon him one day but also that there was always the possibility that someone else could enter that area owned by the state.

Faced with these facts, the Connecticut Supreme Court turned to an analysis of constitutional law to determine whether David Mooney could legitimately claim Fourth Amendment protection against the search and seizure of his personal property.

B. The Opinion

Though Mooney based his claim on both the Fourth Amendment of the Constitution of the United States and article 1, § 7 of the Connecticut Constitution, the court limited their consideration to Mooney's claim under the federal Constitution. Mooney made two claims in his appeal. First, he claimed that his Fourth Amendment rights were violated when the police invaded his "home" without a warrant—a claim based on his condition of homelessness. Second, he asserted a more narrow claim that he had a reasonable expectation of privacy in his duffel bag and cardboard box, located under the bridge abutment, that the police violated when they searched through his personal effects without first obtaining a warrant.

In Connecticut, as elsewhere, successful invocation of Fourth Amendment protection requires a defendant to establish that the area the defendant wishes protected can support a legitimate expectation of privacy. Courts look at each case to determine whether this expectation legitimately exists. The Connecticut Supreme Court used a two-part inquiry to make the determination of whether Mooney could establish a legitimate expectation of privacy: "first, whether the individual has exhibited an actual subjective expectation of privacy, and second, whether that expectation is one society recognizes as reasonable." The court acknowledged that Mooney had manifested a subjective expectation of privacy in the actions he took. The question then became whether Mooney could establish the second prong of the test, an expectation of privacy that society is prepared to recognize as reasonable. The court looked at a number of cases that each examined the place that was searched in a fact-specific inquiry to determine whether the defendants' expectation of privacy was reasonable.

Propounding a theme from *United States v. Taborda*[4] to which they would repeatedly refer, the Connecticut Supreme Court emphasized that for a place to be protected by the Fourth Amendment, society must be prepared, because of its *code of values* and its *notions of custom and civility,* to give deference to a manifested expectation of privacy. The court also thought that this determination of what is reasonable may involve a balancing of conflicting interests. After establishing these initial influences, the court then proceeded to examine, first, the broad claim of Fourth Amendment protection in the area under the bridge abutment, and second, the narrower claim of Fourth Amendment protection in the duffel bag and cardboard box.

Expectation of Privacy in the Bridge Abutment Area

Mooney's broad claim of Fourth Amendment protection in the area in which he lived rested solely upon his homelessness. Mooney argued that he had "exclusive possession" of the area during the time he lived there, given that he departed from the spot each morning to wash in a nearby reservoir, taking care not to be seen whenever he left. He left behind his Walkman, his cassettes and hundreds of dollars in coins he kept in his duffel bag—money, he said, that came from tips that his girlfriend earned at a nearby restaurant. He claimed that his property was always undisturbed when he returned. Mooney asserted that he was therefore entitled to no less privacy under the Fourth Amendment than more fortunate members of society. The state countered that since the area falls under the "open fields doctrine,"[5] and because Mooney was in effect a trespasser on state land with the area in which he lived accessible to anyone who happened along, the area was incapable of sustaining the privacy interest that Mooney asserted.

The court stated that they did not need to decide whether the area under the bridge abutment in which Mooney lived could reasonably support a legitimate expectation of privacy, presumably because the court had established a way to resolve the case based on Mooney's other claim of a reasonable expectation of privacy in his closed containers. Nevertheless, the court spent a great deal of effort analyzing the issue, and even went so far as to say that they assumed the state's arguments that Fourth Amendment protection of the area *must* fail.

The court identified two factors from a variety of cases that would indicate circumstances when society would not be prepared to recognize a defendant's expectation of privacy in a particular place: where the person is a trespasser, and when the area is readily accessible to animals, children, scavengers, snoops, and other members of the public. Though the above factors were relevant, the court stated that they were "helpful guides" and were not to be "undertaken mechanistically" as "ends in themselves." The court insisted that society would look at all the circumstances of each case, with these factors simply to be considered among the totality of the circumstances, to determine if the expectation of privacy is a reasonable one.

Because the court found for Mooney on the basis of the narrower claim, they did not expressly decide whether Mooney's broad claim in the bridge abutment area's protection was valid, although they assumed it was not. By developing the discussion in the manner that they did, however, the court left open the possibility that under a different fact-specific inquiry, they might find that a homeless person's "home" came under Fourth Amendment protection from warrantless searches.

Expectation of Privacy in the Containers

Mooney's narrower claim that he maintained an expectation of privacy in the closed containers, namely the duffel bag and cardboard box, found merit with the court. The court held that the Fourth Amendment applied to the unique factual circumstances of this case, where the closed containers were found by the police in a secluded place that they knew the defendant regarded as his home, where the defendant's absence from that place at the time of the search was due to his arrest and custody by the police, and where the purpose of the search was to obtain evidence of the crimes for which he was in custody. This narrower claim did not rest solely on Mooney's homelessness, as his broader claim did, but also relied on the nature of the containers and the circumstances surrounding their search.

Before establishing their holding, however, the court spent a fair amount of time delineating what the claim did *not* involve: (1) claims of reasonable expectation of privacy in any of Mooney's effects except his duffel bag and cardboard box, from which the evidence used at trial was obtained; (2) claims of expectation of privacy of homeless people in goods and effects that they have on their person or "under [their] immediate control"; (3) claims for Fourth Amendment protection of goods and effects of all the homeless, regardless of circumstances; (4) whether the police, with probable cause, were entitled to seize and preserve the containers while they secured the warrant; and (5) under what circumstances the police may search closed containers discovered in public places for purposes other than searching for evidence.

a. Container Cases. *Mooney* relied on a line of cases establishing that when a person places personal effects inside luggage or other appropriately closed containers, the individual manifests an expectation of privacy in the contents of these containers. The court felt confronted with a tension to balance the deference typically afforded by society to privacy in appropriately closed containers on one hand, and on the other, the principle that property left in public places generally cannot sustain Fourth Amendment protection.

The court examined a number of cases in which defendants claimed to have Fourth Amendment protection in their containers.[6] The court concluded that the Fourth Amendment affords protection to containers that are intended as repositories of personal effects. The "place" invaded, therefore, is the interior, the contents.

Nevertheless, the Connecticut court, though acknowledging that a broad reading of these cases would provide "conclusive support" of Mooney's claim, chose not to rely on them. Instead, the court distinguished them because in each of those cases, when the challenged search occurred, the owner was either accompanying the container, or the owner had entrusted the container to someone for safekeeping or for another particular purpose, or the container was left in a place that had a reasonable expectation of privacy.

The court stated, however, that though these cases do not compel a conclusion that Mooney had a reasonable expectation of privacy in the contents of his box and bag, neither do they preclude such a conclusion. At this point, the court referred back to the tension it felt it must resolve, and then tipped the scales toward the deference, the "weighty interest," society has in the expectation of privacy in the contents of luggage and other closed containers.

b. Abandonment Cases. The court then turned to a line of cases discussing abandoned property. The court affirmed that abandonment in the search and seizure context is essentially the abandonment not of the property itself but of the reasonable expectation of privacy in that property.

The court cited a number of cases[7] to support the proposition that it is relevant whether the defendant manifested by conduct an intent to "shed, albeit temporarily," the expectation of privacy in the property. The court admitted that, at first glance, these cases throw weight to the state's arguments against Mooney's claim of privacy in his containers. As with the line of container cases, however, the court insisted that these cases do not compel the conclusion that Mooney retained no expectation of privacy in his duffel bag and cardboard box. The court distinguished these cases from the facts of *Mooney* because, first, none involved a homeless defendant's luggage in a secluded area that the police knew the defendant took to be a home and searched after defendant was in custody; second, none gave any indication that the defendants raised or that the courts considered the independent question of privacy rights in the interior of the containers; and third, most of the abandonment cases involve an element of conduct on the part of the defendant that manifested the defendant's intent to relinquish any expectation of privacy in the luggage.

Further, the court distinguished *Mooney* from *United States v. Oliver* because the *Oliver* Court declared that open fields—or the marijuana plants growing in them—were not "effects" within the meaning of the Fourth Amendment, and effects were at issue in *Mooney*. The court also distinguished *Mooney* from *California v. Greenwood* on the simple principle that in *Greenwood* the defendants had exposed their property— trash bags—to the public by placing them at the curb *for the express purpose of conveying it to a third party.*

The court made the observation that the balancing of interests—society's fundamental interest in preserving the constitutional right to privacy when weighed against society's legitimate interest in law enforcement— tipped the scales in Mooney's favor as well. The court noted that there would have been "no significant impairment" of the law enforcement interest by requiring the police to have obtained the warrant before searching Mooney's effects.

In its summary, the court returned to the question of whether, under the fact-specific inquiry into the circumstances of Mooney's case, society would be prepared, by virtue of its code of values and notions of custom and civility, to grant Mooney an expectation of privacy in his duffel bag and box. The court concluded that, given the conditions of homelessness and the other circumstances in Mooney's case, notions of custom and civility dictated that society was indeed ready to take such a step.

C. The Dissent

The dissenting judges did not support the majority's holding that Mooney could have a reasonable expectation of privacy in his belongings under the bridge. First, the dissent explained their agreement with the majority's assessment that there was no expectation of privacy in the abutment area. The dissent emphasized that what has been knowingly exposed to, or is readily accessible to, the public does not carry any Fourth Amendment protection from unreasonable search and seizure.

Because the public had ready access to the area under the bridge, and because they viewed Mooney as a trespasser on state property, the dissenting judges concluded that Mooney could have no reasonable expectation of privacy there.

In turning to the issue of whether Mooney could have a reasonable expectation of privacy in the containers, the dissenting judges asserted that this issue was closely linked to whether he could have had any expectation of privacy in the abutment area itself when he left the containers there. Unable to separate the container issue from the area issue, the dissent concluded that because Mooney had no legitimate expectation of privacy in the area under the bridge, he could not have had any legitimate expectation of privacy in anything he left there unattended, whether a closed container or not. Finding no support for adding a "circumstances of the searched" prong to the analysis, the dissent dismissed the fact-specific circumstances of Mooney's case that the majority had used to distinguish his situation from the line of abandonment cases.

II. CONTRASTING THE MAJORITY AND MINORITY OPINIONS

The majority and dissenting opinions, in essence, split on the issue of abandonment. Did Mooney, in voluntarily departing the area—concededly public property—and in leaving all his worldly goods behind, also voluntarily relinquish his expectation of privacy in those personal effects? The dissenting judges found no merit in Mooney's claim because when they considered the abandonment issue they were unable to keep separate, as the majority opinion had done, Mooney's two claims: one for Fourth Amendment protection of the bridge abutment area and the other for Fourth Amendment protection of the closed containers.

The dissent felt it was a necessary conclusion that because the bridge area was a public place, Mooney could not have had a reasonable expectation of privacy there, and consequently could not have had a reasonable expectation of privacy in the closed containers he left there. The dissenting opinion did some fast backpedaling on this issue, however, albeit buried in a footnote. The minority acknowledged that some containers left unattended in an area to which the public has access may warrant Fourth Amendment protection. Referring to *Kelly v. Florida*,[8] a case in which a defendant was found to have a reasonable expectation of privacy in a backpack attached to a bicycle left for ten minutes in a parking lot near some people, the dissent inferred that the circumstances of the *Kelly* case made it so unlikely that the backpack would be disturbed that an objectively reasonable expectation of privacy might arise. The dissent, however, did not provide any rationale as to why they would consider a backpack on a bicycle left for a short time in a public parking lot to hold any more an objectively reasonable expectation of privacy than a closed cardboard box hidden under a bridge abutment, hoisted up on the steel girders, for a long period of time.

The dissenting judges in *Mooney* would have been willing to concede that the circumstances of the items and public area may be considered in finding an objectively reasonable expectation of privacy; however, the majority took the analysis of the circumstances even one step further, specifically taking into consideration Mooney's *homeless state.* The minority argued that relying on Mooney's circumstance of homelessness would create a situation in which a homeless person leaving items at "home" would receive greater Fourth Amendment protection than someone who had a home but placed articles under the bridge abutment for other purposes. One wonders if the dissenters had to swallow hard before making such an ironic statement, ignoring the fact that the person with the home could simply leave the item at home and claim the same privileges the dissent argued they would be denied under the bridge abutment, an option not available to the homeless.

III. CONTRADICTIONS IN HOMELESS RIGHTS

The court in *Mooney,* in reaching its conclusion of law, asserted their unwillingness to reach a decision that would be premised on "the majestic equality of the laws which forbid rich and poor alike to sleep under bridges, to beg in the streets, and to steal bread."[9] In seeking to do justice by its decision, however, the court has also raised questions in the minds of advocates for the homeless regarding the effect that *Mooney* will have on the rights of the homeless.

A. *Mooney* As A Double-Edged Sword

While the Connecticut Supreme Court was deliberating *Connecticut v. Mooney,* many homeless activists hoped the court would establish a precedent that would extend Fourth Amendment protection to the makeshift homes of the homeless. Even though the court did not go quite that far, the finding that Mooney had an expectation of privacy in his personal possessions did expand rights of the homeless at a time when the United States Supreme Court had decided a series of cases tending to restrict Fourth Amendment protections. "It's a breath of fresh air to be going in the other direction," Mooney's attorney commented when the court's decision was announced. "It sends a message that the Constitution applies to everyone. The police here thought they could act with impunity because it was a homeless person, but the court said, no, that this was a human being and he was not without rights just because he couldn't afford a house."[10]

Some advocates for the homeless, however, even though they support Mooney's cause, see it as a double-edged sword, finding its broader impact disturbing. Many advocates for the homeless consider a freeway embankment—or an alleyway, a secluded heating grate, an obscure park bench—an unacceptable symbol of a home. Tim Harris, director of Jobs With Peace in Boston, a group that advocates more money for housing, health care, and education, has said, "It's a double-edged question: if it's not a home, the guy has no rights; if it is a home, we're saying it's okay for people to live under freeways. I don't think either of those answers are morally justifiable. It's a no-win situation."[11] Robert M. Hayes, founder of the National Coalition for the Homeless, considered the *Mooney* decision legally correct but called it a "miserable, wretched right to win" because of its suggestion of the social acceptance of homelessness as a fact of life, a fact that Hayes said "should be resisted to the grave."[12] Hayes recognized that the decision will protect some from further violations beyond those caused by homelessness itself, but felt little comfort in knowing that homeless people's possessions hold some Fourth Amendment protection when, as he puts it, "both the people and the possessions should be inside."[13]

Still other commentators asserted that for the court to conclude that Mooney's expectation of privacy in his makeshift home was illegitimate was to conclude that "only propertied people, who can afford to purchase or rent a residence, can legitimately expect the Government to respect their constitutional right to privacy in their abode by obtaining a search warrant before entering. The constitutional right to be free from illegitimate searches should not have to be purchased with mortgage payments or rent."[14]

B. Anti-Homeless Legislation

Police in cities across the country enforce legislation which prohibits people from sleeping on the streets or sidewalks, or remaining in public parks after hours. Consider, for example, *People v. Davenport*.[15] In *Davenport*, the county of Santa Barbara sought to uphold the constitutionality and enforcement of a municipal ordinance that provides: "It shall be unlawful for any person to sleep in (1) Any public park during the period of time from 10:00 pm to 6:00 am; (2) Any public street; (3) Any public parking lot or public area, improved or unimproved; or (4) Any public beach during the period of time from 10:00 pm to 6:00 am." The court of appeals overturned the municipal court's finding of unconstitutionality, stating, "it is clear that the sleeping to which this ordinance was directed was of the general kind, which enjoys no peculiar constitutional advantage. ... [T]he government can constitutionally prohibit overnight sleeping in public areas as part of its broad police powers." In effect, the ordinance bans sleeping in public in a manner effectively criminalizing homelessness.

Enforcing anti-homeless legislation, however, provides only a temporary solution to the perceived problems that the legislation seeks to assuage. Police arrest the homeless for minor offenses like sleeping in the park, but they generally release them after several hours. Enforcing these laws actually avoids solving the problem of homelessness because enforcement merely encourages the homeless to relocate from one city to another. Some cities have actively sought to further the relocation of the city's homeless onto someone else's shoulders by offering the homeless free, one-way airplane and bus tickets.[16]

The types of constitutional issues raised in cases like *Davenport* have received inconsistent judicial treatment. One approach is that of the *Davenport* court. Other courts have found such ordinances unconstitutional and struck them down as vague and overbroad.[17]

C. *Mooney* And Its Progeny

Connecticut v. Mooney was the first case that addressed the precise issue of Fourth Amendment protection in the personal property of the homeless. Other states' courts—such as Pennsylvania, Colorado, Washington, and New York—have cited *Mooney* only for the principle that there could be no legitimate expectation of privacy in a public area (*Mooney*'s first claim of privacy in the bridge abutment area). However, two different federal courts have cited to *Mooney* as a means of furthering the Fourth Amendment rights of the homeless.

In *United States v. Gooch*[18] the Ninth Circuit Court of Appeals held that a man whose only residence was a tent on a state campground had a reasonable expectation of privacy such that the warrantless search of the tent violated the Fourth Amendment. The court reached this result by analogizing the tent to a large movable, closed container, citing to *Mooney*, and relying on the same line of cases as had the *Mooney* court. The *Gooch* court went even further, holding that the closed tent itself, even though on public ground, was a "non-public" place for Fourth Amendment analysis purposes and as such was analogous to the defendant's residence. The court held that Gooch had a legitimate, if temporary, interest in his privacy even in this short-term dwelling.

In *Pottinger v. City of Miami*[19] the plaintiffs, in a class action suit on behalf of the city's 6,000 homeless, sought to stop the continual harassment and arrests of the homeless in downtown Miami. The complaint alleged that, immediately preceding a high-visibility event in the Miami area, the police for aesthetic purposes customarily arrest the homeless under the city's anti-homeless legislation, although the charges are never processed. The homeless also alleged that the police by custom and practice "sanitize" the city through the seizure and destruction of the personal property of the homeless, including identification, clothing, medication, food, bibles, and bedding. Though the court granted a preliminary injunction proscribing the destruction of the homelesses' property, the police continued in the practice. The court held the city of Miami in civil contempt for the burning and destruction of the homelesses' property that the city had performed in the name of "cleanup." And the court did not stop there.

The *Pottinger* plaintiffs did not challenge the facial validity of the ordinances themselves but instead contended that the city applied these laws to the homeless as a practice of driving them from public places. In addition to holding that the city's enforcement of the ordinances for the innocent conduct of the homeless violated the Eighth Amendment's prohibition against cruel and unusual punishment, and enforcement of such overbroad ordinances violated the homelesses' due process rights and infringed upon the homelesses' fundamental right to travel, the *Pottinger* court addressed the question of whether the homelesses' subjective expectation of privacy in their personal belongings was also objective.

In other words, did the homeless have a legitimate, reasonable expectation of privacy in their personal property such that these items were protected from unreasonable search and seizure under the Fourth Amendment. Relying heavily on an analysis of the *Mooney* decision, the court found that the interior of the homelesses' containers for their personal property—the last trace of privacy that the homeless have—did indeed warrant an expectation of privacy under the protection of the Fourth Amendment.

IV. CONCLUSION

As the *Mooney* court emphasized in their opinion, their holding applies to the unique factual circumstances of the case, where the closed containers were found by the police in a secluded place that they knew the defendant regarded as his home, where the defendant's absence from that place at the time of the search was due to his arrest and custody by the police, and where the purpose of the search was to obtain evidence of the crimes for which he was in custody. This decision is hardly a primer on expansive constitutional interpretation. Because the court tied the decision so specifically to the circumstances of the case, the impact for other homeless people in Connecticut and nationally over the long term remains unclear. Nevertheless, the opinion has received judicial notice by courts across the country and, at least in *Pottinger,* has been wielded as a sword for justice.

The *Mooney* court could have gone further, as the *Gooch* court did, if they had found a constitutionally protected interest in the bridge abutment area, or if they had specifically established that, although not applicable to Mooney's situation, they would be willing to concede other fact-specific situations in which the homeless would have Fourth Amendment protection in their "homes." Advocates for the homeless, however, fear that if society takes the step of finding acceptable that an alleyway or a space under a bridge abutment is a "home" deserving of privacy, then by corollary society will find homelessness acceptable and no longer seek a solution.

Connecticut v. Mooney asserted that the constitutional right to be free from unreasonable searches and seizures need not be purchased with rent or mortgage payments. Though homeless rights advocates may legitimately fear that the *Mooney* decision is a further indication of society's acceptance of homelessness as a cultural norm, one can argue that the role of the courts in this area is the protection of civil rights and not the resolution of the social problem of homelessness. Given that mandate, *Connecticut v. Mooney* was correctly decided. The major success of the case was in taking one small step toward refining individual civil rights apart from property ownership principles, helping to chip away at an obstacle the law tends to impose on the property-poor homeless.

ENDNOTES

1. This essay is an adaptation of a previous Note, *Connecticut v. Mooney and Expectation of Privacy: The Double-Edged Sword of Advocacy for the Homeless,* 13 *B.C. THIRD WORLD L.J.* 87 (1993), used with permission.

2. 218 Conn. 85, 588 A.2d 145, *cert. denied,* 502 U.S. 919 (1991).

3. "The right of the people to be secure in their persons, houses, papers, and effects, against unreasonable searches and seizures, shall not be violated, and no Warrants shall issue, but upon probable cause, supported by Oath or affirmation, and particularly describing the place to be searched, and the persons or things to be seized." U.S. CONST. amend. IV.

4. 635 F.2d 131, 138 (2d Cir. 1980) (holding that identifying items or activities inside a home by use of a telescope when those items or activities could not be identified from outside without the telescope impaired a legitimate expectation of privacy).

5. In *Oliver v. United States,* 466 U.S. 170 (1984), the United States Supreme Court reached the conclusion that open fields outside the immediate enclosure of a dwelling house could not hold a reasonable expectation of privacy because of their open, visible nature.

6. E.g., *United States v. Chadwick,* 433 U.S. 1 (1977) (striking down warrantless search of footlocker seized from automobile at time of arrest); *Ex Parte Jackson,* 96 U.S. 727 (1878) (holding sealed packages in mail cannot be opened without warrant); *Connecticut v. Edwards,* 214 Conn. 57, 570 A.2d 193 (1990) (holding backpack located in a temporary residence protected from warrantless search).

7. *California v. Greenwood,* 486 U.S. 35 (1988) (holding no reasonable expectation of privacy in trash bags left at curbside for trash collection); *United States v. Thomas,* 864 F.2d 843 (D.C. Cir. 1989) (holding no expectation of privacy in gym bag left in apartment building hallway); *United States v. Brown,* 473 F.2d 952 (5th Cir. 1973) (holding suitcase buried under chicken coop on abandoned farm was discarded and therefore fell within open field doctrine).

8. 536 So. 2d 1113 (Fla. App. 1988).

9. Quoting Anatole France's *The Red Lily,* 91 (Winifred Stephens trans., 1925).

10. Sean P. Murphy, *Ruling Recognizes Privacy Rights of Homeless: Connecticut Court Throws Out Murder Conviction,* Boston Globe, Mar. 19, 1991, at 19.

11. John H. Kennedy, *Is A Homeless Man's "Home" His Castle?,* Boston Globe, Jan. 13, 1991, at 29.

12. David Margolick, *Poverty and Privacy: Home, Sweet Niche?*, *N.Y. Times,* Nov. 17, 1990, at 25.

13. Kirk Johnson, *Property of a Homeless Man Is Private, Hartford Court Says, N.Y. Times,* Mar. 19, 1991, at B1.

14. Deborah A. Geier's Letter to the Editor (Assistant Professor of Law, Clev. St. U.), *N.Y. Times,* Dec. 4, 1990, at A30.

15. 176 Cal. App. 3d Supp. 10, 222 Cal. Rptr. 736 (App. Dep't. Super. Ct. 1985), *cert. denied,* 475 U.S. 1141–42 (1986).

16. Michele DiGirolamo, *Plan to Bus Homeless Out of Town Questioned,* UPI, Dec. 5, 1989, *available in* LEXIS, Nexis Library, UPI File (citing an Atlantic City, N.J. councilwoman's plan to give one-way bus tickets to homeless people); *Suburbs Shipping Their Homeless to Philadelphia,* UPI, Feb. 12, 1989, *available in* LEXIS, Nexis Library, UPI File (asserting that suburbs send homeless to Philadelphia against their will); Sally Johnson, *Homeless Get Ticket to Leave, N.Y. Times,* Nov. 20, 1988, at 52 (describing Vermont property owner's offer to fund one-way tickets for the homeless to leave town).

17. See, e.g., *Florida v. Penley,* 276 So. 2d 180, 181 (Fla. Dist. Ct. App. 1973), *cert. denied,* 281 So. 2d 504 (Fla. 1984) (striking down ordinance prohibiting sleeping upon or in any street, park, wharf, or other public place).

18. F.3d 673, 677 (9th Cir. 1993). The defendant in *Gooch* is not described as homeless, but the opinion states that the tent was his *only* residence.

19. 810 F. Supp. 1551 (S.D. Fla. 1992), *remanded for further clarification of Order for injunctive relief,* 40 F.3d 1155 (11th Cir. 1994).

Chapter 5

POLICE: THE FORGOTTEN SERVICE PROVIDER

Martha R. Plotkin and Tony Narr

A woman calls the police dispatcher to complain that her children came home frightened by several homeless men sitting on the benches or talking to themselves in the public park.

A local business owner calls police to complain that the homeless woman who sits on the public bench in front of his store makes his customers uncomfortable; he wants her moved.

Though the plight of those who live in our back alleys and parks rarely makes national headlines on a regular basis, scenarios such as these are common in even our smaller U.S. cities. And while shelters, food services and other agencies try to meet the demand for services that will benefit the homeless, police are still routinely called to "do something" about people living on the nation's streets.

Police encounter homeless people in many situations—when a homeless individual is victimized, intoxicated, in need of food or shelter, the subject of a nuisance complaint, or even a crime suspect.[1] Merchants often prod police to move the homeless away from their businesses, even when the homeless have violated no laws. Some members of the public expect police to drive the homeless from libraries, municipal parks and their own front walks, primarily because of citizens' fear of crime. Yet advocates for the homeless, some politicians, and those who live on the streets demand that police allow the homeless to share public spaces without fear of harassment. Police must often respond to these situations without adequate resources to properly meet the needs of the homeless person, and without clear authority. There is probably no better example of how complex the police function has become than the police response to the homeless. Police are expected to be problem solvers, social workers, employment counselors, order maintenance workers, fear-reduction experts, and mediators. Yet, they often lack the community resources and direction to adequately assume these roles.

58

How did the police become so involved with homeless-related matters? As the economy, political pressures and other forces have worked to reduce social services in most communities, police are called upon with increased frequency to fill the gaps in service provision. Whether or not police choose to be, they are routinely drawn into situations that involve the homeless. Police are often the only 24-hour emergency service providers in a community, and by default they must address these calls for assistance. When someone is concerned about the safety of a person who is homeless, or feels threatened by his or her presence, they often call the police first. Some police respond willingly, while others resist being immersed in situations that they feel would be better addressed by social workers or others who have the resources and training to properly handle a homeless-related problem.

But one has to question whether police are the best first responders when their role in the service provision network has been so poorly defined. It is unclear how far citizens, or even their own agencies, expect officers to go in solving problems or simply referring parties to social services. And how will the police response be viewed and shaped when the community has inadequate resources to support a proper response? Police are expected to uphold the law and to respond to the needs of the community. But when dealing with people who are homeless, these goals often conflict. To which segment of the community should they be most responsive? To politicians who advocate ordinances to ban panhandling or loitering but support liberal enforcement policies? To citizens who want the homeless moved out of their neighborhoods, even when no crime is committed? To advocates of the homeless who believe homeless people should be able to sleep in parks and use any other public space if they do not conduct illegal activity? As Melekian (1990) indicates, police officers are positioned between two opposing demands: "The demand for compassion often conflict[s] with the demand for enforcement."[2] Even when police define their role as helper or enforcer, they are often stymied by inadequate resources such as the lack of available shelters, food banks, mental health programs, and detoxification centers. It is not uncommon, for example, for shelters to require that clients be sober and not disruptive, leaving the police with few options for dealing with people who are homeless and under the influence of drugs or alcohol. And even when resources are available, their capacity, hours of operation and admittance rules all serve to limit police access to needed services.

This article is meant to clarify the conflicts and issues that police face, and to reveal some of the means that agencies use to address them. To understand the police response to people who are homeless, it is necessary to examine the political and legal climates in which police operate, their perceptions of the problem, and their current means for dealing with calls for service involving the homeless.

POLITICAL AND LEGAL CLIMATES

The public's tolerance for homeless-related problems has fluctuated widely over the last decade, evidenced by the enactment of ordinances banning loitering, panhandling and camping in common areas, followed by cycles of liberal then strong enforcement policies. Traditionally, police have dealt with strong enforcement policies by instituting "bus therapy"—that is, moving homeless people from one area or jurisdiction to another. But this practice has been widely criticized and minimized by police executives' orders. Some displacement still occurs, though on a smaller scale, to move street people from one area of the city to another. Today, police are developing more creative responses that address the underlying causes of calls for service. These responses, discussed in later sections, are developed despite the conflicting mandates police receive from citizens, elected officials and even their own agencies.

While police agencies are being encouraged to strictly enforce aggressive panhandling, public drinking and loitering ordinances by some segments of the community, other citizens are complaining that such enforcement is inhumane and in violation of homeless people's civil rights. Caught in a legal tug-of-war, police agencies and individual officers who enforce such ordinances are being criticized—even sued—for violating the rights of people who are homeless. In addition, in cities such as Santa Monica, prosecutors in the past have refused to prosecute offenses "related to economic status." Police actions against violators of ordinances related to life necessities, such as shelter and food, may not be supported by prosecutors. What message does it send police when they must enforce these ordinances but the charges will not be prosecuted? While lawsuits and lack of prosecutorial zeal may have a chilling effect on enforcement efforts, at the same time police are being pressured by some segments of the community to arrest the homeless who violate ordinances.

The political and legal realities of each community influence how police respond to calls involving people who are homeless. One reason why it is so difficult to study the police response is that the political and legal climates fluctuate often, prompting new police responses or suppressing old ones. The media often drives these changes by publicizing the plight of the homeless or by documenting a case in which a homeless person committed a crime. The police response is largely shaped by these mandates and expectations, as well as by police professionals' own vision of what their role should be.

POLICE PERCEPTIONS

To determine whether homeless-related police policies, practices and programs are successful, one must first understand the perceptions that drive police agencies' decisions to implement them. In 1991, with funding from the Robert Wood Johnson Foundation, the Police Executive Research Forum (PERF) began a study to properly gauge police perceptions about people who are homeless, the nature and extent of homeless-related problems and the police response.[3] The study included a survey of all municipal, county and consolidated law enforcement agencies serving populations over 50,000 or employing 100 or more sworn officers.[4] More than 520 agencies participated in this information-gathering effort.[5] Fourteen jurisdictions were then selected for further on-site study, based on their self-reported survey findings that they met several criteria including large numbers of homeless-related calls for service, the perception of homelessness as a major one for police in that jurisdiction, and a working program, policy or training program that specifically addressed the needs of people who live on the street. The survey's major findings are detailed in the discussion that follows.

POLICE CONTACTS

Many of the perceptions that police hold about the homeless and about their response to that population are based on the type and number of contacts they have with homeless people. The survey respondents held a wide range of perceptions about the homeless—from seeing homeless people as victims of a bad economy and other environmental factors to seeing them as lazy and homeless by choice. These perceptions were formed largely through encounters with the types of homeless people who are most often brought to police attention: victims, suspects, offenders, people exhibiting unusual behavior, and subjects of nuisance calls.

When asked to rate how frequently their departments came into contact with homeless people exhibiting certain characteristics such as substance dependency, physical or mental disabilities, and other traits, respondents indicated that their more frequent contacts were with alcohol-dependent (66.9%) and drug-dependent (51.3%) street people, followed by those who appeared to have mental disabilities (48.0%). More than 40 percent of the respondents also indicated that they came in contact with the homeless as offenders (41.7%), while only 27.9 percent of the respondents dealt with homeless people as victims. Homeless families, physically disabled street people, and juveniles had far fewer frequent contacts with the law enforcement respondents.

The police perception of a proper *law enforcement role* in responding to homeless people may also be driven largely by the kinds of contacts police have with that population. When asked for the three most common reasons police make contact with the homeless, the vast majority of respondents indicated calls from citizens (92.3%). These calls may be complaints of nuisances, panhandling, public drunkenness, trespassing, or loitering, or they may involve concern for the safety of the homeless person or others. The second and third most common impetuses for police action included officer observations (82.3%) and calls from the business community (74.3%). Each type of call may dictate a different police response. As for the business community, several respondents raised concerns such as:

> [Homeless people represent] nuisance complaints and a thorn in the side of downtown merchants who expect us to somehow make them go away and not panhandle customers.

> I am very concerned about the relationship that has developed between the business community, the [rest of the] community, and the homeless. The homeless community is growing, as is the rift between the [rest of the] citizens and the homeless. The police are often caught in the middle. The anger seems to be growing to a head in my community. I am quite concerned about this aspect.

Only 16 percent of all survey respondents indicated that contact was initiated by homeless people, far less than by the business community. This raises questions about whether police are perceived as being in a position to provide necessary resources, whether the homeless have a fear of reporting or fear of being institutionalized, and whether there are other issues regarding police/street person relations that inhibit street people from initiating contact. Less than 10 percent of all respondents felt that contact was made largely because of observations from other officers, observations by superiors or observations by elected officials. Additional comments indicate that contact was occasionally made because of an officer's personal experiences, requests from families, or calls for assistance from emergency medical and ambulance workers.

The following reports from follow-up site visits illustrate the nature of police contacts with the homeless and how police in various jurisdictions have dealt with sometimes conflicting messages from businesses, politicians, residents and advocates for the homeless.[6]

"Skid row," concentrated in an area known as Central City East, is located within the Central Police Area of **Los Angeles.** An analysis of Los Angeles' downtown population estimated that the rate of homelessness per 1,000 in the vicinity of Center City East was 271.47. According to this analysis, the homeless population in this 55-square block area was mostly male and exceeded 15,000 people.

More than the lack of funds, unemployment, domestic disputes and mental illness, the greatest cause of homelessness was reported to be substance abuse. Even with 5,300 short-term housing units available in the Central City East vicinity, some estimates indicated that over 7,000 people slept on the streets nightly.

Assigned to the Central Police Area, a team of one sergeant and nine police officers made up the "East Side Detail." The team had one responsibility: coordinating the department's response to incidents related to street people in the "skid row" area. These officers recognized that there were many locations where the homeless congregated within their area; however, they felt the number of homeless people sleeping in the streets was often exaggerated. One location, predominately a warehouse area, had the largest concentration of people sleeping in the streets. Officers estimated that the number of homeless people sleeping in "skid row" usually did not exceed 500 per night. Downtown merchants complained of the impact on business caused by the presence of these street people, and employees in the warehouse district felt threatened by homeless encampments.

The movement of large groups of homeless people was often politically charged. Homeless encampments were not dispersed but were moved from one location to another. The East Side Detail enforced movements only on the approval of several city officials reacting to considerable "not in my back yard" pressure from the area business owners.

The East Side Detail was directed to support street maintenance crews in their cleanup efforts, handle calls for service related to homeless people, provide referrals and transportation, curtail open-air drug sales and generally keep the peace. However, the police response to complaints about the presence of the homeless had changed over time. Judgments against the police department for destruction of homeless people's personal property while removing encampments led to a city regulation that no encampment could be disbanded until an in-depth approval process was complete. Although the East Side Detail maintained a positive presence in the area, unit officers were somewhat limited in their ability to intervene unless criminal activity was involved.

The enormity of homeless-related problems in the skid row area dictated the level of enforcement action that could be taken. For example, little could have been accomplished by enforcing code violations like "blocking a driveway." However, each weekday, officers assisted city maintenance crews by moving encampment residents from one side of the street to the other, allowing workers to collect and haul away the daily accumulation of debris. Drug interdiction was limited to observed sales. Stopping the large number of suspected dealers and individual users was a near impossible task.

In contrast, police in **Joliet, Illinois,** where the number of homeless people and the extent of homeless-related problems were significantly lower than in Los Angeles, made an arrangement with local businesses to allow merchants to make complaints without leaving their shops. The department also made arrangements for business owners to sign agreements that allowed officers to enforce "no trespassing" ordinances without the store owner signing a complaint form each time someone was on business property. Eventually, the number of homeless people living in the downtown area dropped.

In **Santa Monica, California,** the police department created the Office of Special Enforcement and its Homeless Enforcement Liaison Program (HELP) to address the police response to homeless people from both the enforcement and treatment perspectives. During its first month of operation, the unit responded to 231 homeless-related calls.

HELP unit members established relationships with merchants, social service providers, citizens and others who could provide information useful in addressing homeless-related concerns. Increased police presence reduced the conflict between the business community and the panhandlers. Street people avoided privately owned doorways of businesses in hopes that they would not be moved until midnight, when officers began enforcement of a "no camping" ordinance. PERF study team members noticed a significant difference in the congregation of street people when officers were in the area. That is, police presence affected the group's behavior. Once the community realized there was a special unit to handle homeless problems, the HELP unit received more calls for service.

Two business communities in **Montgomery County, Maryland** approached the homeless problem in quite different ways. Officers recall that in 1980 there was one known homeless person. By 1992, the county's homeless population was estimated to be nearly 1,000.

A Community Services Officer (CSO) was assigned to each of the department's district stations to coordinate homeless issues. That position was established to coordinate the flow of information among the police district, homeless service providers and the homeless. CSOs were required to attend all community meetings regarding the homeless.

In one district, relationships among the CSO and members of county agencies, community support and outreach groups, and service providers (soup kitchens, etc.) were reported to be outstanding. The degree to which the CSO was involved in problem solving and the availability of a wide range of resources in that district led to numerous success stories about homeless people who were helped by various county and community programs and services. However, it was noted that in that district, the commitment, involvement and contributions of the religious and business communities as well as the general public were significant. The CSO was only one of a number of active players in the community who were committed to resolving homeless-related problems.

In a neighboring district also in the county, the concerns of the business community regarding a large concentration of street people in a commercial area led to a different police response. Due to the availability of shelter, food and services in this district, the area attracted a large number of homeless. The district commander estimated that in 1989, there were over 400 people, mostly younger men, living on the streets of the district. In response to complaints of citizen fear, declining business activity and illegal conversion of vacant buildings to housing by the homeless, a task force was formed to address the problem. A temporary team of twelve officers formed the Special Combined Action Team (SCAT). In 30 days, this high-profile unit made contact with 340 street people. These contacts, and subsequent "wanted checks," identified several wanted individuals. Many other homeless people, who were not originally from the district but were drawn from other jurisdictions because of the quality of services, no longer frequented the area. Forty-four vacant buildings were boarded up as a result of the team's effort, and a permanent substation, housing nine officers, was established in the area frequented by homeless people. The substation was reported to be a disincentive for the criminally inclined to remain in the area, and served as a location where others could obtain information about county programs and services. The number of homeless people in this downtown area dropped to about 100, largely through displacement.

Police Descriptions of Street People and Related Issues

"The overwhelming majority of street people in this city have at least one of the [conditions listed in the survey]. Many have numerous addictions and utilize the shelters when they haven't been able to steal enough property or money to purchase whatever they need to entertain their habit. They mix with the truly homeless and mentally disabled so they have a place to hide after committing their crimes."

Survey respondents were asked to rate their level of agreement with some stereotypical statements about street people and crime. Table 1 details their responses.

Nearly 69 percent of the respondents believed that street people in their jurisdictions are viewed predominantly as a police problem by the public. This finding is important given the results of other survey questions that indicate police believe the community does not understand the police role and that police are unclear of their role in non-enforcement situations. The survey results also indicate that nearly 65 percent of the respondents felt that the police department is expected to remove street people from the streets. Removal may be requested absent the commission of a crime. "We frequently fail to meet public expectations [in removing street people from the streets]. We believe in behaving legally. At times policing requires an anti-majoritarian, pro-individual rights bias," said one respondent.

Police respondents overwhelmingly agreed that street people are generally viewed as a public nuisance (92.4%). One respondent stated, "The [survey] statements [about street people] are broad generalizations and do not apply to all street people. Many are alcoholic, drug abusers, or mentally ill, but not all. Some are involved in crime, but most complaints are nuisance-related."

Nearly 75 percent of the respondents felt that street people pose a health hazard in the community due to their living conditions. It is

Table 1
POLICE PERCEPTIONS OF STREET PEOPLE AND RELATED CRIME

	Agree	Disagree	N
The street people in my jurisdiction are regularly involved in property crimes.	46.6%	53.5%	490
The street people in my jurisdiction regularly appear to have alcohol abuse problems.	88.1%	11.9%	496
The street people in my jurisdiction are regularly involved in drug abuse.	59.3%	40.6%	487
The street people in my jurisdiction regularly appear to be mentally disabled.	64.9%	35.1%	492
The street people in my jurisdiction are viewed predominantly as a police problem.	68.9%	31.1%	495
The police department makes a concerted effort to locate street people in my area.	34.7%	65.3%	495
The police department is expected to remove street people from the streets.	64.1%	35.9%	494
Street people are generally viewed as a public nuisance.	92.4%	7.7%	496
Police are the only agency in my jurisdiction responsible for street people.	31.5%	68.5%	492
The presence of street people increases the fear of crime among citizens.	92.7%	7.2%	498
Street people pose a health hazard in the community due to their living conditions.	74.6%	25.4%	495
Street people are generally ignored in this jurisdiction.	27.7%	72.3%	491

Note: Percentages reflect the proportion of respondents answering each question.

unclear whether the respondents felt that the quality of life sustained by people living on the streets is a public health hazard to the homeless population alone, to the greater community or to the officer. In any case, perceiving the homeless as a public health risk adds to the fear and misperception about this group. One respondent commented, "Their lifestyles attract rats, lice, and other vermin." Another respondent suggested, "[I]t is a perception of some of the public that a health hazard is very real, especially in places transients hang out." Another commentator stated, "Contagious diseases such as [t]uberculosis and AIDS seem to be of chief concern to the officer on patrol as he or she is dealing personally with the homeless on a day-to-day basis."

Another factor that bears on police perceptions about the homeless, and the proper law enforcement response, is citizens' fear of crime. More than 90 percent of the respondents agreed that the presence of street people increases the fear of crime among citizens. That fear may or may not be based on actual incidents or genuine threats to the public. The fear of crime is not limited to personal harm but to fear of theft and burglary by street people, though over 50 percent of the respondents to this survey disagreed that street people are regularly involved in property crimes in their jurisdictions. Anecdotal data revealed that many of those victimized are within the homeless community. "While many are involved in property crimes, what we see is usually crimes against other street people," said one respondent. The following site visit reports illustrate the ways that homeless people are often victimized.

> In **Seattle, Washington,** conservative estimates of the homeless population were between 3,000 to 3,500 on any particular day. Homeless people seemed to congregate in the downtown and waterfront areas, and other locations close to social service agencies. Over half of the homeless population was believed to be single adults. These people often became targets of crime. Homeless single women and elderly men were reported to experience particularly high levels of victimization from street predators.

> The homeless population in **Broward County, Florida** was reported to include a much greater number of women and children than many cities. After a police study confirmed that conditions in public housing were contributing to the county's crime problem, a problem-oriented policing (POP) unit was created to step up law enforcement in these developments. What began as a specific attempt to address crime in public housing evolved into a concern for both the housed poor and homeless. In the words of one sheriff's office official, "the homeless program undertaken by the POP Unit [in 1989] was the result of increasing concern for street persons, citizen complaints, and the suicides committed by street persons in a densely wooded area of Pompano referred to as The Jungle." The Jungle, an area located near railroad tracks and a labor site that provided daily work, became a major concern of the POP Unit. The magnitude of the problem became evident when it was discovered that nearly 100 individuals could be found residing, without basic necessities, in this heavily vegetated area. In addition, over the following months, a dozen street people were found dead on the railroad tracks bordering the Jungle.

The great majority of respondents (88.1%) also indicated that street people in their jurisdictions appear to abuse alcohol and nearly 60 percent believed that street people in their jurisdiction appear to be regularly involved with drug abuse. In addition, nearly 65 percent of the respondents stated that the street people in their jurisdictions appear to have mental disabilities. But, it appears that street people who do not have substance abuse problems or mental illness simply do not have as much contact with police as those who do. This would certainly skew the respondents' perceptions.

POLICE RECORDS ON STREET PEOPLE

In determining how survey respondents formed their perceptions of the scope and nature of the homeless problem, it became apparent that they were largely based on experience and personal beliefs, rather than record-keeping. Most specific crime or victim statistics do not identify the number or percent of crime victims or accused that are homeless. Police perceptions of homeless people are often formed in the absence of data on calls for service or other departmental record-keeping. That is not to say that police perceptions are not accurate, only that they are rarely confirmed by statistical information. The information about victims and accused people that is recorded when crime and arrest reports are taken may reflect that a person has "no fixed address," but after data are entered into the departmental records system, homelessness is not usually distinguishable.

Of all agencies responding to the survey (521), 200 reported that they do not collect data on the calls they receive regarding the homeless. Over 40 percent of those agencies that reported that the data were not available believed that homelessness was not a police problem, or was a minor problem. It is possible to construct a circular argument that agencies do not collect data because they perceive the problem to be minor, and they perceive the problem to be minor because they do not collect data. Over 100 agencies did not answer the question regarding whether they collect data on calls for services related to the homeless.

Barriers to collecting data are reflected in the following comments:

"Rarely if ever are homeless people identified as such in official department records."

"Not tracked as such. May be researched for specific needs, normally using 'transient' for address or one that is known to be used by homeless people to collect mail."

"All records are kept but people are not categorized as 'street people'; they are categorized as victims, suspects, witnesses. . . . "

"We just don't keep specific 'street people' records. I'm afraid someone would sue us for labeling these people."

"There is no CAD [Computer-Aided Dispatch] designation for street people; therefore, all figures are estimated."

"Calls for service type codes (i.e., drunk, loitering, trespass, mental distress, and other similar order maintenance calls) are generally associated with street people—especially in the downtown area."

"Records are maintained when an officer writes a report and not all contacts with street people result in a report."

Record-keeping varies from department to department. Some police agencies are not yet fully automated. Others use coding systems and descriptive data that are not readily retrievable to analyze police contacts with the homeless. Many of these problems were addressed more fully during the site visits to selected police agencies.[7]

Some departments do undertake informal, yet valuable, non-statistical record-keeping efforts. For example, in Montgomery County, Maryland, one officer initiated a labor-intensive method of tracking homeless people who stay in the district.

An officer observed, on the 1990 death of an elderly street person, that this population is rarely in possession of adequate identification, making notification of next of kin nearly impossible. Moreover, because they have few family and neighborhood ties, homeless people are not missed when, in fact, they are missing.

To overcome these problems, the officer began to maintain a file on each homeless person in the district who was interested in participating in an identification program. Unlike traditional police files, the existence of this information was predominantly for the benefit of those about whom the files were developed. By explaining the value of being in this "directory" and never taking photographs of unwilling participants, the officer was able to compile a fairly comprehensive "directory of the homeless" in the district. Photographs were accompanied by a field interrogation report that provided additional information (aliases, date of birth, physical description, violent or strange behavioral traits, known medical problems, and hangout locations) about each person. Any future field reports documenting the activities of directory participants were included in the files. Over time, these reports have proven to be useful, both in providing service to the homeless individuals and to police officers in search of individuals wanted for criminal activities.

POLICIES AND TRAINING

Whether police develop policies and training to respond to street people is largely based on their perceptions of the needs of that population and their own authority and ability to respond to those needs. *Of the 521 respondents, 184 (35%) stated that they had no policies specifically related to incidents involving street people.* Many additional respondents did not answer the questions regarding policies. Police policies that affect street people generally cover responding to and referring people who are substance abusers, mentally disabled, or a danger to themselves or others.

Many police policies advocate that officers refer the homeless to proper resources. Police commonly refer homeless people to shelters. When respondents were asked whether officers are regularly informed about the availability of shelters for street people, more than 65 percent answered affirmatively. It is clear from respondents' comments, however, that just because a shelter exists in the community does not mean that there is available space. Many of the respondents expressed frustration with the limited capacity and strict entry requirements of some of the facilities in their jurisdictions. Most respondents indicated that officers are not regularly informed about the capacity of shelters. This lack of information regarding capacity may be due to the constantly changing numbers of clients, particularly during bad weather; the perception that shelters are always full; or a genuine lack of communication between the police and shelter care facilities.

Half of all respondents (49.9%) indicated that their agencies provide no special training concerning the homeless. "To the extent the homeless person falls into other categories (e.g., responding to [people with mental disabilities], etc.) they would be covered." This sentiment was corroborated by the site visits to selected agencies.

THE POLICE RESPONSE

It is clear from the survey and on-site studies that despite the complexity of the problem, police agencies across the nation have responded in many ways to homeless people in their communities. Some have created special units to deal exclusively with homeless people, while other agencies have simply handled homeless-related problems as they arise during normal calls for service. Other departments have worked on the homeless problem through cooperative efforts with other agencies.

A number of departments have created units to cope with homelessness. These units not only refer the homeless to appropriate services but often take an active role in ensuring that those services are attained. Some police programs help bring social services to areas where the homeless congregate; others try to locate family members, treatment facilities and other resources that require long-term effort. Some police agencies use non-sworn personnel to follow and coordinate cases with non-police service providers. Because some police agencies have units that deal almost exclusively with the homeless, they are involved in solving the underlying causes of calls for police service. Some police agencies have even engaged in formal agreements with non-police agencies or have sought legislative solutions to better serve the needs of communities grappling with homeless-related problems.

Interagency committees are another method law enforcement agencies employ to coordinate efforts to resolve homeless problems.[8] In several jurisdictions police have joined with other service providers to better define the roles of those in the network, improve coordination and cooperation, and ensure that resources are being used to best serve the community. The range and complexity of police responses are beyond the scope of this paper. The bottom line is that most police officers entered the profession to help their communities. On site visits, PERF researchers repeatedly saw examples of individual officers who went beyond department policies and programs to ensure that a homeless person they encountered had food, clothing or some other comfort, even if it came from their own pocket or home. Those individual stories are rarely retold and are not captured in the survey data but should not be overlooked nonetheless.

There are also numerous new programs emerging around the country since the completion of the mail survey. There are many police agency responses worthy of further study that are either outside the original survey sample, have emerged since that phase of the project, or were simply not reported by the individual completing that agency's survey.

PROGRAMS AND PRACTICES

Police agencies must assess, at one time or another, whether one or more individuals should be selected to deal solely with incidents involving the homeless, or whether it is best left to patrol officers. Of all respondents, 83 percent indicated they had no individual or unit assigned to deal with the specific needs of the homeless. Approximately 12 percent of the respondents employed a full-time person to respond to homeless people, while only 5 percent had a part-time assignment of this type.

Even those departments that have personnel assigned to handle incidents involving street people do not necessarily have special programs to address the needs of that population. In fact, 96.7 percent of all respondents indicated that they do not have a formal program that focuses on the needs of the homeless. Of the 16 agencies that did report special programs, several were participants in citywide coalitions or cited the multidisciplinary efforts of community service providers as a special program from which their agency benefitted. A few of the agencies had programs that entailed photographing street people or taking a census of that population for a discrete period of time. Many of the other agencies that cited special programs were selected for further on-site study.[9] One of those programs is highlighted here.

> Among the agencies that served as study sites, the **New York City Transit Police Department** (now merged with the **New York City Police Department**) was recognized as having developed one of the most comprehensive programs to respond to street people. The transit police were charged with enforcing the laws and keeping the peace on the city's transit system property, trains and vehicles. Officials realized that the number of homeless people seeking shelter in transit system facilities was reaching unmanageable proportions. Street people found that the transit system stations and trains offered a warm, dry environment in which to sleep 24 hours a day, at no cost.

> Unlike most police departments, the transit police found that calls for service related to homelessness consumed an overwhelming amount of officer time. As a result, in 1982 the department joined forces with the Human Resources Administration (HRA) of New York City to develop a transit system outreach program. The program was designed to eliminate barriers to shelter care and other services by creating an outreach team that patrolled the locations where the homeless were most concentrated and by providing free

transportation for the homeless to shelter services. However, not all homeless people accepted shelter services.

Transit police officials estimated that as many as 80 percent of the homeless were mentally ill and/or chemically addicted. Some ventured beyond the station into the track and tunnel system where they could enjoy some personal privacy and less risk of ejection by transit officers. Not only did the risk of injury by the trains and unsanitary conditions pose a significant danger to the homeless, but passengers were aware of the situation and long expressed concern that the system was out of control and had become a less desirable mode of travel.

While transporting large numbers of homeless people from the transit system to shelters was successful, each year an increasing number of people were killed in the track and tunnel system. Having encountered 79 such deaths in 1989, the department created the "Tunnel Team" to rescue those people deep in the tunnels and bring them to available services.

Despite all efforts, the homeless population continued to grow. It is estimated that in 1989 there were approximately 5,000 homeless people living in the various facilities and other locations operated by the transit system. This increase in homeless people and homeless-related problems in the transit system, coupled with the realization that HRA would not be able to further increase its contribution of resources, resulted in the Transit Police Department creating its own Homeless Outreach Unit in 1990. The primary purpose of this unit was to ensure that homeless people found in the subway system were offered shelter and services before being removed, and that the process did not deny any individuals their dignity. By the time a homeless person is "keeping house" in a subway tunnel, personal dignity may be all they have left. This is a theme that was repeatedly voiced by many of the officers assigned to the unit. It was in this spirit that employees of the Transit Police Department, at their 1991 Christmas Party, collected donations and purchased a television set for the waiting room at the Bellevue Shelter, where many of the homeless referred by transit officers waited before being admitted.

Maintaining its commitment to better the quality of life of the homeless found in the transit system and the quality of the system's environment for passengers, the Metropolitan Transit Authority initiated numerous other programs. Seven community-based organizations (CBOs) were given contracts to provide outreach and referral services at Grand Central Terminal, Pennsylvania Station and at 29 subway stations. Also, a Station Enhancement Program (SEP), specifically aimed at elimination of rule violations, was put in place at 13 stations.

The effect of the many programs and initiatives in which the transit police participated is impressive. The number of homeless estimated to be living in the transit system declined to approximately 1,000. It is believed that as few as 80 to 100 homeless people actually continued to live in the tunnels. The number of homeless deaths in the transit system dropped to 54 in 1991. From 1982 to 1992, over 55,000 homeless contacts were made and more than 30,000 offers to provide service were accepted. Just through the efforts of the Transit Police Department's own Homeless Outreach Unit, nearly 9,000 people were transported to city-run shelters from November 1990 to November 1992. The number of contacts made and services accepted, as reported by the outreach teams, should not be confused with the actual number of homeless people present in the subway system, as many of the homeless had repeat contact with the New York Transit Police Department's programs.

The Transit Police Homeless Outreach Initiative (Bus Programs) was a multiagency effort (New York City Transit Authority, Long Island Railroad and Metro North). This was the department's first winter (November 1990–April 1991) outreach initiative. An updated initiative has been activated each following winter. The program provided additional transportation to homeless people who were being removed from the system and were interested in city shelter care. The Transit Authority allocated four out-of-service buses that were refurbished into "police vehicles" by the Transit Police. Additional vans were eventually added, so that during cold weather emergencies, five vehicles could be deployed.

For 24 hours a day and seven days a week, police officers operated the buses that responded to any transit site location where an officer located a homeless person desiring transportation to a city shelter. Upon accepting services and entering a bus, homeless people were provided with a boxed meal and drink. In the winter of 1990–1991, homeless people were transported to shelters 1,403 times. For the same period in 1991–1992, 4,044 such transports were made.

Building on the success of the winter operation, a modified version of the program continued to operate throughout the summer months. From April through November 1991, homeless people were transported to shelter facilities 1,305 times. The program was reestablished in April 1992.

The Homeless Emergency Liaison Project (HELP), under the aegis of the city's Health and Hospitals Corporation, was a mobile, emergency psychiatric, medical and social service expressly for the mentally ill homeless. Operating from radio-dispatched vehicles, a team of a psychiatrist, nurse and social worker responded to locations where officers had come into contact with severely mentally ill persons. Since 1990, the unit has been staffed with 40 personnel.

The HELP team was empowered by New York State Mental Hygiene Law to obtain mental evaluations with or without the patient's consent. In order to appropriately refer those people found to be impaired, but not admissible to psychiatric treatment facilities, the teams maintained close relationships with other outreach programs and services.

Under Operation Last Stop, transit officers were positioned at the four "end of the line" locations to inspect trains before they were taken out of service for rule violators hiding or sleeping in the cars. When violators were removed from the cars, those believed to be homeless were offered transportation to city shelters and outreach services.

Station Enhancement Program (SEP), also referred to as Operation Enforcement and the Operation Enforcement Task Force, called for aggressive enforcement of all violations of rules and regulations. The SEP was aimed at improving the system's overall environment, and officers' enforcement actions were not limited to violations committed by the homeless. As a result, data collected on rule violations by homeless people was maintained separately. Rule violations included obstruction, soliciting/begging, unlawful commercial activity, non-transit uses, disorderly conduct and restricted area violations.

The Homeless Outreach Unit, operating department-wide, was staffed by one lieutenant, three sergeants and 37 transit officers. Officers selected to work in this unit were well-informed about the problems they would encounter. Recognizing that officers may feel a moral responsibility for the homeless they ejected from the system, the department felt that it was essential that officers realized that a full range of services were available and offered to the homeless population.

WORKING WITH NON-POLICE SERVICE PROVIDERS

Because the police response to homeless-related incidents often involves a wide range of non-law-enforcement service providers, the survey asked respondents to rate their satisfaction with social service resources that exist in their jurisdiction. Adequate resources and positive working relationships may well influence how police respond to calls for service involving the homeless. It is important to remember that ratings of dissatisfaction may be due to lack of available space or services, rather than the quality of existing services.

Overall, survey respondents were most satisfied with food services

(79.8%), medical assistance (69.8%) and shelter resources (69.6%). More than half also expressed satisfaction with child care services, clothing resources, alcohol abuse care, and mental health aid. Those services receiving the lowest ratings included job referral services, psychological aid and skill training. Note that these services are more long term in nature and are not available in many jurisdictions. Drug abuse treatment also received unsatisfactory ratings by more than half of all respondents. Table 2 provides detailed results.

Table 2
POLICE RATING OF COMMUNITY RESOURCES
FOR NEEDS OF STREET PEOPLE

	Satisfied	Moderately Satisfied	Dissatisfied	Moderately Dissatisfied	Resource Not Available	N
Alcohol Abuse Care	18.7%	43.1%	20.0%	12.4%	5.9%	476
Child Care	21.6%	41.1%	17.3%	9.6%	10.3%	467
Clothing	21.8%	42.8%	18.6%	8.0%	8.9%	463
Drug Abuse Treatment	10.9%	38.8%	28.5%	15.2%	6.6%	467
Food	32.1%	47.7%	12.7%	5.7%	1.9%	474
Job Referral	7.3%	24.9%	33.6%	16.7%	17.6%	450
Medical Assistance	24.3%	45.5%	17.8%	9.5%	3.0%	473
Mental Health Aid	16.4%	37.8%	26.5%	16.0%	3.4%	476
Psychological Aid	9.4%	30.5%	31.6%	18.1%	10.5%	459
Shelter	21.6%	48.0%	19.8%	8.0%	2.5%	485
Skill Training	4.7%	14.3%	29.8%	17.5%	33.6%	446

Note: For this study, a *shelter* was defined as a place where a person may be admitted to receive food and a place to sleep without cost. The shelter may also provide counseling, medical care, or other services. All respondents were given this definition on the survey. Percentages reflect the proportion of respondents.

SHELTERS

The call for more shelters, increased capacities and specialized services has been the subject of great controversy in the national media, Congress and town meetings across the country. Because of the tremendous amount of attention paid to this resource, the survey addressed several shelter issues that pertain to police.

Most of the respondents indicated that their officers informally refer street people to shelters (53.9%). Less than 40 percent refer them as a matter of policy. Only 16.5 percent do not refer them to shelters at all. More than 60 percent of the respondents will also transport street people to shelters if there is a special reason, while 22 percent transport on a regular basis. Decisions on how police make referrals are sometimes made with input from other service providers. At least 40 percent of the respondents indicated that their agency had been contacted by shelter operators for advice on matters of referrals. Most of these contacts are informal, as confirmed by the site visit findings. There were, however, 23 agencies that indicated they had a formal agreement with a shelter for making referrals.

Many of these shelters have strict limitations, only permitting access for battered women (54.1%), runaway or throwaway youth (32.4%), alcohol-addicted individuals (32.2%), men (27.4%), drug addicts (19.0%), or mentally disabled people (16.3%). Other types of shelters include facilities for those unable to work, families, homeless only, and abused or neglected children. As indicated earlier, many of these shelters have limited capacities, are accessed by people not necessarily living on the streets, and have regulations regarding conduct. Shelters may also bar individuals who have used the facilities more than a permissible number of times in the past year or have created disruptions in the past.

> "We are sometimes at a loss in what to do with street people we come in contact with who are repeaters that have been blackballed from area shelters because of various reasons such as having caused trouble, found drinking alcohol or using drugs, or not helping an organization in some monetary way or work effort."

POLICE/SOCIAL SERVICE RELATIONS

Though police officers express frustration over the social service system, the site visits confirmed that problems between police and community social workers are not as widespread as one might think. Certainly individual personalities and styles come into play, but on the whole, both the survey and site visits suggested, there are generally good police/social service worker relationships, particularly when all players have taken the time to fully communicate the limitations of their authority and resources. Over 75 percent of the respondents disagreed that there were strained relations between the social service agencies and police departments. Those respondents who voiced some dissatisfaction with social service agencies expressed frustration at the limitations of the systems rather than bad relations. One respondent suggested, "people that are shipped to the mental health facilities are generally released too soon. Their problems cannot be corrected in the short amount of time they stay in these facilities." Another respondent indicated that the police/social service tensions are "due to lack of funding." One respondent added, "Our jurisdiction has an extremely strong and well-directed mental health association that provides excellent assistance as needed. Our major shortcoming is a limited number of indigent beds for those individuals in need of immediate service delivery."

Another "myth" that appears to be dispelled by the survey is that police are unaware of resources in the community. While self-reported, respondents indicated that law enforcement officers are largely aware of the available resources for responding to street people (70%). There is, of course, the possibility that they are unaware of resources but believe they have sufficient knowledge of community support services.

PERCEPTIONS OF THE POLICE RESPONSE AND ROLE

"Too often the police don't understand what the community expects in responding to street people."

To further determine how the police define their role in providing services to the homeless and enforcing the law, survey respondents were asked to rate their level of agreement with some general statements about how the police relate to street people. Those ratings represent a wide diversity of views regarding access to non-police resources, as well as the current police role in responding to homeless people. They are included in Table 3. Additional comments and findings of special note from Table 3 follow.

"I feel that given the magnitude of the problem in some jurisdictions the police may be getting into a problem that has the potential to overwhelm our capacity. Our experience has shown that this problem is largely one that has been thrust upon us by social service and mental health agencies because they too are overburdened."

Respondents overwhelmingly agreed that police agencies need referral arrangements with other service providers to effectively respond to street people (96.6%). These responses support the belief that police are called to address the non-criminal, social problems of homeless people. The resources are not always available to meet that need, however, according to many of the survey participants.

"The growth in the numbers of homeless (street people) has increased in recent years. There has been, and continues to be, a lack of service

Table 3
PERCEPTIONS OF THE POLICE RESPONSE TO STREET PEOPLE

	Agree	Disagree	N
There are too many street people in my jurisdiction for my department to effectively handle alone.	38.7%	61.2%	498
Police departments need some type of referral arrangement with other agencies to effectively respond to street people.	96.6%	3.4%	502
There are insufficient referral agencies in my jurisdiction to respond to the problem.	59.3%	40.7%	501
There are no facilities or services available to respond to the needs of children of street people.	32.2%	67.8%	500
On weekends and after working hours, it is difficult for the police to get help for street people.	65.0%	35.0%	500
It is difficult for the police to get emergency medical care for the street people in my jurisdiction.	22.8%	77.2%	500
It is difficult for the police to get mental health care for the street people in my jurisdiction.	54.5%	45.5%	501
The community does not understand the police role in responding to street people.	76.9%	23.0%	499
There are strained relations with the social service agencies that could help the street people in my jurisdiction.	23.6%	76.4%	493
Officers in my jurisdiction are not aware of the available resources for responding to street people.	29.7%	70.4%	502
The police do not have a clearly defined responsibility in dealing with non-criminal problems of street people.	67.9%	32.1%	501

Note: Percentages reflect the proportion of respondents answering each question.

agencies and funding to specifically target this group, except to the extent that they are represented in other service populations."

Over 50 percent of the survey respondents indicated that there are insufficient referral agencies in the jurisdiction to respond to the problem. Even those agencies with access to referral organizations suggest that their mere existence is not enough. Common complaints, as discussed previously, were the lack of available space in existing facilities and the restrictive entry requirements that must be met by clients.

More than half of the respondents indicated that they have difficulty finding mental health care for street people in their jurisdiction. Yet, only 23 percent found it troublesome to get emergency medical care for street people. Sixty-five percent of respondents agreed that one of the more difficult problems was getting help after regular working hours.

"Social service agencies work Monday to Friday 9 a.m. to 4 p.m. Emergency crisis team intervention in real life means the social service agency is available after 9 a.m. *next* Monday. The alcohol treatment centers only take sober drunks. The entire system is oxymorinated."

"During day hours we have abundant resources to deal with the problems of street people. After hours, we run into every problem imaginable. . . . We have had instances of street people needing a place to stay who will break a window downtown to qualify for a bed in jail. Providing families with shelter after hours is a real challenge."

SOME CLOSING THOUGHTS

Several completed surveys had comments peripherally related to the questions on the instrument that are of special interest in assessing the police response to street people. They provide insight into the police perception of the problem and into the problem-solving efforts of several agencies. For example, a common fear expressed by respondents was that increased services to the homeless actually create a greater demand by attracting street people from other jurisdictions.

"I don't believe cities should provide too much shelter space for the homeless. If a city takes in many homeless, other jurisdictions will ship their homeless to that city."

"Although no study has been done . . . our street people population seems to have increased significantly with the opening of each new service."

"We find it difficult to provide adequate help for our street people without encouraging the homeless from other jurisdictions to congregate in our city. This problem of encouraging outside transients has not been properly addressed by our city government or non-police service providers."

Another issue that emerged in reviewing survey respondents' comments was dealing with people who refuse assistance.

"Beyond having food, clothing, shelter, and emergency health care available for all street people—not a small task with shrinking public and private budgets—the problem becomes how to deal with those people who refuse the offered assistance."

Part of the problem concerning those who refuse care seems to be the number of individuals who require mental health care and substance abuse treatment but may not be easily admitted to a facility or institutionalized.

"Our most frequent problem, which is not adequately addressed in this community, is repeated contacts with a small number of street people who get categorized by the criminal justice system as not mentally competent to be tried for criminal offenses (or at least not mentally appropriate for charges) and by the mental health system as not dangerous enough for continued confinement. The typical person would be one whom all agree is mentally ill ... and whom most would agree does on occasion present a threat to him- or herself or others sufficient to warrant commitment to an institution. The person is committed for a short time; behavior is brought under control by medication; and the person is released. Upon release, without supervision, the person stops taking medication prescribed, and again starts acting in a bizarre and threatening or criminal manner, at which time he or she is again committed."

"In some cases, street people are perpetrators of petty crimes which cannot be prosecuted due to their mental condition. Lacking mental health facilities (and legal means to mandate participation) these individuals must be released into the same environment. In a few rare cases, municipal judges won't even allow these individuals to be charged any longer, effectively preventing even their arrest for petty crimes."

Finally, survey respondents offered some comments about the police role in dealing with the homeless and suggestions for addressing related issues.

"Homeless and street people should not be stereotyped and must be treated as individual cases. The image of the community and its police department can either be enhanced or damaged by the way in which the less fortunate are handled. . . . If no one else wants to or cares to, the police will handle the problem. Police resources in this community are strapped to their maximum and all of our service-oriented programs are in jeopardy."

"The real problem facing this department and many others appears to be how to legally and morally deal with them in an acceptable fashion."

"The homeless should not be a police problem, but like anything else, the police ultimately become the problem solver. This is a problem society has to deal with. The police are always called upon as social workers. We must come to some solutions."

"Police contact with street people is inevitable, unavoidable. They will, simply stated, respond when compelled to. Otherwise, as with the majority of other institutions, police will ignore the plight of the street person. There is just too much happening around police. They will do what they think society expects them to address. We are great at doing surveys and reports and forming commissions. But unfortunately, the dirty, day-to-day grinding effort to resolve, assist, or rehabilitate remains for a relatively few committed people."

"I believe the problem needs to be addressed; be it by special training for officers, written policies . . . , or a special position created to deal with both the people and agencies that can help them."

WHERE DO WE GO FROM HERE?

Work in this area is far from over. Many large police agencies across the nation are grappling with very complex homeless-related concerns. They are using means that range from tailored, department-wide responses to more traditional enforcement and displacement approaches—often within the same agency.

If there is one conclusion that can be made from this project, it is that police need guidance and assistance in addressing agency and community concerns related to homelessness. The survey and site visits confirm that police are frustrated and uncertain about what their tasks should be in responding to street people. Officers and deputies stated that the public does not understand the police role in responding to incidents involving homeless individuals.

The state of confusion and frustration must be addressed in a series of multidisciplinary approaches. There are encouraging signs that indicate that police are particularly receptive to new approaches.

First, there is increasing realization among progressive police leaders that officers must do more than simply respond to calls for service. Police must take a proactive approach that focuses on the underlying causes of calls for assistance. Instead of responding to the same nuisance complaints in the same neighborhoods for weeks on end, police are meeting with citizens, community leaders, service providers, health care professionals, and others to get at the root causes for these complaints. By addressing underlying concerns, police are reducing repeat calls for service and improving the quality of life for all citizens. This problem-oriented, community-based approach is sweeping the nation's police agencies. Police are more receptive than ever before to effective means for addressing social problems—homelessness being no exception.

Second, there is a trend among some police and other service providers to recognize homelessness as a problem that impacts public health, susceptible to the same complications and remedies as other health concerns. The implication of this trend for police is the increased opportunity to draw on the experiences and resources of health care professionals and others to deal appropriately with homeless people.

Third, there is greater recognition among elected and appointed officials that the police will continue to be first responders to incidents involving street people. In some communities, particularly small jurisdictions, police may be the only 24-hour emergency providers available. Police must be given proper guidance, through training and comprehensive written policies, to provide a quality response to homeless people.

Police are also learning to better deal with a politically charged community agenda. Police officers and their agencies cannot act independently to achieve effective responses to homeless people. Police in some jurisdictions have begun working closely with political and community leaders, other government agencies, and nonprofit organizations to establish viable networks to respond to the needs of street people.

Police cannot achieve lasting reform without the support and cooperation of others on the national and local levels. During this period of fiscal strain in which many human service organizations have difficulty maintaining their levels of service, coordination and cooperation is essential. Funding entities such as city and county councils, national charities, foundations, and the federal government should adequately fund police and multidisciplinary programs, and require evidence of coordination of services as justification for continued support. There is also a need for government and community leaders to set standards and higher expectations for coordination of services among those agencies and organizations responsible for meeting the needs of homeless people.

With so much more work to be done to help police assess and improve their response to street people, it is easy to overlook what has already been accomplished. Some excellent approaches have already been identified. Most of the agencies participating in this project recognized that police officers play an important role in the delivery of services to street people. It is a modest beginning to what promises to be a long-term effort to improve the police response to homeless-related issues. But this beginning has demonstrated that police are concerned with the plight of individuals on the streets of this country and that they are willing to do something about it. We must ensure that police do not face that challenge alone.

ENDNOTES

1. For the purposes of this chapter, the terms "homeless" and "street people" are used interchangeably. When providing services, police do not generally distinguish between the truly homeless and those people who spend the majority of their time on the street, but have regular housing arrangements.
2. Melekian, Barney. 1990. "Police and the Homeless." *FBI Law Enforcement Bulletin,* 59, 11 Nov: 1–7.
3. This chapter is based on the Robert Wood Johnson-funded report, The Police Response to the Homeless: A Status Report, published in 1993 by the Police Executive Research Forum (PERF), a Washington, D.C.-based membership organization of progressive police professionals.
4. David Carter from Michigan State University and Allen Sapp from Central Missouri State University helped develop the mail survey, collect the data and analyze sites for follow-up visits. Their work was completed under PERF's Research Fellowship Program.
5. PERF sent 650 chief law enforcement officers (chiefs, sheriffs, public safety directors, etc.) who serve populations of 50,000 or more people a survey on issues related to police perceptions of the homeless and on agency operations. Surveys were most often completed by agency personnel familiar with the topic, or by staff assigned to compile information and respond to all agency surveys. A total of 525 responses were received, though four were eliminated from the analysis because they were incomplete, incorrectly completed or received after the submission deadline. Though the findings assess the views of police in the largest jurisdictions in the country, data should not be generalized to the police profession at large. There are about 17,000 U.S. police agencies. Only about 700 serve jurisdictions with populations of 50,000 or more. Readers who are interested in a more detailed discussion of the methodology and participant demographies can refer to the full PERF report (see: Martha Plotkin and Ortwin Narr, "The Police Response to the Homeless: A Status Report," Washington, D.C.: Police Executive Research Forum, 1993).
6. Site visit descriptions are based largely on self-reported activities. PERF staff did not evaluate these programs, only reported them as accurately as possible. No program or approach is endorsed by inclusion in this chapter.
7. Plotkin, Martha and Ortwin Narr. 1993. *The Police Response to the Homeless: A Status Report.* Washington, DC: Police Executive Research Forum.
8. Zudak, Catherine. 1992. "Fragmented Approach to Homelessness: Addressing the Causes and Service Needs." *Public Management,* 9–15.
9. Those agencies reporting special programs or practices, policies, procedures, special units, training were considered for site visits under the PERF project. After factoring in geographic representation and staff logistics, the following sites were chosen for site visits: New York City Police Department, New York City Transit Police Department, Montgomery County (MD) Police Department, Broward County (FL) Sheriff's Office, Miami Police Department, West Palm Beach (FL) Police Department, Joliet (IL) Police Department, Chicago (IL)

Police Department, Kansas City (MO) Police Department, Overland Park (KS) Police Department, Tulsa (OK) Police Department, Seattle Police Department, Los Angeles Police Department, and Santa Monica Police Department. Information on data collection, policies and procedures, training, interagency cooperation, special programs, special units, perceptions and legal issues were collected from each jurisdiction (see: Martha Plotkin and Tony Narr, "The Police Response to the Homeless: A Status Report," Washington, D.C.: Police Executive Research Forum, 1993, Chapter 3).

Chapter 6

HOMELESSNESS: COMPASSIONATE ENFORCEMENT

Daschel E. Butler

As the chief of police of the city of Berkeley, a city known for its compassionate treatment of the downtrodden and disenfranchised, I have often grappled with exactly what our role should be in dealing with the many facets of the homeless problem. Certainly I have no comprehensive answers that solve the problems of homelessness in the urban environment. However, I can help to identify the problems as I have observed them and some programs and philosophies that have worked for the Berkeley community.

The homeless are human beings, Americans, and (in some cases) veterans and, as such, deserve the same consideration and respect as any other citizen. Having worked in the community for better than twenty-five years, I do not see the homeless as faceless entities; they are young people whom I have seen grow up, and then at some point their lives took a tragic turn—a turn that may have left them deeply involved in alcohol or drug abuse, or they may have just fallen upon hard times.

The homeless have specific needs and problems, each of which requires a different approach from law enforcement, government, and social services providers. We must also balance this against the problems of urban blight and decay that have taken over many of our cities and the rather significant role that the proliferation of homeless persons on our streets may play in this deterioration. Certainly citizens have a right to walk the center city, any city, without fear of being set upon by overly aggressive panhandlers, having to walk over sleeping bodies on the sidewalk, or suffer the fetor of dried urine. For many the fear of being robbed or assaulted by persons approaching from the shadows is very real, and the homeless person panhandling poses a real threat to some. Very seldom does this actually occur, but the threat is nonetheless real.

It would be far too easy to simply make the problem of managing the homeless in any jurisdiction a law enforcement problem. To simply throw police resources at the problem will simply serve to move the homeless around and will simply force them to be more clever in establishing the encampments. Further, using law enforcement to *control* the homeless may result in constitutional problems, since law enforcement may, in responding to pressures exerted from residents and the business community, act in ways that are not well thought out. Policing/law enforcement is only part of the equation—not the final solution.

I feel that there are at least six categories of homeless individuals, with each requiring a different tact to be taken in both approach and handling by police. For any municipality, the most difficult category of homeless persons to deal with are those individuals who are service resistant—that is, the individual who does not want to go to a shelter or transitional, publicly owned housing but, rather, chooses to reside in doorways and illegally on private property. These individuals must be convinced that they need public and community-based services, then suitable services must be found to work with these individuals. The service-resistant individual is often both an easy and accessible victim of crime. The service-resistant individual will not fit well within the culture of a community-run shelter. Often the service resistant have dropped out and are distrustful of services and service providers.

There is also substantial crime and degradation in the community associated with these service-resistant individuals. Specifically, service-resistant individuals seem to be more apt to survive by theft and/or inappropriate street behavior (aggressive panhandling and the assaultive street behavior that often accompanies same).

The city of Berkeley utilizes both public and private providers to help resolve some of the problems faced in dealing with a service-resistant homeless population. The Homeless Outreach and mental health workers, part of the city of Berkeley's Health and Human Services Department, work closely with the police department and respond to locations at the request of the beat officer, citizens, or the dispatcher. A significant effort was made to educate officers and dispatchers as to the capabilities and guidelines of both programs. The city of Berkeley's Mobile Crisis team responds to calls in dealing with people experiencing psychiatric emergencies and mental health crisis situations. The mental health teams are available from 10:30 a.m. and 11:00 p.m. every day of the week. They attend patrol briefings at 11:00 a.m. and 4:00 p.m. daily to interact with beat officers and work mutually to solve problems.

The second category of homeless persons who often present an even more significant public safety problem for law enforcement and the community as a whole are the mentally disabled homeless persons. Law enforcement personnel throughout California perceive that the streets have become the asylums of the nineties.

The complete dismantling of the public care system in California has been a public policy disaster. Public psychiatric care facilities do not have to be run like a prison, but there are those who need full-time care. Individuals wander our streets who are, in some cases, virtually helpless and who, prior to the passage of legislation that made mental health treatment community based (although never adequately funded), would have been institutionalized. Society does not stand in the paternal relationship that it once did, and our cities are suffering as a result.

The mentally ill on our streets have also been a significant problem for the business districts in my jurisdiction and in others throughout America. The inappropriate street behavior problem has certainly been a source of consternation for virtually every police department and city government in urban environments. Over the last few years there have been random acts of violence perpetrated by mentally ill homeless persons that have received national news coverage.

Even if appropriate services were funded and available, the mentally ill may not be totally aware of what is available to them and may not be inclined to avail themselves of those programs. The mentally ill may panhandle or accost individuals on the streets, certainly making the business districts less attractive, and in many cases perpetuating the citizen backlash that we are beginning to see in cities across the nation.

In the city of Berkeley, mental health clinicians are mobile on the streets and available for dispatch on the police radio frequency. As law enforcement, we are certainly appreciative of this effort, as it provides an option to the traditional law enforcement response. The mental health workers can perform emergency psychiatric committals and provide for those on the streets who may be unable to ask for services. The city of Berkeley also has homeless outreach workers to help provide for the needs of the homeless population, to further help fill the void between needs and services. Both the mental health program and Homeless Outreach provide mobile services directly to the target populations. Taking the services to the community has greatly helped the police department in dealing with the problems of the mentally ill homeless.

A third group exists that simply wants to live outdoors. This group may avail themselves of other city and community services, but will probably not choose to live in a shelter or transitional housing. This group causes no particular criminal problem other than the obvious sleeping/trespassing on private property, the attendant sanitation issues, and the occasional petty crime issues. However, this too adds to the general degradation of the urban environment and has a disquieting effect on communities throughout America.

A fourth and even more tragic group of homeless persons are families with children. It is not uncommon to find entire families living in an automobile, as this is most often the last remnant of the life that once was. Often women find themselves on the streets with their children as a result of domestic violence, the loss of employment by the female head of household, or severe cases of substance abuse. We have in the last few years seen more women living with children in the most dire circumstances as a result of rock cocaine and other substance addictions.

Certainly, families or women with children have many more services available than other categories of homeless persons. In Berkeley, there are shelters run by community-based organizations, city services, and county social services available to help. Therefore, this group, although tragic to see, is usually not in the bad situation as long as other homeless persons. Due to the fact that homeless families are in a more service-rich environment, families and women with children do not present as significant a problem for law enforcement, other than the issue of how to make sure that the target population is made aware of the community resources at hand. Most of the homeless who fall into this category do not commit antisocial acts, nor are they panhandlers; it has been our experience that for the most part they are too ashamed to beg. The combination of city, county, and community-based organizations has certainly proven successful in dealing with families and children.

The fifth category of homeless persons is of significant concern in every major city—the proliferation of substance-addicted homeless, many of whom are dually diagnosed. The term *substance addicted* refers to both alcohol and drug abuse. This is certainly a major problem for cities, since there is substantial crime and degradation of the inner cities connected with this large population of substance-addicted homeless persons. I have observed substantial petty crime, aggressive panhandling/behaviors, and the general degradation of business districts and adjoining neighborhoods as a result of the growth of the substance-addicted homeless population.

There is also the issue that if the substance-addicted homeless population panhandles in an area to get money, then this will invariably bring drug traffickers into the area and encourage the proliferation of open-air drug markets.

The problem is exacerbated by the fact that long-term detox centers are not readily available due to the cost of such facilities, especially in light of the tremendous need in most urban centers. At this time, I see a tremendous need for drug and alcohol detox centers, and in meetings with the community we encourage public funding of same.

Estimates of the proportion of homeless who may have substance abuse problems range as high as 100 percent. A sample of fifty-one homeless persons was taken in the city of Berkeley in 1993, and the results were startling. Of the fifty-one homeless persons interviewed, 100 percent reported substance abuse and/or mental health problems. I think that this was certainly an aberration, but from my own observations I know the percentage to be quite high.

The sixth category of homeless persons would be the professional panhandler posing as a homeless person. We have encountered another whole class of individuals who pose as indigents and panhandle in the commercial areas. Certainly, this is not illegal, but it certainly adds to the problems in the commercial areas. There is no real tactic to deal with this group, since they do not make for a criminal problem per se, but they do contribute to the deterioration of the commercial areas.

The aforementioned study, with some fifty-one homeless persons in Berkeley interviewed, revealed the following baseline demographic information:

BACKGROUND INFORMATION

Cause(s) of Homelessness
Family/Personal Reasons (23%)
☐ Eviction
☐ Loss of employment (9%)
☐ Combination of events (9%)
☐ Earthquake-displaced

Length of Time Homeless
Median length of time (3.5 years)
☐ Homeless longer than 5 years (chronic) (43%)
☐ Repeat Homeless (42%)

Demographic Information
Mean Age (36 years)

☐ Age Range (19 years to 53 years)
☐ Median Time in Berkeley (5 years)
☐ Place of Origin:
  • Berkeley (14%)
  • Bay Area (20%)
  • California (18%)
  • Other States (45%)
  • Other Countries (2%)

Rather than strictly a law enforcement response to the problem, we in Berkeley look to community-directed efforts. We look at efforts where the police are part of the overall solution to the problem and equal partners in the community problem-solving process. The city of Berkeley, not just the police department, has taken a holistic approach to dealing with homelessness and all of the peripheral issues.

The city of Berkeley, like many cities, has distributed services throughout the city to service the indigenous homeless populations and their particular needs. A successful team was created by linking the police department with the mobile crisis unit and homeless outreach (previously mentioned) to deal with some of the problems of the mentally ill and indigent communities.

A new city of Berkeley funded support center is functioning and offers an array of services at one location. The shelter is a cooperative effort between a community-based organization (CBO) and the city of Berkeley. The CBO is Berkeley-Oakland Support Services (BOSS) and it provides the following services at the Multi-Agency Service Center:

Benefit Advocacy
☐ Money Management
☐ Shower, Respite, & Socialization Services
☐ Information/Referral & General Case Management
☐ Alcohol/Drug Abuse Counseling & Education
☐ Health Care for the Homeless On-Site Referrals
☐ Acupuncture Clinic Referrals
☐ Housing Advocacy
☐ Employment Services by Jobs Consortium

These services are provided Monday through Friday. The Multi-Agency Service Center is too new to assess its overall effectiveness; however, this does provide the officer on the beat with another referral for indigents who are in crisis or desire help.

Officers are also armed with lists of resources for homeless persons to provide them with food, shelter, and the other basic necessities. In dealing with the homeless population, enforcement of the law has been the last resort. Rather, warnings are stressed. If the homeless must be moved, officers try to give them alternatives—officers try to provide them with somewhere to go.

As was previously stated, there are those individuals who simply do not respond to offers of help, availability of services, nor a "kinder and gentler" approach taken by the police. Those individuals continue to aggressively panhandle, harass passersby, and trespass on both private and public property. In Berkeley, the community felt more was needed to address "quality of life" issues in the commercial districts directly related to the homeless issues. Citizens were concerned about the degradation of the downtown and the fact that many citizens were taking their business out of town to suburban malls and shops. To address the concerns most commonly expressed by residents, an ordinance was prepared that might deal with the comfort level of shoppers and those conducting business in the commercial districts.

However, before the ordinance was prepared, tremendous research was done regarding other cities that had enacted such behavior-regulating legislation. The city of Berkeley, in collaboration with community groups, very carefully crafted an ordinance; however, an agreement was struck that any ordinance proposed would be inextricably tied to a battery of new services and treatment. The ordinance would be crafted in such a way as to de-emphasize the enforcement side and to emphasize treatment, choice, services, and long-term solutions. After months of research and community input, including meetings with homeless advocates, Measure "O" took shape.

The services attached to Measure "O" were designed to target "hard to serve" populations, especially those who are prone to engage in what came to be known as "problematic street behaviors" and who might require intensive support services as well as an alternative program setting. The services were distributed on both a citywide and regional basis so as to promote a fair share and equitable distribution of such services and to address the needs of homeless subpopulations residing throughout areas of the city. Local churches were full participants in the planning to provide services to the homeless. The services were considered as a pilot and were subject to intensive external independent monitoring and evaluation. The services are to be evaluated and realigned as needed to guarantee that the services are delivered in the most efficient and effective means possible. The city provided almost a quarter of a million dollars to make the services a reality.

Thus, the city took a holistic approach to dealing with the "problematic street behaviors." The approaches, strategies and resources that went into Measure "O" are as follows:

Community Policing—Bike/Foot Patrol
☐ Berkeley Guides Program
☐ Measure "O" Services
☐ Existing Support Services—Homeless Outreach, etc.
☐ Community Norm-Setting
☐ Special Needs—Housing and Shelter
☐ Regional Sobriety Placement Center

The challenge was to develop an ordinance that would be compassionate, effective and would withstand constitutional scrutiny. The law was crafted to be minimally intrusive on the rights of all who might fall under its purview.

A *Police Department Training and Information Bulletin* (#227) was prepared to explain the ordinance to police department staff, and the first part of the ordinance, "sitting and lying," is here quoted:

CITY ORDINANCE PROHIBITING
SITTING AND LYING ON PUBLIC
SIDEWALKS IN COMMERCIAL DISTRICTS
BETWEEN THE HOURS OF 7:00 A.M.
AND 10:00 P.M.

PURPOSE: The purpose of this training and Information Bulletin is to explain a new City ordinance which was enacted to keep the public sidewalks in commercial districts clear and free for foot traffic.

A VIOLATION OF THIS ORDINANCE IS AN INFRACTION OF THE LAW: B.M.C. section 13.36.015

    A. Prohibition. No person shall sit or lie down upon a public sidewalk, or upon a blanket, chair, stool, or any other object placed upon a public sidewalk, within six feet of the face of any building fronting the right-of-way in any commercial zone in the City of Berkeley between the hours of 7:00 A.M. and 10:00 P.M.

    B. Exceptions. The prohibition in Subsection A shall not apply under the following circumstances:

1. *to any person sitting or lying down on a public sidewalk due to a medical emergency:*
2. *to any person who, as the result of a disability, utilizes a wheelchair or similar device to move about the public sidewalk;*
3. *to a child who is utilizing a stroller or similar device to move about the public sidewalk;*
4. *to a person authorized to ride a bicycle on the sidewalk pursuant to section 14.04.130 of the Code;*
6. *to any person who is a proprietor, patron or employee of an establishment or vendor, duly authorized by the City to conduct business in the public right-of-way.*

Nothing in any of these exceptions shall be construed to permit any conduct which is prohibited by any other provision of law.

C. *Citation. No person shall be cited under this section unless the person engages in conduct prohibited by this section after having been notified by a law enforcement officer that he or she is in violation of the prohibition in this section.*

The second portion of the ordinance addresses panhandling, "solicitation for the immediate payment of money or goods." Again a training and information bulletin was prepared to inform officers of the law and is here quoted:

CITY ORDINANCE REGULATING THE TIME, PLACE AND MANNER OF SOLICITATION FOR THE IMMEDIATE PAYMENT OF MONEY OR GOODS IN PUBLIC PLACES

PURPOSE: The purpose of this Training and Information Bulletin is to explain a new City Ordinance which was enacted to protect the public from coercive, threatening or intimidating solicitation of money in public places; and to prohibit solicitation for immediate payment of money or goods at certain times and in certain places.

A VIOLATION OF THIS ORDINANCE IS AN INFRACTION OF THE LAW: *B.M.C. section 13.37.020*

A. *It is unlawful for any person to solicit another in any public place at the times, locations and in the manner specified below:*
1. *In any manner which coerces, threatens, hounds, or intimidates the person solicited;*
2. *From any person entering or exiting from an automotive vehicle;*

> *Within ten (10) feet of any automatic teller machine in the City of Berkeley;*
> 4. *Within six feet of the face of any building fronting the right-of-way in any commercial zone in the City of Berkeley;*
> 5. *After dark as defined in this ordinance;*
> B. *No person shall be cited under subsections 13.37.020 A (3), or A (4) unless the person engages in conduct prohibited by those subsections after having been notified by a law enforcement officer that the conduct violates those subsections.*

For each section, a complete set of definitions was attached, which thoroughly defined what is meant by the words and terms used in each section. The definitions and clarifying statements were written in such a way as to make sure that the sections were clearly understood.

The philosophy of the Berkeley Police Department is that although we realize there is intrinsic tension between the residents of the city and the homeless community, the use of police power must be reserved for clear-cut violations of law. Poverty should not be criminalized, but there are certain breeches of public order and sanitation that are almost exclusively deeds of the homeless and indigent population. There is a famous quote that addresses just this issue:

> *The law, in its majestic equality, forbids the rich as well as the poor from sleeping under bridges, to beg in the streets, and to steal bread.*
>
> — Anatole France

It is clear that the rich man is quite unlikely to have occasion to sleep underneath the bridge. Certainly the goal of Measure "O" is not to criminalize the "have not" status but simply to restore order and provide some comfort zone for those using the commercial areas. There is tremendous toleration of those who do not buy into the social norms established by the community, and that is certainly evident in the last iteration of Measure "O." The goal is to never have to use the enforcement section but, rather, to inform and gain voluntary compliance.

Measure "O" was put to the ballot and was passed by the community. But prior to any enforcement of the ordinance, all of the promised services had to be put in place. However, prior to the effective date of implementation of the ordinance, homeless advocates submitted the issue to the district courts for constitutional review. The first court struck down all but one section of the ordinance, with a stay on enforcement put in place. The matter is currently on appeal by the city with a higher court, and due to the fact that litigation is pending I will reserve further comment.

Measure "O" may be on hold at this time, but it is an excellent effort to establish a community norm—a community norm with all of the local stakeholders, politicians, service providers and law enforcement involved. Law enforcement must participate on every level to handle the complex problems of homelessness in the urban environment. Law enforcement will on occasion find itself in an advocacy role for the homeless in order to protect their constitutional rights. Homelessness is inherently a social problem, with no *constitutionally legal* enforcement solution. Certainly specific behaviors can be addressed, but homelessness, in the broader sense, is not against the law.

Collaboration to provide services and alternatives for the homeless community will be an important part of the law enforcement function in the future. We will certainly need to look for non-traditional solutions to this problem. As previously mentioned, we will need to evaluate the various subcategories of homeless persons and prescribe the appropriate services and, as a last resort, enforce laws against specific behaviors.

Chapter 7

POLICE ON THE HOMELESSNESS FRONT LINE: A POSTMORTEM OF SAN FRANCISCO'S MATRIX PROGRAM

ANTHONY GARDNER AND PETER LINDSTROM

INTRODUCTION

Imagine you are laid off from your job with a large San Francisco employer. Your family and friends help you out, but soon you are evicted from your apartment, and eventually you become homeless. You go down to the local homeless shelter in search of a bed for the night. When you get there, the staff tell you that there are no beds available (there are less than two shelter beds for every ten homeless people in San Francisco[1]). "Come back another night," they say.

While at the shelter, you decide you would not want to stay there anyway because three people tried to sell you crack on the street outside, it seems dangerous inside too, and there are too many rules about how to act, when to go to sleep, when to get up, when to shower, and when to leave. You are an adult after all and used to making these decisions for yourself.

You must sleep somewhere, but the streets are too dangerous. Instead, you find yourself a place to sleep tucked away deep in Golden Gate Park. When you get there, you see that there are already many other homeless people living there, but they are all quietly minding their own business so there are no problems.

You stay in the park without trouble (except for two "camping" tickets) for the next couple of months until you wake up one morning and find out that three of your fellow park dwellers had been shot in the middle of the night. San Francisco Mayor Frank Jordan originally got elected on an anti-homeless stance, but his popularity is now sagging. Another tough election is around the corner and he hopes to shore up his political support by drumming the anti-homeless beat again. The shootings provide the perfect opportunity. There is an immediate flurry of city hall activity, and then, to the glare of press lights, Mayor Jordan unveils his new "get tough" plan. Although the *victims* of the crime were homeless people, the mayor announces that homeless people have now made the park too dangerous for "San Francisco residents" and that the city will now use the police to "take back our park."[2] Anyone caught sleeping there will be arrested. Matrix II has been born, the heavily hyped sequel to the original political extravaganza, Matrix.

Before sending in the police, the mayor does plan to send a handful of social workers around the park to offer shelter beds and referrals to fleabag, single-residence-occupancy hotels (SRO's); remember, however, that you are repulsed by such dangerous, unsanitary places, and you have trouble trusting the social workers because police officers are always lurking in the shadows behind them. Instead, like many of the other park dwellers, you leave the park even before the social workers arrive and find yourself a new place to sleep in another park or neighborhood.

This vignette describes a typical homeless person's experience of San Francisco's highly publicized Matrix program, which put police officers at the front line of the city's response to homelessness. Although Mayor Jordan has since been unseated and the new mayor, Willie Brown, has said Matrix would be ended,[3] the program was so controversial and emulated by so many cities in the San Francisco Bay Area, and elsewhere, that it deserves a thorough postmortem examination aimed at preserving any lessons. This article provides that postmortem by looking at the history behind Matrix, what Matrix actually was, what its impact was, ethical and legal issues it raised, and conclusions to shape future homelessness policy.

HISTORICAL BACKDROP

Matrix was the most systematic, far-reaching criminal justice strategy ever devised by a San Francisco government (perhaps by *any* American municipal government) to control its ever-increasing homeless population. Since the 1970s, continued economic sluggishness in California accompanied by high unemployment; the steady decline in the purchasing power of the employed and explosion of a minimum wage economy; cuts to public benefits programs for poor people; the large-scale release of mentally ill patients from state hospitals with no arrangements made for their continued treatment or lodging; the shrinking of affordable housing stock through the destruction of SRO's and general escalation of rents (the median rent for a two-bedroom apartment in San Francisco is now $1,004 per month); and the repeated slashing of federal housing program funding, have all contributed to steep increases in the numbers of homeless people in San Francisco—now up to 10,000 or more on any given night.[4]

These rapidly rising numbers of homeless people have created undeniable social pressures, as we have all been forced daily to confront more and more people who have no choice but to sleep, store their belongings, and otherwise conduct their lives on our streets and in our parks. Pre-Jordan city responses to this phenomenon were at best inconsistent, flip-flopping between treating homelessness as a social malady requiring complex social solutions and as a criminal issue demanding tough police enforcement. Thus, while money was poured into supportive service and housing programs to end homelessness, and these efforts were centralized under a newly instituted office of the city homeless coordinator, the police were, at the same time, instructed to enforce so-called "quality of life" criminal ordinances, homeless people were periodically "swept" out of various neighborhoods, and city architectural features such as park and bus benches were redesigned so that homeless people could not sleep on them (i.e., homeless-proofed).

The most enlightened approach came during the 1987–1991 term of Mayor Art Agnos, who promised to end homelessness in the city with a "Beyond Shelter" plan to move homeless people into newly created permanent affordable housing through a network of "multi-service centers" that provided short-term emergency shelter and referrals to the new housing and supportive services.[5] Although this plan was potentially successful, providing permanent housing is very expensive and limited funding had to be diverted away from emergency shelter, resulting in a continuation, and even growth, of visible homelessness around the city.

This perceived failure of policy, and voter frustration with continued homelessness, contributed, in large measure, to Mayor Jordan's election in 1991. Early in his campaign, Jordan, a former city police officer and police chief, had talked tough about "discouraging new vagrants from migrating to San Francisco," sending homeless people to a work camp in San Bruno, and running periodic warrant checks at shelters.[6] Toward the end of the campaign, however, he mellowed his rhetoric with a call for providing some services for homeless people. "San Francisco's diverse homeless populations deserve better help than they are getting. My plan will see to it that they get it. At the same time I will . . . see to it that our streets are clean and safe and that they are free from aggressive pan-handling."[7]

Once he was elected, it took time for Mayor Jordan's criminalization strategy to fully coalesce. Although he supported voter propositions to ban aggressive panhandling and to fingerprint general assistance (GA) recipients, he continued Agnos's "Beyond Shelter" strategy and even signed a U.S. Mayors Conference on Hunger and Homelessness Task Force report that recommended banning "laws which discriminate against homeless people until adequate shelter and other services are provided."[8]

In April 1992, Mayor Jordan's Office of Economic Planning and Development had issued a report hinting at Matrix by blaming home-less people for a claimed loss of $170 million in sales to San Francisco businesses, and recommending ordering police to aggressively enforce "quality of life" offenses and sending mobile teams of social workers and police to refer homeless people to social services.[9] Why Mayor Jordan took 16 months to adopt these recommendations is not clear; he may have been trying to reverse a growing public perception in the summer of 1993 that he was an ineffective mayor, or he may have wanted to use the U.S. Conference of Mayors Conference Task Force on Hunger and Homelessness meeting in San Francisco that summer as a political spring-board for his new "get tough" policy. Whatever the reason, he eventually turned to the police, whom he knew and trusted, and in August 1993, Matrix was born.

WHAT WAS MATRIX?

Much has been said and written about Matrix, but few have taken the time to define what it actually was. Mayor Jordan called Matrix "a multi-departmental city effort to help people living on the streets obtain shelter and other services (such as psychiatric and drug and alcohol treatment), while at the same time protecting the general public from certain offenses committed in public."[10] However, because the police enforcement dwarfed the social service efforts in impact, costs, and personpower expended (as described below), Matrix was, in reality, a large-scale police dragnet with small social service outreach appendages. Large numbers of homeless people were cited or arrested, but relatively received help in escaping homelessness.

The institutional structure of Matrix, consisting of the Police Enforce-

ment Program, the Matrix Outreach Program, and the Night Referral
Program, is described below.

The Police Enforcement Program

This was defined by a set of police department operations orders
instructing all police officers at all stations to aggressively enforce a list
of "quality of life" offenses and to search out and take action against
"concentrations of individuals" committing such offenses. The first public hint of this strategy came in the August 1, 1993 edition of the neighborhood newspaper *The New Fillmore,* in which Captain Cairns of the
Northern Station (which covers Union Square, Market Street and Civic
Center Plaza) announced that a host "quality of life" offenses, such as
aggressive panhandling, urinating in public, and blocking sidewalks,
would be "targeted for enforcement" and that a "no tolerance policy for
the officers will be in effect and all violations will be enforced."[11] The
following month, the "success" of this plan led Mayor Jordan to extend it
to all other stations, where officers were ordered to "vigorously" enforce
the following offenses against "concentration[s] of individuals who on a
regular basis create quality of life problems for neighborhoods":

> Lodging in public
> Trespassing (various types)
> Public inebriation
> Willful, malicious obstruction
> Public consumption of alcohol
> Obstructing a sidewalk
> Remaining on private or business property
> Urinating or defecating in public
> Possession of shopping carts
> Soliciting on or near a highway
> Sleeping in vehicle on the street
> Sleeping in parks
> Erecting tents or structures in parks
> Obstructing a sidewalk with an object
> Aggressive panhandling[12]

Panhandling near an automated teller machine was added later by voter
proposition. Officers were told to take a "proactive posture," and "discre-
tionary decisions by officers" were to "weigh towards an enforcement

disposition rather than tolerance." Officers were allowed to warn first offenders, but any subsequent offenses required a citation or arrest. "Supervisory personnel" were to "identify problem areas within the district, assign officers to abate the situations and follow up to ensure tasks have been accomplished." The latter provision shows that the enforcement program was more than just a set of orders to aggressively enforce certain offenses, but a broad plan for police command to target homeless people and then "sweep" them out of neighborhoods (although Mayor Jordan maintained that the enforcement program was targeted at "observable violations of the law" rather than "any person based on appearance or status as a homeless person," and police policy bulletins were issued to that effect.[13])

The Matrix Outreach Program

Started three months after the police enforcement program, this was a mobile team of outreach workers that attempted to connect homeless people primarily to SRO housing, but also to emergency shelter, substance abuse treatment, and mental health treatment.[14] The team included two Department of Social Services (DSS) social workers, one substance abuse counselor, and two Department of Public Health (DPH) mental health workers empowered to "5150" people, i.e., involuntarily hospitalize them for severe mental illness under Section 5150 of the California Welfare and Institutions Code. The team operated between 7:00 a.m. and 4:00 p.m., Monday through Friday, and four of the above workers were usually available on any given day. One or two police officers always accompanied them on rounds but stayed "in the background" unless team members felt threatened or needed them to physically take control of a person involuntarily hospitalized.

The team focused on areas where the police were conducting Matrix operations. The social workers approached individual homeless people and encouraged them to participate in the city's voluntary Modified Payments Program, through which the homeless person's $345 monthly GA or other benefit check was paid to the Tenderloin Housing Clinic (THC), which in turn paid rent on an SRO room for $280 or less and remitted the remainder to the homeless person. Interested homeless people qualified for GA were transported to the Mission Hotel, where they received Matrix set-aside rooms until the THC found permanent space in another SRO. Those not interested were offered information about emergency shelter, food, income, and medical resources, and sometimes given other informal help, such as clean socks. If a homeless person seemed "under the influence," the substance abuse counselor would offer detoxification and treatment services. The mental health workers would offer mental health treatment services to anyone who seemed mentally ill, or would "5150" anyone seeming extremely mentally ill.

The Night Shelter Referral Program

In December 1993, the police department started this program carried out in neighborhoods where large numbers of homeless people were sleeping.[15] Between 6:00 p.m. and 10:00 p.m., officers approached homeless men and offered them vouchers to the Salvation Army Lifeboat Lodge men's shelter, which set aside beds every night for Matrix referrals. Those who accepted these vouchers were offered transportation to the shelter via DSS mobile assistance patrol van. Homeless women were told about the women's shelter at Saint Paulus Lutheran Church (which burned down in November 1995).

IMPACT OF MATRIX

The Mayor's Objectives

According to Mayor Jordan, the purpose of Matrix was to reduce crime and improve the "quality of life."[16] Although enforcement of "quality of life" offenses did increase, there is no evidence that serious crime was reduced. Indeed, to the extent Matrix diverted officers' time, serious crime may have increased. Many San Franciscans would be infuriated to know, for example, that while they were being mugged or their cars broken into, three police officers were standing around in Golden Gate Park citing one homeless person for sleeping.

San Francisco Police Commander Dennis Martel has said that enforcing "quality of life" offenses is a form of early intervention that deters people from committing later, more serious crimes. Beat cops, he said, believe that 70 percent of vehicle break-ins are committed by people with no address.[17] There appears to be little validity to these statements, and what little there is requires distinguishing among the Matrix offenses.

Serious crimes might be traceable to alcohol-related offenses (of which the city's Matrix statistics include many non-homeless people) but seem unconnected to life-sustaining activities, such as sleeping or urinating in public. Thus, even under Commander Martel's own theory, enforcing many Matrix offenses made no sense.

As for "quality of life," Matrix made almost no improvement because it failed to attack the root cause of the problem: homelessness, not the homeless. Homeless people conduct their private lives publicly—sleeping, storing their few belongings, sitting on sidewalks, and urinating—because they have no other choice. The "quality of life" problems that result may be irritating to the rest of us, but we must accept them unless we are willing to commit the resources needed to end homelessness.

Rather than solving the root cause of these problems, police enforcement merely moved them from neighborhood to neighborhood. For example, by "sweeping" homeless people out of Civic Center Plaza, that area became cleaner, but since the homeless people living there had to go elsewhere, "quality of life" in other neighborhoods worsened correspondingly. Likewise, when the nighttime closing of Golden Gate Park forced homeless people into surrounding neighborhoods, residents of these neighborhoods reported increasing "quality of life" problems. Thus, Matrix did not improve *overall* "quality of life" but merely redistributed it around the city. Some neighborhoods were even worse off than they had been before. This may be why a *San Francisco Chronicle* poll conducted shortly before the Jordan-Brown runoff election indicated only 28 percent of San Francisco voters thought Jordan would do a better job on homelessness than Brown:[18] voters wanted a real end to homelessness and its associated problems; criminalization did not provide it.

Even the small Matrix outreach components failed to markedly improve "quality of life," mainly because there were insufficient services underlying the referrals. For instance, a great many homeless people were referred to emergency shelters, but the shelters were always full, and to the extent a Matrix referral was given set-aside space, someone else had to sleep on the street, causing continued "quality of life" problems. The same is true regarding referrals for substance abuse and mental health treatment (many public inebriates were simply dumped back on the streets after their arrest with no substance abuse treatment offered). The case of 5150'd people is particularly illustrative; after release from the psychiatric ward they were cycled back to the streets, where they typically received no follow up psychiatric treatment until they were again 5150'd. No wonder "quality of life" failed to improve.

Recent DSS statistics do show that as of October 16, 1995, Matrix referrals did result in about 252 homeless people receiving permanent housing, primarily in SRO's.[19] This is a qualified success, but tempered by the realities that on any given night there are 10,000 or more homeless people in San Francisco, that the Matrix outreach team contacted over 9,000 homeless people, and that many of these people may have cycled back into homelessness. Given these facts, Matrix housing referrals may have marginally improved "quality of life" but to only a minor extent in relation to the overall scale of the problem. And the question is raised: Is there a more efficient way to get people into permanent housing than provided by Matrix outreach?

Commander Martel has also said that Matrix accomplished the "modification" of homeless people's behavior.[20] This is probably true for some (although there is no evidence that homeless people are typically more badly behaved than others); after a two-year reign of citations and arrests, homeless people may have been intimidated into behaving more politely toward merchants and the housed, whom they worried might turn them into the police. Some might consider this a positive result of Matrix—but was it worth the cost?

Costs of Matrix

Matrix cost San Francisco taxpayers a whopping estimated minimum of $7,633,995 (breakdown provided below)! This does not include court costs to process Matrix warrants and court cases; city attorney costs to process and prosecute Matrix cases and defend the Matrix-inspired *Joyce v. City and County of San Francisco* litigation; police overhead costs (supervisory time, administrative processing, officer training, gasoline, and the like); police overtime and "special events" costs; all police costs for Matrix II; police salaries and expenses for the night shelter referral program; DSS and DPH overhead relating to the Matrix outreach team; board of supervisors' costs for Matrix hearings and action; and mayor's office costs to develop, implement, publicize, and defend Matrix. Adding $1,500,000 for these expenses (admittedly a rough guess), the overall cost of Matrix was probably closer to $9,133,995. Taxpayers must ask if the key results of Matrix—"modification" of homeless people's behavior and

SRO housing of perhaps 252 people—were worth this cost. The mayoral election results might indicate otherwise.

Police officer salaries and benefits were the highest known cost. Based on an analysis of the police department operations orders, an October 5, 1993 *Tenderloin Times* news article reported that at least 1,320 officer hours per week were spent enforcing "quality of life" ordinances.[21] At the average police compensation rate of $30.17 per hour (salary and benefits), this totals $4,619,630 over the 116 weeks between the beginning of Matrix in August 1993 and November 1995. Adding to this an estimated cost of $195,501 for one or two full-time officers riding with the Matrix outreach team over the 108 weeks between the team's October 1995 inception and November 1995, yields a total of $4,815,131!

Matrix jail booking costs were also very high. "A Housing Status Assessment of County Bookings" by Alissa Riker of the Center on Juvenile and Criminal Justice found that of the average 138 people who are booked into San Francisco County Jail every day, 21 percent, or 29 people, are homeless.[22] Of these homeless bookings, 42 percent, or about 12.2 people per day, are for Matrix-type misdemeanors. At a sheriff's department cost of $87 per booking, this totaled $861,866 between August 1993 and November 1995. This does not include booking costs for the marginally housed, who make up 18 percent of all bookings and who are often Matrix targets.

Incarcerating homeless people was also very expensive. A February 1994 board of supervisors' budget analyst report estimated that 12 to 15 homeless people are in jail on any given day, primarily for "quality of life" offenses[23] (although Riker feels this figure is low). At a cost of $63.10 a day per prisoner (much higher than the shelter bed cost of $11 per night![24]), this totalled $768,558 between August 1993 and November 1995.

Jail overcrowding fines were another cost. Due to past jail overcrowding, a federal court had imposed on San Francisco a fine of $300 per day for each inmate exceeding the mandated maximum capacity.[25] Assuming 15 homeless people in jail per day for Matrix offenses, this could total $135,000 per month for jail overcrowding. Because the monthly fines exceeded $135,000 only once ($238,000 in March 1994), virtually all the fines were attributable to Matrix prisoners! Using the sheriff's department's own statistics, Matrix-related fines totalled $635,400 between August 1993 and November 1994, when a new jail opened eliminating overcrowding.

The Matrix outreach team was also expensive. The February 1994 board of supervisors' budget analyst report put this cost at $266,264 per year: $80,100 for the salaries of three DSS social workers and $186,164 budgeted for the DPH component.[26] Extrapolating this amount over the 108 weeks between the October 1993 beginning of the Matrix outreach program and November 1995 yields an overall cost of $553,010.

All Matrix costs are summarized in Table 1.

Table 1
OVERALL ESTIMATED MATRIX COSTS TO TAXPAYERS
AUGUST 1993–NOVEMBER 1995

Cost Item		Amount
Police Compensation		$4,815,131
Jail Bookings		861,866
Incarceration		768,588
Jail Overcrowding Fines		635,400
Matrix Outreach Program		553,010
	Subtotal:	$7,633,995
Other Costs		$1,500,000?
Court Costs		
City Attorney Costs		
Police Overhead Costs		
Police Overtime and "Special Events"		
All Police Costs for Matrix II		
Police Night Shelter Referral Program		
DSS and DPH Overhead Costs		
Board of Supervisors Costs		
Mayor's Office Costs		
Estimated Overall Matrix Taxpayer Bill:		$9,133,995

Cost to Homeless People

Taxpayers paid a hefty bill but not nearly as high as that paid by homeless people themselves, especially psychically. Calculating the total number of citations and arrests suffered by homeless people is difficult because the police department distorted its Matrix statistics by lumping in a range of serious non-Matrix misdemeanor and felony offenses, such as narcotics arrests.[27] Also, as Sister Bernie Galvin of Religious Witness with Homeless People showed through municipal court research, the police underreported minor Matrix infractions, such as obstructing a sidewalk or sleeping in a park.[28] Moreover, Commander Martel consistently refused to vouch for the accuracy of the police numbers, stating they were kept only for internal police control purposes (although they were widely publicized).

Galvin's independent municipal court-derived statistics are most accurate, but they only cover some of the offenses listed in the Matrix operations orders.[29] Without further intensive court research, the most that can be done is to subtract all non-Matrix offenses from the police department's statistics and replace police department numbers with Galvin's numbers where available. This method yields an estimated 39,454 Matrix citation and arrest figure from August 1993 through September 1995, including 34,132 citations and 5,322 arrests. With an estimated 10,000 homeless people in San Francisco, that totals almost four Matrix citations or arrests per homeless person—a true reign of terror! And for doing what?—engaging in life-sustaining behavior over which they had no control by virtue of their homelessness—in essence for being homeless. True, many of the citations were for "open container" or public inebriation, but these numbers lump in many non-homeless people, and homeless people, unlike the rest of us, have nowhere but public spaces in which to drink.

Initial Matrix fines at $76 a piece cost homeless people at least $3,014,084, but this was just a starting point. If the initial fine was not paid (what homeless person could afford to?) or the person failed to appear in court, a court computer automatically issued an arrest warrant with an increased fine of $180. If the person failed to appear for any further court date, the court issued a "bench" warrant with a further fine. The total of all these additional fines is unknown.

The case of a hypothetical homeless man, stopped by the police for obstructing a sidewalk, illustrates how this system affected individual homeless people.[30] Assuming the man had no previous arrest warrants, he probably received a citation (unless he had no identification or was uncooperative, in which case he was arrested and booked). After being cited, he had 21 days to appear in municipal court or pay the $76 fine. If he appeared, charges were usually dismissed (sending him back to square one) because the already overcrowded court had no time for Matrix cases. If he neither appeared nor paid the fine, a court computer automatically spit out a $180 arrest warrant.

A month later he was awakened by police while sleeping in Golden Gate Park. A warrant check found the arrest warrant for his previously unpaid citation. The officer then had a choice between making a custodial arrest or simply ignoring the warrant and issuing another citation. (Officers usually ignored warrants, unless there were several, to save themselves the trouble of a custodial arrest.)

If the arrest was made, he was booked and then released on "citation" with an order to appear in court. If he did appear, charges were usually dismissed (again sending him back to square one). If not, a bench warrant for his arrest was issued with an increased fine.

Assuming all this happened several times and his fines accumulated to over $1,000 (often the case), he was no longer eligible for release on citation and remained in jail until his court date, when he was dismissed with credit for time served (again sending him back to square one).

Or was he really at square one? Rather than being merely homeless, he was now homeless with a criminal record, which made it harder for him to find housing or work. His self-esteem, already shattered by homelessness, was made worse by his inability to control the circumstances leading to his repeated citations and arrests and the sense that he was somehow a bad person. Any services he had been receiving were physically disrupted by the citations and arrests and psychically disrupted by the undercutting of his self-esteem. Fear of police encounters may have deterred him from seeking services needed to help end his homelessness. When he was arrested, his few belongings in a shopping cart were probably seized and destroyed. "Looked like garbage to me," the arresting officer probably said, even though officers who work around homeless people know they often keep their property in shopping carts. Mindlessly and repeatedly he was cycled through an already overburdened justice system, with no penological or juridical sense because the acts being punished were involuntary and any such cases that went before a judge were dismissed. All this at great cost to taxpayers, yet homelessness and its associated problems continued to spiral out of control. This obviously was bad policy, but it also raised pressing ethical and legal issues striking at the core of our identity as members of a civilized society.

ETHICAL AND LEGAL ISSUES

Ethical Issues

The critical ethical issue centered on the morality of punishing the types of personal behavior criminalized by Matrix. Mayor Jordan's position was that there are certain minimum acceptable standards of street behavior required of everyone, and anyone who violates these standards should be punished.[31] As an ethical stance, this begged the question of exactly where those minimum standards should lie. Few would disagree that there are minimum standards; for example, virtually everyone agrees that murder is unacceptable street behavior and should be punished. The real issue thus was whether specific Matrix-punishable acts were unacceptable behavior, especially considering the conditions under which the acts were committed; in effect, was it right to punish homeless people for publicly engaging in activities, such as sleeping, sitting, standing, urinating, and storing belongings, when it appeared they had no other choice. Mayor Jordan's enforcement program said yes.

The list of San Francisco organizations which took strong moral stands against Matrix is long and includes the Anti-Poverty Coalition, the American Civil Liberties Union, the Lawyers Committee for Civil Rights, the Homeless Advocacy Project, the San Francisco Neighborhood Legal Assistance Foundation, and the Coalition for Civil Rights. Of particular importance was the San Francisco Coalition on Homelessness, which spoke loudly and often against Matrix through press statements and articles in its own monthly newspaper, the *Street Sheet.* Among its anti-Matrix actions were the formation of a "Street Watch" program to videotape police abuses against homeless people, constant negotiating with the city to ameliorate the effects of Matrix, and organization of political protests. The role the coalition and these other organizations played in ending Matrix cannot be understated, but unfortunately, a full description is beyond the scope of this article.

From a purely ethical perspective, however, the work of the powerful Religious Witness interfaith movement deserves special note. The 2,700 Jewish, Christian, Islamic, Buddhist, and other faith members of Religious Witness were motivated by what they saw as an unbridgeable moral chasm between the systematic repression of homeless people practiced under Matrix and the teachings of their own religious traditions—and the United States Constitution, United Nations Charter, and United

Nations Declaration on Human Rights—about how to treat poor and homeless people.

Ethically, Religious Witness distinguished between "threatening conduct and other violations of public safety" and unavoidable life-sustaining conduct, like sleeping.[32] Enforcement against the former was acceptable, but punishing the latter was cruel and inhuman because it penalized acts over which homeless people had no control by virtue of their homelessness and which do others no harm. In essence, it made the status of homelessness a crime, which was morally wrong because it violated principles of basic human dignity and the inalienable right of all people to provide for their own basic life needs. "All our spiritual traditions," according to Religious Witness, "affirm that poor and homeless people are our brothers and sisters—not criminals to be arrested, nor untouchables to be shunned."[33] Rather, "all faith traditions teach us to comfort the afflicted, feed the hungry, and give justice and shelter to the homeless poor. Our society will be judged as to whether we housed the homeless or arrested them, and whether we fed the hungry children or abandoned them."[34] As put in the Bible, "Woe betide those who enact unjust laws . . . , depriving the poor of justice, robbing the weakest of my people of their rights."[35]

Putting principle to practice, Religious Witness members answered a call to actually stand with and bear witness for homeless people, which they did through well-publicized civil disobedience actions, including a sleep-in on city hall steps, a white tablecloth Sunday dinner in Civic Center for homeless people, rallies at city hall and in Union Square (where 62 members were arrested), the dumping of 19,000 Matrix citations at city hall, and a 411-person fast which immediately preceded the city's celebration of the fiftieth anniversary of the United Nations founding in San Francisco. In perhaps its greatest practical success, Religious Witness, working in concert with the San Francisco Coalition on Homelessness, convinced the county board of supervisors to adopt a resolution strongly condemning Matrix by a vote of 9–1.[36] Mayor Jordan continued to defend Matrix until the end of his tenure, and his staffers blamed Religious Witness members for being out of touch with the citizens and for spending their time protesting rather than providing food and shelter to homeless people[37] (even though Saint Anthony's Foundation, Glide Memorial Church, Hamilton Methodist Church, Saint Vincent de Paul Society, and the Salvation Army are the largest providers of food and shelter to poor people in San Francisco).

Legal Issues

As the ethical drama was unfolding, so was a legal battle in federal district court. In *Joyce v. San Francisco,* a lawsuit conceived by the San Francisco Coalition on Homelessness Civil Rights Working Group, homeless plaintiffs charged that Matrix violated various federal and state constitutional protections, including the rights to be free from cruel and unusual punishment, to equal protection of the laws, to travel freely, to due process of the law, and to be free from unreasonable seizures of property.[38]

Judge Jensen rejected all of these arguments in a summary judgment ruling. His reasons are almost unimportant; the order showed that courts are just as conflicted as the rest of society about the implications of homelessness, and that success in homeless litigation often depends more upon the personal attitudes of the judge hearing the case than upon the merits of the legal arguments made.

This explains why, on the critical Eighth Amendment cruel and unusual punishment claim, the court reached precisely the opposite result as the court in *Pottinger v. Miami* on nearly identical facts. In *Pottinger,* the district court held (among other things) that because homeless people have no choice but to sleep in public places, punishing them under a statute prohibiting sleeping in public places constituted cruel and inhuman punishment.[39] The *Joyce* court distinguished *Pottinger* on the highly technical grounds that the corresponding San Francisco ordinance prohibits "lodging" rather than "sleeping," although the difference is far from obvious and entirely disappears when you consider that police guidelines allow lodging arrests merely for being somewhere for an extended period of time. "Sleeping is a necessary part of life," but "lodging" (at least in Judge Jensen's opinion) is "conduct that even people who have no residence can control," and "can be abstained from without immediate physiological resistance."[40] He also upheld the ordinance prohibiting sleeping in parks between 10:00 p.m. and 6:00 a.m. because he found essentially that homeless people need not sleep at night. Individuals do "control when they sleep," said the judge. "Only round-the-clock prohibitions on public sleeping prevent . . . the necessary life activity of sleeping."[41] One wonders what the ruling would have been had the plaintiffs been homeless children.

Whether Mayor Brown's ending of Matrix renders the appeal of this ruling moot is not clear at the time of this writing.

CONCLUSIONS

Homelessness is not insoluble. Solving it requires the substantial infusion of resources into affordable housing, income and employment programs, and supportive services, organized into a "continuum of care" strategy that prevents homelessness before it happens, provides emergency shelter and services when it does, moves people quickly into transitional housing with in-house services of the type they need to end their homelessness, and then moves them into permanent housing and stable employment with continued services to make sure they remain housed and employed. While Matrix was happening, Mayor Jordan was also working with community groups to create such a continuum of care homelessness plan (Mayor Brown's adoption of this plan is still uncertain at the time of this writing).[42] The plan is well conceived but will fail like its predecessor, "Beyond Shelter," if sufficient implementation funds are not found. To avoid this fate, Mayor Brown should divert the substantial resources that went to Matrix toward continuum of care housing, jobs and income, and supportive services programs. This alone would not solve the money problem, but would certainly help and would go much farther toward improving "quality of life" than did Matrix.

The success of continuum of care strategies requires not only the infusion of substantial resources but also homeless people who are mentally prepared to fully benefit from these resources. Criminalization undercuts continuums of care because it physically destabilizes homeless people and erodes their self-esteem, which reduces their ability to help themselves and to access the service delivery system. For this reason, guaranteeing civil rights must be co-equal with the provision of housing, jobs and income, and supportive services in any continuum of care strategy. The San Francisco continuum of care document contains a civil rights action plan that was the product of tough negotiations between the city and homeless advocates. While guaranteeing civil rights ultimately depends on the attitude of city government and the police, the negotiating process by which this action plan was reached serves as a model for other communities desiring to create a welcoming atmosphere, conducive to the success of their continuum of care plans.

Regarding the Matrix outreach team, there is always room in a homelessness plan for outreach, but the key to its success is the existence of underlying services. Where services are missing, limited money is better spent on buying those services. This is true with Matrix. Rather than funding outreach with nowhere to send anyone, the city should use the money for increased shelter, housing, substance abuse treatment, and mental health services. If outreach is conducted, police should not participate because they defeat the purpose of the outreach by scaring homeless people away. Also, because of the potential for abuse of the 5150 power, the terms of its use should be subject to review by homeless advocates representing homeless peoples' interest; use of the 5150 power should certainly be supported by sufficient mental health treatment services.

As a final note, cities considering Matrix-type programs should beware: voters want a real end to homelessness, and criminalization cannot provide it.

ENDNOTES

1. HomeBase, "Homelessness in the Bay Area: Transform Basic Causes; Meet Human Needs," 1994, pp. 4, 9.
2. "S.F. Mayor Wants Park Campers Out," *San Francisco Chronicle*, August 22, 1995, p. A13.
3. Although Mayor Brown has promised to end Matrix, it is not certain at the time of this writing how this promise will be implemented.
4. For a general discussion of the causes of increasing Bay Area homelessness, consult "Homelessness in the Bay Area."
5. Mayor A. Agnos, "Beyond Shelter: A Homeless Plan for San Francisco, Statement of Need," August 1989.
6. "Homeless Talk About Jordan," San Francisco *Chronicle*, December 12, 1991, p. A26.
7. "Jordan Unveils Friendlier Plan for S.F. Homeless," San Francisco *Chronicle*, December 6, 1991, p. A1.
8. U.S. Conference of Mayors Task Force on Hunger and Homelessness, "Ending Homelessness in American Cities: Implementing a National Plan of Action," July 1993, preface and p. 12.
9. "S.F. Plan to Get Tough on Homeless," San Francisco *Chronicle*, April 27, 1992, p. A1 (citing a report by the Mayor's Office of Economic Planning and Development).
10. *Id.* at p. 26.
11. J. McIntyre and A. Riker, "From Beyond Shelter to Behind Bars," Center on Juvenile and Criminal Justice, San Francisco, December 1993, p. 3 (citing *New Fillmore* newspaper quoting Captain Cairns of the Northern Station).
12. San Francisco Police Department Memorandum to all Personnel, Mission Station, from Captain G. Kowalski, September 1, 1993.

13. Mayor F. Jordan, "Responding to Homelessness in San Francisco," February 1994, pp. 29–30.

14. *Id.* at pp. 27–28.

15. *Id.* at pp. 28–29.

16. "Mayor F. Jordan, Responding to Homelessness in San Francisco," February 1994, p. 30.

17. Interview with Commander Dennis Martel, San Francisco Police Department, August 18, 1995.

18. "Homelessness No. 1 Problem, S.F. Voters Say," San Francisco *Chronicle,* October 30, 1995, p. A1 (citing Chronicle/KRON–TV poll).

19. San Francisco Department of Social Services, "Matrix Weekly DSS Report: A Report of Outreach and Assessment," October 16, 1995.

20. Interview with Commander D. Martel, San Francisco Police Department, August 18, 1995.

21. J. McIntyre and A. Riker, "From Beyond Shelter to Behind Bars," Center on Juvenile and Criminal Justice, San Francisco, December 1993, p. 3 (citing an October 5, 1993 *Tenderloin Times* article regarding police officer compensation and time spent on Matrix).

22. A. Riker, "A Housing Status Assessment of County Bookings," San Francisco County Sheriff's Department, San Francisco, 1994.

23. San Francisco Board of Supervisors Budget Analyst, "Survey of the City's Current Programs and Services Affecting the Homeless Population," February 1994, pp. 14–15.

24. J. McIntyre and A. Riker, "From Beyond Shelter to Behind Bars," Center on Juvenile and Criminal Justice, San Francisco, December 1993, p. 8.

25. Telephone Interview with Eileen Hurst, San Francisco County Sheriff's Department, November 11, 1995.

26. San Francisco Board of Supervisors Budget Analyst, "Survey of the City's Current Programs and Services Affecting the Homeless Population," February 1994, pp. 7 and 9.

27. Telephone interview with Commander D. Martel, San Francisco Police Department, November 6, 1995 (in which Commander Martel provided up-to-date department Matrix statistics).

28. "No justice, no sleep," *San Francisco Bay Guardian,* May 24, 1995, p. 10.

29. Sister B. Galvin, "Matrix Statistics," Religious Witness with Homeless People, San Francisco, September 1995.

30. For an excellent description of how individual homeless people experience the criminal justice system through Matrix, see J. McIntyre and A. Riker, "From Beyond Shelter to Behind Bars," Center on Juvenile and Criminal Justice, San Francisco, December 1993.

31. Mayor F. Jordan, "Creating Exits From Homelessness," San Francisco *Chronicle,* November 30, 1995, p. A25.

32. Telephone Interview with Sister Bernie Galvin, Religious Witness with Homeless People, December 14, 1995.

33. Religious Witness with Homeless People, "A Call for Justice and Compassion

for Poor and Homeless People" (a statement signed by over 2,700 members of the interfaith community).

34. Religious Witness with Homeless People, "The Human Tragedy Behind Matrix Statistics."
35. "Homily Delivered by the Rev. Dr. Robert McCafee Brown." Interfaith Service Sponsored by Religious Witness with Homeless People, March 20, 1994 (citing the Bible).
36. San Francisco Board of Supervisors Resolution 207-94-21.
37. "Religious leaders bring clout to protests of city's Matrix program," *S.F. Weekly,* February 2, 1994.
38. *Joyce v. City and County of San Francisco,* No. C-93-4149 DLJ (N.D. Cal. Aug. 18, 1995).
39. *Pottinger v. Miami,* 810 F. Supp. 1551, 1564–65 (S.D. Fla. 1992).
40. *Joyce,* Slip Opinion at pp. 8–9.
41. Slip Opinion at pp. 9–10.
42. City and County of San Francisco, "Continuum of Care: A Five Year Strategic Homeless Plan, 1995–2000," October 1995.

Chapter 8

DOMESTIC VIOLENCE AND HOMELESSNESS

MICHELE OSTRANDER

A 23-year-old woman living in northern Harris County, Texas, found herself and her two small children fleeing from their home after her husband had beaten her up and threatened to kill her. She had no relatives with whom she and the children could stay. She could not go to her in-laws because they were prominent and wealthy members of the community and the situation was an embarrassment to them. This young woman and children were homeless. Luckily she found refuge at a battered women's shelter. She and the children were able to stay in the emergency shelter for 30 days. By that time, the woman's in-laws had convinced their son to move out of the home so that his wife and children could return. The woman, wanting to believe his sincerity and having no housing alternative, returned to her home. Once again, she began her job in a nearby restaurant. One evening soon after she returned to her home, her husband went to the restaurant, waited until her shift was over, and beat her up. She again fled to a battered women's shelter with her children and obtained a protective order that would order her husband to stay 200 feet away from her home and her place of work. She returned to her home. This woman has since obtained a divorce from her husband; however, she continues to live in terror. She is virtually a prisoner in her own home. A knock on the door is enough to create hysteria in herself and her children. Both she and her children continue to receive counseling. Even though this woman's life is consumed with fear, she is one of the lucky ones—she did not end up living on the streets.

The need to provide safe emergency shelter for battered women is great. Unfortunately, on any given night in Houston, there are 500 homeless battered women and children who are unable to find emergency safe shelter.[1] These women and children have fled their homes due to the overwhelming fear of their batterers. They feel safer on the

118

streets than in their own homes. In Houston/Harris County there are
only three shelters for battered women and children totaling 139 bed
spaces. In many parts of the county, especially in outlying areas, there
are no safe refuges for battered women and children. On an average
night in Houston/Harris County, 361 battered women and children are
left without a safe place to stay. The lack of emergency shelter has forced
more women and children to be turned away than helped. These women
and children are forced to live in their cars, from relative to relative, on
the streets, or end up murdered.

Once a woman and her children are homeless, the problems faced by
the family increase dramatically. Not only must the mother confront the
effects of the violence in their lives, but also confront the effects
homelessness has on the physical, psychological and emotional well-
being of herself and her children. A mother cannot adequately provide
for her children's psychological and emotional needs if all her energy
must be expended on providing safety, food and clothing—none of
which a homeless mother can guarantee. Recent research also shows that
one long-term effect of homelessness on children who experience "multiple
placements" in homes of friends or family or in homeless shelters include
the increased likelihood to experience homelessness in their adult lives
compared to children who grow up in stable environments.[2]

One young Houston woman, who was kicked out of her house when
her parents discovered that she was a lesbian, found herself bouncing
between friends' homes. She began to become involved with women who
promised that they would take care of her. Unfortunately, this security
was often obtained at the cost of her safety. The women expected her
submission for payment of financial security. She found herself going
from one abusive relationship to another. She finally found herself at a
battered women's shelter at the age of 21. She had not completed her
education. She had no job training and no means of supporting herself.
Her thirty days had come to an end with no alternative housing in sight.
She contacted her parents who stated that she could return home if she
denied her sexual orientation and followed a strict list of rules. The
woman could not deny this integral part of how she defined herself and
she again entered the streets.

The Houston Area Women's Center (HAWC) is typical of organizations and social service agencies that provide shelter and support services for women and children who are homeless because of domestic
violence. HAWC first began with a hotline established in 1978 by volun-

teers of Women in Action to respond to the changing needs of women, especially the needs of battered women and children. The HAWC hot line was instrumental in collecting information from battered women that helped establish the first shelter for battered women and children in Houston. Currently, the women's center provides emergency safe shelter for almost one thousand battered women and children each year as well as counseling and support services to non-residential battered women and children. Women and children who enter the HAWC shelter are homeless. Sheehan found that 50 percent of the women and children living on the streets are homeless due to domestic violence.[3] Some arrive immediately after fleeing their homes. Some arrive with a Houston police officer who just rescued them from an attack. Some arrive after hiding on the streets for several days or weeks. Some arrive from relatives' homes after the batterers found their hiding places. One study found that domestic violence murders have declined by 18 percent since the advent of safe shelters for battered women which first opened in the 1970s.[4] Safe shelters for battered women provide not only shelter but safety and secrecy.

The importance of having emergency safe shelters where the address is kept secret and security measures are taken cannot be understated. The women's center shelter has an elaborate security system to protect the residents, including: bullet-resistant glass in windows, bullet-resistant security doors, security cameras, and fencing around the building. These measures are necessary to ensure the safety of the women and children residents. The most dangerous time for a battered woman is when she attempts to leave the relationship.[5] If the woman successfully leaves the relationship, the batterer loses the object he has controlled and dominated for the past countless months or years. For women and children who cannot find safe emergency shelter, the threat to their lives increases dramatically. Women and children living on the streets are vulnerable not only to random stranger violence but also intimate violence from partners or husbands/boyfriends and fathers who so often hunt them down.

One 42-year-old woman found herself in a battered women's shelter due to the horrendous physical violence she experienced at the hands of her husband. She had lived in an upper middle class neighborhood in northeast Harris County for over 15 years. Her husband and she owned their home and had raised two children there. The physical abuse had become increasingly severe until one evening she was forced to flee for her life from the home that she had helped purchase, furnish and decorate. She was unable to take anything with her. Due to the severity of violence, she did not dare to return to her home to collect other belongings. Fifteen years of work had been effectively erased. In addition to the battering, this woman was diagnosed with breast cancer while living in the shelter. She entered the hospital for a mastectomy. When she left the hospital, she went to a friend's house to recover. Unfortunately, the batterer located her and began stalking and threatening her. Due to the fear for her own safety and her friend's safety, the woman moved back into a safe shelter. Eventually, the woman was able to leave the shelter and move into her own apartment. The woman has almost finished chemotherapy. So far the batterer has not located her. She has stated that if he finds her again, she will kill him.

In 1994, 1,161 adult battered women called the Houston Area Women's Center hot line seeking emergency safe shelter; however, space was only available to 406 women and 508 children, leaving 755 women and 1,067 children without shelter. In total, the battered women's shelters in Harris County provided 2,682 safe spaces for battered women and children.[6] Of these women, 48% were Anglo, 28% Black, 20% Hispanic, 1% Asian/Pacific Islander and 2% "other." Thirty-eight percent of these women had less than a high school education and only 21% of these women were employed when they entered the emergency safe shelter.

The horrors of domestic violence are becoming increasingly apparent in our society. The maiming and killing of women by their intimate partners is one of the worst forms of misogyny. Domestic violence is now the leading cause of injury to women between the ages of 15 and 44, more common than automobile accidents, muggings and cancer deaths combined.[7] In 1994, 151 battered women residing in Texas were killed by their intimate partners and an additional 163,223 incidents of domestic violence were reported to Texas law enforcement agencies.[8] Domestic violence not only causes physical and emotional injury to women and children victims but also causes great losses to society. The recent National Crime Victim's Survey reports that domestic violence accounts for almost 100,000 days of hospitalization, 30,000 emergency room visits and 40,000 visits to physicians annually.[9] Family violence costs the nation from $5 to $10 billion annually in medical expenses, police and court costs, shelters and foster care, sick leave, absenteeism, and non-productivity.[10]

Ninety-five percent of domestic violence victims are women.[11] Battering occurs in all socioeconomic strata, educational levels, ethnicities, sexual orientations and abilities. Domestic violence is defined as the intentional, repeated acts by an individual's intimate partner which cause physical, sexual, emotional and economic harm to the individual—usually in a predictive cycle. The most obvious form of violence is physical battering including knife cuts, black eyes, broken bones, internal injuries and bullet wounds. Sexual abuse includes rape, forced prostitution and forced sexual acts with others. Emotional abuse includes threats, intimidation, humiliation, constant criticism, accusations and isolation from friends and family. Economic abuse includes controlling family resources and denying access to education, job training or employment.

CYCLE OF VIOLENCE

Domestic violence occurs when one partner wants to control and dominate the other partner. This control and domination usually occurs in a predictive, repetitive cycle. The cycle of violence contains three phases: (1) tension-building phase; (2) acute battering phase; and (3) calm or honeymoon phase.

1. Tension-Building Phase. The tension-building phase is marked with increasing verbal/emotional abuse and decreasing appropriate communication. Women often report they feel as though they are "walking on eggshells." They try to control the environment (e.g., house is extra clean, children are kept quiet, arriving home from work at exactly 5:15 p.m.) in an attempt to placate the batterers and reduce the chance of the batterers becoming angry. Regardless of what women do, however, batterers find fault.

2. Acute Battering Phase. This tension continues to escalate until the acute battering phase erupts. During this phase, the most serious injuries occur and lethality can result. The police are often called to intervene during the acute battering phase.

3. Calm or Honeymoon Phase. Immediately following the acute battering phase, the batterer becomes very apologetic and sorry for his actions and the calm or honeymoon phase is entered. During this phase, the survivor is very emotionally vulnerable. Her sense of reality is in question as the batterer seeks to make her feel in control of his emotions. Her damaged self-esteem—resulting from the abuse—is bolstered by his admitted need for her and the lavish attention showered on her during this phase. Women often state that they do not want the relationship to end—only the abuse. The women want to believe the batterers' promises that the abuse will never happen again. She begins to believe that maybe she is partly to blame and if she changes her behavior the abuse will not occur. This denial on the part of both the batterer and the victim makes the repetition of the cycle of violence inevitable.

OBSTACLES TO LEAVING A VIOLENT RELATIONSHIP

The most commonly asked question of battered women and of advocates for battered women is "why don't they just leave"? This question can be answered in part by the cycle of violence but also through examination of the obstacles battered women and children must overcome to achieve independence. The truth is that women do leave over and over again, only to run headway into barriers. Some of these obstacles include: fear of death; finding a safe place to live; achieving financial independence; shame, denial, and self-blame; insensitive police intervention; lack of laws that punish batterers for their actions; lack of child care; and lack of legal assistance.

FEAR OF DEATH

The most immediate obstacle a battered woman must overcome is the fear of being murdered by her batterer. One of the most common threats heard from a batterer is "if you leave me, I will find you and kill you." Every day in the United States, four battered women are killed by their intimate partners. The threat of death is real to battered women because they know that their batterers are capable of murder. Research has demonstrated that separated or divorced women were 14 times more likely than married women to report having been victims of violence by their spouses or ex-spouses. Although separated or divorced women comprise 10 percent of all women, they reported 75 percent of the spousal violence.[12] The most dangerous time for battered women is when they attempt to leave the relationship.

The *Houston Chronicle* reported that in March 1995, Loren Jones kicked in the door of his estranged wife's residence, critically wounding her and fatally shooting a male friend who was visiting in her apartment.[13] Again in July 1995, Duane Buck crashed into the home of Debra Gardner, his former girlfriend, carrying a pistol. He first shot a male friend of Debra's in the chest, fatally wounding him. He then shot a female friend of Debra's, critically wounding her. He then chased Debra, who had run out of the house, and gunned her down. During this attack, both Debra's two children and her niece were in the home.[14] Last year, according to the Houston Police Department, 20 Houston women were killed by their intimate partners. The number of friends, relatives and children murdered is unknown.

FINDING A SAFE PLACE TO LIVE

The second major obstacle that battered women must overcome is locating a safe place to live. A battered woman cannot safely stay with her mother, sister, aunt or other relative, because the batterer will know where to find her. Staying with relatives not only puts the woman at risk but also her family. In order to maintain her own safety, the safety of the children and the safety of her family, a battered woman must find a safe emergency shelter. The number of battered women and children needing safe emergency shelter, however, greatly exceeds the number of bed spaces available.

If a woman is fortunate enough to locate space in a battered women's shelter, she generally has 30 to 60 days to locate more permanent housing. In Harris County, there are 515 family spaces in transitional living centers. Families can often live in a transitional living center between 18 to 24 months. Since the space is limited and the stay is an extended length of time, openings are rarely available. According to the city of Houston's Housing and Community Development Program, there are three other types of housing assistance programs: Section 8, Public Housing, and Project-Based Section 8 HUD Subsidized Units. For section 8 housing, 9,000 certificates or vouchers are currently being issued, with a waiting list of 20,000 families for a wait of four to six years. There are 4,443 low-rent housing authority units with 9,000 people on the waiting list and a three- to four-year wait. There are 7,500 project-based section 8 subsidized units representing 50 separate projects, each with its own waiting list. The National Alliance to End Homelessness found that over the past twenty years the supply of housing available to low-income people has declined.[15] In 1970, there were twice as many low-cost units available as there were low-income households. By 1983, this number had been reversed—there were two households competing for every available unit.

FINANCIAL INDEPENDENCE

In addition to locating a safe place for herself and her children, the battered woman must obtain financial independence. When a battered woman leaves a violent relationship, she generally leaves with nothing but the clothes on her back. This woman is fleeing for her life. There is no time to pack clothes, toys, household items or anything. A battered woman not only must leave her home but often must be prepared to leave her job. A safe shelter will be of no use if the batterer can locate his partner at her place of work. The *Houston Post* reported in February 1995, Charlie Wamget walked into a convenient store where his ex-girlfriend worked and fired at her four times, killing her.[16] Again, in June 1995, the *Houston Chronicle* reported that Clinton Dillard fatally shot his ex-girlfriend as she was leaving the Texas Commerce Bank building where she worked.[17] In 1992, approximately twenty percent of the women killed in the workplace were murdered by a husband or male partner, current or former.[18] So not only is a woman losing her home, she is often losing her source of income due to fear of the batterer finding her and killing her. Since it is virtually impossible for a woman to find a new job and save enough money in 30 days to pay a security deposit, first month's rent, and electricity deposit, women are often forced to turn to public assistance to survive or else return to the batterer.

In 1994, 89 percent of the women safely sheltered in Harris County had an annual income of less than $10,000.[19] In Texas, Aid to Dependent Children maximum benefits are $163 per month for one woman and one child, $188 per month for one woman and two children, and $226 per month for one woman and three children. Maximum food stamp benefits are $212 per month for one woman and one child; $304 per month for one woman and two children; and $386 per month for one woman and three children.[20] With this money, a woman must feed her children, pay for child care so that she can search for work, purchase furniture upon which to sleep and sit, find transportation, and pay legal fees if custody, support, or divorce are in process.

The average cost of child care in Harris County is $79 per week for an infant or toddler, $72 per week for preschoolers, and $39 dollars per week for afterschool programs.[21] If a woman has little education or work experience, she will average $5 an hour or $200 a week. After paying child care, transportation costs, rent and utilities, little or nothing will be left for food or clothing. Filing fees for a divorce in Harris County are

$140—which for a woman struggling to pay rent, child care, utilities and other expenses is impossible. With no divorce, the likelihood of obtaining child support is small. The obstacles continue to mount and the challenge to obtain financial independence can become overwhelming which is one reason why a woman is often forced to return to her batterer.

RECOMMENDATIONS

The homelessness caused by domestic violence can only be eradicated by many agencies, government entities, and individuals working together. The provision of shelter alone will not solve this complicated problem. The solution must include provisions for prevention of domestic violence as well as services to current survivors. The recommendations to prevent homelessness of domestic violence survivors include: (1) adoption of zero-tolerance policies; (2) access to financial assistance; (3) increased job training and educational programs; (4) provision of subsidized child care; (5) increased numbers of safe emergency shelters; (6) increased numbers of transitional living centers; and (7) increased numbers of affordable permanent housing options.

(1) **Adoption of Zero-Tolerance Policies.** Communities must adopt zero-tolerance domestic violence policies. This zero-tolerance policy includes: (1) improved laws concerning family violence, stalking and harassment; (2) harsher penalties for perpetrators; (3) court-mandated batterers' intervention and prevention programs for perpetrators; (4) protective orders that are easily obtained and enforced; (5) mandated education about domestic violence for lawyers, district attorneys, judges, law enforcement personnel, social workers, doctors, teachers, counselors, and child abuse investigators; and (6) mandated reporting of domestic violence and referral to domestic violence programs.

(2) **Access to Financial Assistance.** Departments of human services must provide access to financial assistance for battered women and their children. Currently, welfare reform legislation would place severe restrictions on women who need financial assistance during their transition from violence to independence. Restrictions such as time limits, financial caps, and including sponsors' incomes for immigrant women would increase the likelihood of the battered woman remaining in an abusive relationship. Welfare reform should give the states the flexibility to recognize and address the issue of violence against women and their

families, particularly when it affects poor women's ability to gain economic independence through work and education.[22]

(3) **Increased Job Training Programs.** Departments of human services must work with vocational schools, community colleges and universities to increase job training and educational programs for women. The effects of domestic violence on completion of job training and education programs have been documented.[23] One study which surveyed numerous welfare job education programs around the country found that the majority of women in these programs were currently experiencing domestic violence or were past victims of domestic violence. Women reported that their abusers were intimidated by the potential of their partners' economic self-sufficiency. Many had dropped out of the job training programs due to physical injury and threats that they received from their abusers. The importance of economic self-sufficiency cannot be understated. If a woman cannot support herself and her children, she is much more likely to return or stay in an abusive relationship. Job training must be provided in non-traditional, higher-paying jobs as well as traditional pink collar jobs. As Professor Susan Deller Ross stated: "Denying women economic power and independence is a major cause of violence against women because it prolongs their vulnerability and dependence."[24] Job training programs that encourage women to enter pink collar, low-paying jobs provide little assurance of financial independence. Non-traditional job training programs would increase the likelihood of battered women becoming financially independent.

(4) **Provide Subsidized Child Care.** Federal, state and local government must increase subsidies for child care for low-income families. The child care centers must provide safe, quality, affordable child care. The child care workers must have the skills to provide appropriate care, supervision and education to the children. Women with small children cannot succeed in job training programs if child care is unavailable. Nor can they put their skills to use if, upon completion of vocational programs, there are no affordable child care centers in which to place their children while they work. Subsidized child care is a necessity for women who are just beginning the journey to financial independence.

(5) **Increased Number of Emergency Safe Shelters.** In order to provide more safe shelters, money from federal and state grants, corporations, and individuals must be available to support battered women's programs. The average cost per day per client in HAWC's safe shelter is two dollars. Monies are needed to support residential, non-residential and outreach

programs. The emergency shelters must provide shelter, food, clothing, transportation, child care, counseling, legal advocacy and safety. The security and safety required by battered women and children is tremendous. The shelters must be located at undisclosed locations and have adequate security measures to keep batterers from harming their partners.

(6) **Increased Numbers of Transitional Living Centers.** Funding must be made available through the Department of Human Services and the U.S. Department of Housing and Urban Development (HUD) that would allow for increased numbers of transitional shelters that provide a secure base to allow for stabilization, job training and education. Increased number of emergency shelters will be of no benefit if after the 30-day stay women and children are faced with the choice of returning to their batterer or living on the streets.

(7) **Increased Numbers of Affordable Permanent Housing Options.** The U.S. Department of Housing and Urban Development (HUD) must increase the number of permanent housing options available to low-income families. The dramatic increase in families needing affordable housing units will, in all likelihood, continue over the next few years due to the federal cuts in moneys and programs that serve low-income families.

CONCLUSION

The prevention of homelessness caused by domestic violence depends on numerous variables including safe living conditions, financial assistance, job training and education, subsidized child care, advocacy and support. This assistance is needed by women and children who have or currently are experiencing domestic violence. The goal of the battered women's movement, however, is prevention of domestic violence. Prevention can only be achieved through education about domestic violence. This education needs to occur at all levels including: elementary, intermediate and high schools; colleges; trade schools; law schools; medical schools; youth groups; churches; corporations; individual businesses; and all other places where individuals live, learn, work and play. Young people need to grow up knowing that domestic violence is unacceptable in any situation. Domestic violence results in horrible consequences. The tragedy is that domestic violence and the resulting homelessness is preventable.

ENDNOTES

1. McKinsey & Company, Inc. (1989). *Addressing the Problem of Homelessness in Houston and Harris County.* Houston, TX.

2. Roman, N.P. & Wolfe, P.B. (1995). *Web of Failure: The Relationship Between Foster Care and Homelessness.* Washington, D.C.: National Alliance to End Homelessness.

3. Sheehan, M.A. (1993). "An interstate compact on domestic violence: What are the advantages"? *Juvenile and Family Justice Today, 1*(4), 12–19.

4. Fox, J.A. (1994). *Supplementary Homicide Reports 1976–1992.* (ICPSR No. 06387). Washington, D.C.: U.S. Department of Justice.

5. Harlow, C. (1991). *Female Victims of Violent Crime.* Washington, D.C.: U.S. Department of Justice.

6. Texas Department of Human Services. (1995). 1993 and 1994 Family Violence Shelter—Client Information. Austin, TX.

7. Koop, C.E. (1989). *Surgeon's General Report.* Washington, D.C.: U.S. Public Health Service.

8. Texas Department of Public Safety. (1994). *Family Violence in Texas 1994.* Austin, TX: Crime Records Division, Uniform Crime Reporting.

9. National Victim Center. (1993). *Crime and Victimization in America: Statistical Overview.* Fort Worth, TX.

10. Meyer, H. (1992, Jan. 6). "Seeing the Pain: America's Physicians Confront Family Violence." *American Medical News,* p. 7.

11. Texas Department of Public Safety. (1994). *Family Violence in Texas 1994.* Austin, TX: Crime Records Division, Uniform Crime Reporting.

12. Harlow, C. (1991). *Female Victims of Violent Crime.* Washington, D.C.: U.S. Department of Justice.

13. Bardwell, S.K. (1995, March 29). "Estranged husband held in shooting." *Houston Chronicle,* p. A20.

14. Johnson, S. (1995, July 31). "Gunman kills 2, critically wounds 1 in west Houston." *Houston Chronicle,* p. A11.

15. Roman, N.P. & Wolfe, P.B. (1995). *Web of Failure: The Relationship Between Foster Care and Homelessness.* Washington, D.C.: National Alliance to End Homelessness.

16. Hensel, D.Q. & Klanke, A. (1995, February 13). "Man 66, charged with gunning down ex-girlfriend, 25." *Houston Post,* p. A1, A13.

17. "Ex-boyfriend sought." (1995, June 14). *Houston Chronicle,* p. A27.

18. Bureau of Labor Statistics. (1993). Washington, D.C.: U.S. Government Printing Office.

19. Texas Department of Human Services. (1995). 1993 and 1994 Family Violence Shelter—Client Information. Austin, TX.

20. Texas Department of Human Services. (1995). Aid to Dependent Children Benefit Summary. Houston, TX.

21. Initiatives for Children. (1995). *Child Care Survey 1994.* Houston, TX.

22. Davis, M., Kraham, S., & Reuss, P. (1995, August 16). *Background on Family Violence Waiver.* NOW Legal Defense and Education Fund.

23. Raphael, J. (1995). *Domestic Violence: Telling the Untold Welfare-to-Work Story.* Chicago, IL: Taylor Institute.
24. Deller Ross, S. (1995, April 28). *A Leadership Summit: The Link Between Violence and Poverty in the Lives of Women and Their Children.* NOW Legal Defense and Education Fund.

Chapter 9

PROJECT RESPOND: EFFECTIVE RESPONSE TO THE HOMELESS MENTALLY ILL

JULIE LARSON AND SUE BEATTIE

INTRODUCTION

Take a walk down the street in any urban center. What do you see? There's a shopper with packages, a professional person waiting for the light. A family with a small child window shopping. A woman entering her apartment. These are the scenes you would expect to see in the urban landscape. But what about the man on the street corner making frightening gestures, the woman with her shopping cart piled high with plastic, or the frightened-looking man sitting in the doorway rocking and moaning.

These people are the homeless mentally ill. They do not choose their plight. They suffer from a serious and chronic illness that affects their ability to perceive reality, form relationships, and exercise good judgment and insight. No one chooses to be mentally ill. Mental illness does not discriminate between rich and poor, educated or uneducated. Some of the mentally ill have come from the state hospital, others have become disengaged from family and loved ones.

For many people suffering mental illness medicine and support help to reduce the symptoms. The angry voices that live inside become quieter, thinking becomes clearer and fearfulness becomes reduced. For some, medicine does not help, or it causes unpleasant, potentially permanent side effects. This helps to explain why some mentally ill persons are reluctant to take medications or even speak to a mental health clinician.

They wander the streets. They behave bizarrely. Shoppers are frightened. Business is impacted. Residents are uncomfortable and concerned. No one knows what to do. They call the police and complain to city officials. Police are often frustrated when asked to evict an elderly woman from the shelter in the dead of winter, confront a naked and obviously psychotic man wandering in traffic or arrest the same hungry and home-

131

less man for the crime of stealing food. Most police officers did not enter the police academy to become social workers, yet these are everyday calls to which they must respond. It is not that police officers are heartless or unconcerned, but they do not have the training, resources or time to effectively intervene in a meaningful or lasting way.

In their frustration, many officers and city planners want to know: How did this situation arise? What's wrong with these people? Are they wacko or what? Have state hospitals simply discharged their mentally ill patients to the streets? Where are their friends and families? Where are the counselors and services they need? Why are hospital beds in short supply? When a hospital bed can be accessed, why is the individual out on the streets again after a week?

These were questions that were being asked around the nation and in Portland, Oregon by police officers, government planners, the business community and other concerned citizens who were frustrated and concerned about the increase of homeless and apparently mentally ill persons on the streets. Complaints and requests for help were often fielded by Mental Health Services West, the downtown community mental health center with a mandate to serve the urban poor. In April 1993, Mental Health Services West piloted Project Respond, a mobile crisis and outreach team to respond to the growing number of disenfranchised mentally ill persons wandering the streets and to provide support to the other non-mental health emergency responders. In the two years since its inception, the project has demonstrated its effectiveness and become an integrated part of the emergency service system and a recognized expert in outreaching to homeless mentally ill. In addition, Project Respond staff have provided extensive training and consultation to those having contact with the homeless mentally ill, such as social service providers, businesses, and other concerned community agents. Project Respond will be described in detail later in this chapter.

DEINSTITUTIONALIZATION: FROM THE HOSPITAL TO THE STREETS

Up until the 1950s, most persons with severe mental illness spent the majority of their life in a mental asylum. With the discovery of effective medications to treat the symptoms of mental illness, states began to be increasingly concerned about protecting the civil rights of the newly compensated mental patient and began to discharge their patients back into the community. During the 1960s, state hospital populations decreased by approximately 67 percent.[1]

While the intent of deinstitutionalization was to transfer care to community-based programs, this was not always successful. Resources usually did not follow patients into the community, and community programs were not always prepared to deal with the level of psychopathology exhibited by the newly discharged psychiatric patient.[2] More recently, government has been under enormous pressure to reduce costs. As a result, state hospitals have continued to discharge patients and "downsize" in order to further reduce the states cost of caring for the mentally ill. For example, in the state of Oregon, the 1960 cumulative census in the state's three psychiatric hospitals was about five thousand patients or 293 patients per 100,000 population. Most recently, the state has closed one state hospital, and cumulative census has been reduced to about 780 or 30 patients per 100,000 population.

With deinstitutionalization also came changes in the civil commitment laws. Commitment statutes became more restrictive and required clear evidence of imminent danger to self or others or gross inability to care for basic needs before an individual could be involuntarily detained in a hospital. As a result, more mentally ill persons became visible on the streets, and communities have learned to tolerate, and largely ignore, the mentally ill in their midst. Urban centers often act as a magnet, attracting a sizable homeless and mentally ill population. Not only does the city center typically provide an array of inexpensive housing alternatives, but the urban core usually evidences a greater tolerance for diversity and bizarre behavior than that which is acceptable in smaller neighborhoods and communities.

WHO ARE THE HOMELESS?

In an effort to better understand homelessness, The National Mental Health Association[3] (1988) has identified three broad groupings into which most homeless individuals fall. These include those who are homeless due to an economic crisis, those who are homeless due to a personal crisis (such as battering or abuse) and those who are homeless due to chronic disabilities such as drug or alcohol addiction or mental illness.

WHO ARE THE MENTALLY ILL?

A chronic mental illness, such as schizophrenia, bipolar disorder (manic depression), is a complex and often debilitating disease that affects the brain. Some of the symptoms of mental illness include: difficulty perceiving reality, hallucinations, paranoia, mood swings, confused thought process, and poor insight and judgment. These symptoms often lead to an overall decline in the person's ability to function. Unfortunately, there are no known cures for mental illness, but the symptoms can be controlled by a combination of medications, support, and treatment. Each person is impacted differently by the illness, so treatment must be individualized through an often frustrating process of trial and error.

WHO ARE THE HOMELESS MENTALLY ILL?

To be homeless means more than being without a home. It means being without a bed in which to sleep, a table from which to eat or bathroom in which to tend to grooming and other personal business. Homelessness is challenging and stressful to anyone. Symptoms such as confused thinking, paranoia, and compromised judgment make it even more difficult to cope with and resolve homelessness. Although a mentally ill person with housing may have the same disabling psychiatric symptoms, they have a "home base" from which to operate. They are more likely to meet their basic needs and are more likely to have a support network, either professionals such as a case manager or private psychiatrist, and/or natural helpers such as an apartment manager or family member. Such a support network ensures that there is someone who might provide support, assistance in maintaining basic resources, or at a minimum help to monitor functioning and symptoms and seek assistance for an individual who appears to be in crisis.

There are a myriad of reasons for a mentally ill person to become homeless. Some, like their non-mentally ill cohorts, have fallen victim to an economic or personal crisis. Others have "fallen between the cracks" or have rejected help, believing rightly or wrongly that the help came with expectations or strings attached that were too onerous. Whatever the cause, homeless mentally ill persons are then left to fend for themselves in whatever way they can. Certainly, the stress of homelessness and the constant threat of victimization may exacerbate psychiatric symptoms.

On the street, bizarre behavior and frightening dress may also serve an adaptive purpose, in that it keeps others at a distance. Even a would-be perpetrator is less likely to victimize the man who carries a large stick and curses whenever someone comes near, the woman who slaps herself in the face and screams when men look at her, or the homeless man who sleeps with his belongings in his cart during the day and stays vigilant all night on a park bench. While these behaviors effectively keep others away and reduce the chance of victimization, they also present difficulties to the well-intentioned person or outreach worker who attempts to intervene. Some of the homeless mentally ill have also had previous experience in the mental health system and have grown dissatisfied and distrustful, due to real or perceived mistreatment. In turn, case managers who are already feeling overburdened by a demanding caseload of severely mentally ill persons who present to the clinic for services, may not seek out the person who quietly drops out of services. This can result in a "mutual withdrawal between disaffiliated, distrustful clients and their psychiatric caregivers."[3]

Physical health care represents yet another difficulty for the homeless mentally ill person. The homeless mentally ill are more likely to be without health insurance, they are more likely to have difficulty in making appointments, and when they present for health care are likely to be perceived by most primary health care establishments as less desirable than other consumers. The homeless are also exposed to more extreme conditions in general and as a result suffer more problems with physical health due to untreated infections, exposure to the elements, exhaustion and poor nutrition. In the absence of regular checkups, health problems associated with normal aging go untreated and health complications such as blood pressure, diabetes, or circulatory problems intensify. Physical health problems in turn exacerbate and intensify psychiatric problems, which in turn renders the individual less able to withstand the hardships of being homeless.[4]

WHO RESPONDS TO THE HOMELESS MENTALLY ILL?

Although the homeless mentally ill are most frequently described as "non-compliant," "service resistant" or "non-help seeking,"[5] this designation seems only to apply to their participation in traditional outpatient mental health services. In fact, the homeless mentally ill are frequent consumers of a de facto crisis mental health system which includes police, medical emergency personnel and outpatient providers. It is estimated that up to 80 percent of police time is spent in non-crime-related activities, including responding to mentally ill persons and their social welfare-related problems.[6] When police are called because an older "bag lady" is washing her clothes in a city fountain, or a disheveled man is frightening shoppers with his psychotic ramblings, they can only respond to the immediate crisis. They may cite an ordinance that prohibits the behavior and make a misdemeanor arrest, move the person on, or ignore the situation. As one officer put it, "Bear in mind I'm a walking policeman downtown. We see many street people who have mental illness and we have no place to put them. . . . Police only can arrest people when they act out. . . . We would like to help those who really want it, but our only resource is to lock them up or send them on their way."[7]

The question of who responds to the homeless mentally ill will be pivotal to any planning effort designed to address the problems of this general population. Although the mental health professional may seem like the obvious choice to take the lead in any intervention plan, it is more often the street officer who is left to intervene as a first-line responder. Although some studies find that police officers are ill-equipped to handle the mentally ill,[8] many others consistently describe ongoing frustration faced by police when they attempt to access the mental health system on behalf of this most vulnerable population.[9] One study examined the relationship between the police and the mental health system and identified several essential components which promote, for the police, a positive working relationship.[10] This included an emphasis on availability, which includes ready, consistent and timely on-site response, an ability to formulate and articulate intervention strategies and a willingness to assume ownership for disposition when a call involves a mentally ill person.

SYSTEM DESCRIPTION

On a systems level, developing a coherent and effective response to the homeless mentally ill requires cross-program participation and cooperation. Although every community is to some extent unique with respect to the specifics of community needs and resources, there are also some commonalities across systems that may be productively pursued. Any effective response to the homeless mentally ill will need to coordinate closely with both the emergency mental health responders and the outpatient providers.

Fragmented and frustrated would accurately describe the psychiatric emergency response system in Portland, Oregon in 1985. As is so often the case, tragedy was the catalyst for change. The shooting of a well-respected psychiatrist by a decompensated patient propelled the system to initiate a large-scale planning effort to demystify and coordinate the efforts of the various emergency mental health responders. The process recapitulated what effective planners already know: productive planning requires focusing on a clear definition of roles, a willingness to listen to the concerns and frustrations of one another, a valuing of each responder's expertise, a commitment to work together, and a plan to debrief new incidents as they occur and follow up with regular and ongoing meetings.[11] Out of this planning process emerged PEOT, the Psychiatric Emergency Operation Team. The core membership of PEOT consists of representatives from each mental health crisis program, police representatives from each precinct and local municipality, key hospital personnel, staff from the involuntary commitment program office, the team supervisor for the 24-hour crisis phone line, and representatives from county and state mental health. Although the group answers to a Policy Review Group made up of executive level administrators of the various member agencies, PEOT itself is composed of operational level supervisors who are close to the actual work and able to speak knowledgeably about operational details. The group meets monthly to share information, debrief incidents, problem solve and make recommendations regarding potentially useful changes in policy or procedures. PEOT is a forum to discuss potentially sensitive issues and high-profile individuals. Initially, the group struggled with issues related to confidentiality and specific incident debriefing. While some guidelines were developed to answer specific issues related to confidentiality, concern dissipated as trust developed, and the group remains an effective vehicle for both problem solving and support among the member agencies.

State mental health law authorizes police officers, psychiatrists with admitting privileges to a certified hospital, and certain "mental health designees" to initially cause the involuntary detention of an individual alleged to be mentally ill and dangerous to self or others. In addition to initiating such a petition, state law also requires police to transport allegedly mentally ill individuals to a state-certified facility for evaluation when directed to do so by an authorized mental health designee. If the facility staff (usually a medical doctor) does not concur with the field assessment, the officer is responsible to transport the individual back to the site of the original detention. Although the system provides for adequate due process checks and balances, it also affords ample opportunity for conflict and hard feelings. A forum such as PEOT allows providers to vent and ultimately to problem solve around these most difficult systems problems.

COMMUNITY CONSIDERATIONS

"Policy which is enacted within a community will ultimately reflect the prevailing community attitude."[12] Portland, Oregon is a rapidly growing city of about one million people and is the only true urban community in the state. The city of Portland is fortunate to have an already established coalition of businesses and committed urban partners who have agreed to a voluntary tax in order to enhance the viability of the urban core. Revenues from this tax are administered by the Association for Portland Progress (APP), an independent, not-for-profit organization which employs a network of guides, private security officers, and street maintenance workers who regularly patrol the streets of downtown Portland. Another Portland innovation is the CHIERS Program which is run by the Hooper Detox Center and regularly patrols the streets, removing incapacitated and intoxicated persons to the detox center. The city has also implemented a comprehensive model of community policing which integrates officers into the daily activities of neighborhoods and communities. In the downtown area, this includes the development of many small precincts offices which utilizes citizen volunteers and deploys officers on horseback, bicycles, and on foot, with an expectation that they participate in local planning efforts and attend neighborhood meetings.

As in every large city, there exists in Portland a significant homeless population which includes a relatively large proportion who are mentally ill. Although accurate figures are difficult to come by, local experts estimate that there are approximately one thousand homeless persons, and estimates of the number of mentally ill among this population have ranged from 30 percent to 60 percent. This wide variation is most likely due to the subjective definition of mental illness. The lay community tends to include anyone who exhibits troubling or odd behaviors as mentally ill. This might then include persons with drug and alcohol problems, mental retardation, problems with aging, head injuries, HIV, dementia, and physical handicaps.

Since the mid-1980s, Mental Health Services West, which is the community mental health program located in the downtown area, made repeated efforts to fund and deploy a mobile crisis and outreach team. The agency made numerous attempts to secure government funding, but these attempts were largely unsuccessful due to the difficulty of spending state mental health dollars to serve individuals who may or may not have a bonafide mental illness. With the help of APP and the talent of an agency-employed fundraiser, private fundraising efforts directed to business owners and local foundations succeeded in raising the necessary funds to begin operation. In retrospect, the need to privately raise funds among the constituents most interested in finding a solution to the problems posed by the homeless mentally ill has created an alliance between the business community, other concerned constituents of the urban core and the mental health center. This, in turn, has fostered a deeper, more compassionate understanding of the mentally ill on the streets and has helped in building a broad community consensus as to the appropriate response to this vulnerable and troubling group of individuals.

DESCRIPTION OF PROJECT RESPOND

Project Respond is a crisis response and street outreach program that utilizes a staff composed of 8.4 FTE outreach/crisis workers (masters level mental health professionals), necessary medical support, and the project director. There is a day and evening shift, seven days a week, providing services from 8:00 a.m. to 11:00 p.m., although operating hours are flexible and can be adjusted to meet community needs.

Operationally, each shift pairs two outreach/crisis workers together in a vehicle to provide mobile mental health services to the community. A third team member provides follow-up services to identified clients during the weekday shifts. The staff wear purple jackets or tee shirts that say Project Respond so that they can be readily identified when on the scene of a crisis. Mentally ill persons who might easily be confused or mistrustful of different team members who rotate through shifts have institutionalized their trust when they see someone in the team attire.

Currently, the team responds to crisis calls and does outreach anywhere within the urban core. Calls from police and businesses in other parts of the county are triaged and the team responds as capacity permits. The annual budget for Project Respond is approximately $400,000.

The Project Respond team fulfills three essential functions: (a) crisis response, (b) street outreach, and (c) consultation and community training/networking.

CRISIS RESPONSE

Crisis response is the first priority of the Project Respond team. Community partners such as the police, CHIERS staff, Portland guides, business employers/employees, apartment managers, shelter staff, family members and other concerned citizens or agencies contact Project Respond via cell phone or APP dispatch. These community agents call to report disturbances or concerns that involve a mentally ill person. They also call anytime they encounter a person who appears to be in distress regardless of the individual's mental status. In such situations, Project Respond will travel to the site of the crisis and provide evaluation and consultation.

When the caller reports an *imminent crisis* (such as suicide, bizarre and/or escalating behavior), the Project Respond *crisis/outreach team is immediately dispatched to the scene* (within minutes). If the caller reports a situation which includes a weapon or assaultive behavior, the team immediately notifies the police. In such situations, the police are the primary responders in these situations, although Project Respond staff also arrive on site to provide consultation and evaluation. If the situation de-escalates, the team will accept jurisdiction from the police, as appropriate. When a caller reports a less than imminent risk situation, Project Respond provides an estimated time of arrival, usually within an hour of the initial call.

Project Respond clinicians are broadly empowered to intervene in a variety of situations. When they arrive on site, the clinician assesses the situation, interviews witnesses and other involved parties as well as conducts a mental health assessment of the identified individual. Most often, problematic behavior can be confronted and/or the individual can be directed toward appropriate services. Concerned community agents get a consult and/or relevant information about mental health problems and the resources available to deal with specific situations.

Project Respond staff also have the authority to initiate an immediate petition for civil commitment and cause the individual to be involuntarily transported to a hospital for further evaluation as appropriate and supportable under Oregon law. In such situations, the team follows the police to the hospital and is available to take over in the emergency room and provide information and consultation to the hospital staff. This allows the police to return more quickly to the street.

Occasionally, there arise situations where a permanent and immediate solution is elusive. Most often this occurs when a homeless mentally ill person is initially resistant to contact with mental health professionals. Due to the flexibility of its mobile response in the field and the combination of crisis response and street outreach capacity, Project Respond outreach/crisis workers have the ability to repeatedly return and re-evaluate ongoing situations as they develop.

STREET OUTREACH

When the team members are not engaged in a crisis call, they are a visible presence on the streets as they approach and build trust with the disenfranchised, often homeless, mentally ill population. Project Respond staff identify individuals in need of general outreach services as they respond to crisis requests.

The team regularly visits parks, shelters, freeway underpasses and other locations where homeless people frequent. They offer basic supplies such as warm beverages, food, blankets, dry clothes, meal vouchers and a caring response.

The ultimate goal of outreach is to establish a viable, consistent, trusting relationship which ultimately allows the team to assist an individual in accessing services such as housing, financial support and ongoing mental health services. Some individuals readily respond and accept our services. Others, who harbor debilitating suspicion or who have experienced real or imaged mistreatment, require that we be patient, consistent, respectful and persevering in our initial approach.

Project Respond was developed by Mental Health Services West in response to a repeatedly identified need for expanded outreach services in the downtown core, and Project Respond clients have derived great benefit from the integration of the outreach program into the more traditional services of the mental health center. For example, the team can accompany a mentally ill person to the agency's day treatment program and depend on day treatment staff making a special effort to connect with the person and offer such commodities as a hot meal, a shower, or simply the opportunity to spend time in a safe and supportive environment. To make the transition even easier, the nurse practitioner on the outreach team is also a part-time staff member on the day treatment team. The goal of the team is to transition the individual from outreach-based services into so-called regular case management. This type of seamless transition avoids some of the pitfalls that often occur when mentally ill persons are moved from one provider to another.[13] Transitioning clients into ongoing programs as they stabilize and move into housing also prevents the team of developing an ongoing caseload which might limit their ability to be available to respond to newly identified homeless mentally ill individuals on the street.

CONSULTATION AND COMMUNITY TRAINING/NETWORKING

In the course of outreach, Project Respond staff come in contact with staff of other service providers who are based at locations where disenfranchised mentally ill individuals congregate such as homeless shelters, missions and SRO hotels. These community partners are invaluable in identifying individuals they believe to be mentally ill and in need of services. This regular contact, in turn, provides these community partners with regular, dependable and expert mental health consultation as they attempt to provide the most basic shelter services to Portland's disenfranchised mentally ill population.

In addition, the team provides consultation and training to businesses and concerned groups. In the last year, we have provided consultation and training to shelters, banks, department stores, the mayor's office, apartment and hotel managers (ranging from upscale hotels to SRO's), the police, APP, private security companies, PSU, health clinics, the state employment office, churches and the zoo. These groups all report an increased contact with the mentally ill and especially the homeless mentally ill and are seeking education and information about mental illness and practical advice regarding how to interact, stay safe and be helpful.

Project Respond staff are often asked to serve on specialized task forces that are focused on resolving a community problem. Recently Project Respond staff served on a committee convened by the chief of police to develop a week long intensive training on working with the mentally ill for a specialized group of officers known as the Crisis Intervention Team

(CIT). These officers are function as first-line responders to calls involving the mentally ill and are available in every precinct on each shift. They work closely with Project Respond staff and other mental health providers.

In another effort, the Community Action Office of Multnomah County formed a relocation team to assist the 120 residents of a homeless shelter that was being closed due to funding cuts. The team was composed of specialists from agencies who work with older adults, people with alcohol and drug problems, Hispanic individuals, people with mental health problems, and the general homeless population. In less than three months, this committee interviewed over one hundred of the shelter residents, screened for disabilities, and conducted a "needs assessment." Residents of the shelter were then assigned a case manager from the relocation team whose expertise most closely matched the needs of the individual. Special, one-time-only funding was made available to purchase housing while the assigned agency initiated services and explored other resources. The project was surprisingly effective at connecting long-term shelter residents to alternative housing and services, and the plan is to conduct follow-ups throughout the year to measure the long-term success of the project.

As Project Respond has developed a successful track record of transitioning mentally ill individuals from the streets, more recently we have been able to secure federal support through two separate Housing and Urban Development (HUD) grants. These grants have allowed us to be able to greatly expand the services we are able to provide, including the development of additional mobile crisis capacity, the addition of 50 residential beds and a 24-hour professionally staffed Drop-In program expected to open in the fall of 1995. A second grant recognized the need to "cast a wide net" when providing outreach services and specifically supports linkages and coordination among all the various social service agencies which must necessarily come together to provide the level of assessment and care needed by these most difficult individuals. With the development of a successful local model for delivering outreach services, county government is now actively looking for funding to expand and ensure the availability of resources necessary for the continuation of outreach services throughout the country.

OUTREACH AS A MODEL FOR
THE HOMELESS MENTALLY ILL

The American Psychiatric Association Task Force Report on the Homeless Mentally Ill (1984) strongly endorses the use of assertive outreach as an effective strategy to engage with the homeless mentally ill. In the last ten years, dozens of outreach programs of varying magnitudes, staffing and resources have piloted efforts to address the needs of the homeless mentally ill.[14] Although each program differs according to the specific community situation, the key components of outreach—establishing trust, building rapport and nonjudgmental acceptance—appear to be essential to the process of engaging a homeless mentally ill person.[15] Cohen describes engagement as a process of establishing trust and reducing fear so that the real work can begin.[16] The Project Respond team has found that the amount of time spent in engagement can take anywhere from minutes to months to years. For the homeless mentally ill person living on the street, under a bridge or in the shelter, engagement usually starts with a low-key, non-threatening acknowledgment of the person's presence through verbal and nonverbal communication. The actual approach is individualized based on the person's demeanor, the setting and any safety considerations. Engagement often includes the offering of some basic commodity such as food, a warm blanket or a cigarette. This process of "starting where the client is"[17] initiates an engagement which can be described as an "opening wedge"[18] in which trust is developed by meeting the person's basic needs with no strings attached.

CASE EXAMPLES

- A female outreach worker who is assigned to a large shelter two days a week is referred to a middle-aged woman who has been disruptive at night, talking to herself and then denying it when confronted. She also smells so bad the other women complain and staff believe they will need to ask her to leave in order to keep peace in the shelter. The outreach worker purposely sits one chair away from her casually reading a magazine and occasionally nods in her direction. The worker says out loud, "I'm going to get a cup of coffee, do you want one" and does not press her when there is no response. Instead, she returns with two coffees and places one on the chair between them and goes back to her magazine. In the next minute, the worker hears a low, throaty "thank-you" and notices out of the corner of her eye the woman is drinking the coffee. When the worker leaves, she thanks the woman for letting her sit nearby and says she hopes she sees her again soon. The woman and the outreach worker have a brief moment of eye contact. To many outreach workers this would be considered a successful first outreach contact.

- A man living on a park bench screamed every time the team left him a sandwich. He would then stomp on the sandwich. On the twenty-second day, the man ate the sandwich and from that time continued to accept food from the team. Eventually he told the team his name. After a long period of relationship-building in the park, the man moved indoors and began taking medications. He was later able to share with the team that he originally assumed that the team meant to poison him with the sandwiches, but after seeing other persons eating our sandwiches with no apparent ill effect, he finally decided to try one because he was very hungry.

- Police call the Project Respond team to a parking lot behind a fast-food restaurant where a very disheveled woman is standing in the dumpster throwing garbage at patrons as she digs through it. The woman curses and waves them away when they offer food. The workers ask if there is anything they can do to help. She stops and says she is looking for "a goddamned red button." Miraculously, the team is able to produce a button and she climbs down from the trash bin smiling sweetly, showing a missing button on her tattered sweater, and asking if they have any thread. The team was able to walk her to the day treatment center where there are a number of craft supplies. They were able to produce a needle and thread. She also made use of the program showers, food and other resources. From that point she started coming to the center on her own and was assigned a regular case manager who was then able to help with other resources including housing.

- The team was able to build a relationship with a very disheveled, disorganized, psychotic man who had been homeless for over ten years. After a months of sustained effort, the team was able to secure entitlements for him based on the team psychiatrist's evaluation which was conducted during several contacts in parks and under bridges. The man could not think of anything to buy with his monthly entitlement check, nor did he want housing (too many rules), but he did consistently state he would like an address for people to write him. The team was able to use his entitlements to purchase an "address" with a free room thrown in. The team wrote to him at his address, which was a couple of blocks from the clinic, and left clothes, crackers and juice in his room. When they encountered him on the street, they would tell him he had mail and a surprise waiting for him at his address. Eventually, the hotel manager reported he had begun staying overnight several times a week, especially when the weather was poor. After more than a year of consistent contact with the team, he has successfully moved indoors. To date he continues to decline medications and is quite confused and psychotic. He does, however, participate in several of the programs at the clinic where his needs and symptoms can be monitored.

CONSUMER PERSPECTIVE

The actual consumers of mental health services are an important and newly recognized resource for programs for the mentally ill persons. Consumers have played an important role in the recent crisis intervention training (CIT) for the Portland Police. Groups of consumers voluntarily met with small groups of CIT officers and showed them their homes or attended luncheons to share about themselves and discuss issues of concern. The officers reported that the non-crisis contact with mentally ill persons who were relatively stable and able to share their stories helped dispel myths and raised the officers' comfort level. The following was written by a consumer who facilitated a luncheon with the police:

> As a mentally ill person I would like to address a few comments to the police that hopefully can improve community relationships. My situation is better with police understanding and worse without it.
>
> Most mentally ill people are non-violent. They may be acting out or shouting in public. I have advice on how to talk to someone who is upset. I suggest that the police use a soothing and calming tone, low voices and no shouting. Use phrases that reassure the frightened person such as: "It's going to be alright" or "It's going to be okay." Show you care and establish trust. Tell the victim (and the mentally ill are often victims of their illness and of the community) to "take it easy and slow down." Say that "We are here to protect you and help you." Be polite, as in "Please get into the car." Have patience, as the victims are as frightened as you might be. What you say may escalate the situation.
>
> Use only gentle restraints when necessary. Don't struggle with the victim.

Tell them to "Stay calm, don't panic" and that "we'll soon be there." It works against us both when you rough us up and it badly damages the victim's fragile psyche.

Tell yourselves that you are doing a good job, that I believe in you and that I am proud of you for the way you handled that. I believe these efforts will improve community relationships between the police and the consumers of the mental health system.[19]

CONCLUSION/RECOMMENDATIONS

In order to operationalize the material discussed in this chapter, the authors would like to offer the following suggestions to assist in the development of programs to meet the needs of the homeless mentally ill.

1. Conduct an adequate needs assessment and clarify the problem from a number of different perspectives. Include the police, businesses, local officials at the city, county or state level, politicians who have an interest in or are sympathetic to the plight of the homeless mentally ill, mental health providers, local members of the Alliance for the Mentally Ill (AMI), mental health consumers, legal advocates for the mentally ill, and other relevant participants, given your specific community.

2. Pilot small projects to clarify your data, test system design, and identify barriers and limitations. Arrange for key participants to visit existing programs in cities of similar size and demographics and solicit ideas regarding program design and implementation.

3. Any new programs or protocols should have the support from the top down and vice versa, which requires developing consensus across and within systems.

4. Qualities of lead staff should include competency and familiarity with the population and the larger system, an interest in the homeless mentally ill population, enthusiasm for an outreach model of working, and an interest in gaining increased expertise with the population. An ability to work collaboratively with a diverse group of colleagues is essential. Consider new or young staff who have shown potential and initiative and are looking for a career step. Sometimes new approaches such as the outreach model are more palatable to staff who have not spent years behind a desk.

5. Develop strong linkages to ongoing mental health services. The goal of outreach is to engage the individual and develop linkages to

available resources, including outpatient mental health services. An outreach program must be able to move consumers into regular case management services or risk developing an ongoing caseload which will interfere with their ability to respond to newly identified homeless mentally ill persons on the street.

6. Encourage cross-system contact among line staff. Ride-alongs with the police, spending time in a homeless shelter, or meeting with a consumer group at the local mental health center will educate and help to promote goodwill.

7. Set reasonable timelines to begin new programs and allow systems time to adjust to the changes. Project Respond has taken two years to become fully operational.

8. Undertake frequent program evaluation with measurable outcomes and use the data to inform ongoing program refinement. Promote a "can do" attitude and a willingness to be flexible. Whenever possible, attempt to respond to reasonable requests from other systems.

The question of funding is inevitable. There is a tendency to reallocate funds in times of crisis or when a fresh and exciting project is proposed. It is important to approach such decisions cautiously. Effective case management programs that provide support to currently housed chronically mentally ill persons need to stay intact, as do other traditional treatments, in order to prevent new crisis. Joint federal funding, demonstration grants, foundations and fundraising to businesses and other constituents that benefit from these efforts should be thoroughly explored. If you only fund crisis, crisis is all you get.

ENDNOTES

1. Gilmartin, K.M. The effects of psychiatric deinstitutionalization on community policing. *The Police Chief,* 37–39, December, 1986.

2. Lamb, H.R. (Ed.). *The homeless mentally ill: A task force report of the American Psychiatric Association.* Washington, D.C.: 1984.

3. Chafetz, L. Withdrawal from the homeless mentally ill. *Community Mental Health Journal, 26:* 449–461, 1990.

4. Brickner, P.H., Filardo, T., Iseman, M., Green, R., Conanan, B., & Elvy, A. "Medical aspects of homelessness." In Lamb, H.R. (Ed.), *The homeless mentally ill: A task force report of the American Psychiatric Association.* Washington, D.C.: 1984.

5. Rog, D.J. *Engaging homeless persons with mental illness into treatment.* Alexandria, VA: National Mental Health Association, 1988.

6. Cesnik, B.I., Pierce, N. & Puls, M. Law enforcement and crisis intervention services: A critical relationship. *Suicide and Life-Threatening Behavior*, 7(4), Winter, 1977.

7. Gillig, P. M., Dumaine, M., Stammer, J. W., Hillard, J. R. & Grubb, P. What do police officers really want from the mental health system? *Hospital and Community Psychiatry*, 41:663–665, 1990.

8. Murphy, G.R. *Special care: Improving the police response to the mentally disabled.* Washington, D.C., Police Executive Research Forum, 1986. Police ill-equipped to handle the mentally ill. *Criminal Justice Newsletter*, 1986. Lester D., & Pickett, C. Attitudes toward mental illness in police officers. *Psychological Reports*, 42:888–891, 1978.

9. Cesnik, op. cit. Gillig, op. cit.

10. Cesnik, ibid.

11. Cesnik, B.I. & Stevenson, K.H. Operating emergency services. New Directors for Mental Health, 2, 1979.

12. Karl McDade, Portland Police Sergeant.

13. Goldfinger, S., Chafetz, L. Developing a better service delivery system for the homeless mentally ill. In Lamb, H.R. (Ed.), The homeless mentally ill: A task force report of the American Psychiatric Association. Washington, D.C.: 1984.

14. Marcos, L. R., Cohen, N. L., Nardacci, D. & Brittain, J. Psychiatry takes to the streets: Initiative for the homeless mentally ill. *American Journal of Psychiatry*, 147:1557–1561, 1990. Robertson, M. *Project Care: Final report on the first contract year.* Albuquerque, NM: St. Martin's Hospitality Center, 1988. Lomas, E. & Honnard, R. *Development of a model community mental health program to serve the homeless mentally ill.* Los Angeles, CA: LA Department of Mental Health, 1987.

15. Rog, op. cit. Axleroad, S. E. & Toff, G. E. *Outreach services for homeless mentally ill people.* Rockville, MD: National Institute for Mental Health, 1987.

16. Cohen, M. B. Social work practice with homeless mental people: Engaging the client, *Social Work*, 34:505–509, 1989.

17. Cohen, ibid.

18. Lamb, op. cit.

19. Kerry Hawley, Mental Health Consumer.

Chapter 10

RE-RUNNING A FAILED PROGRAM: THE USE OF SANCTIONS TO SOLVE FAMILY PROBLEMS

J. Howard Finck and Della M. Hughes

HISTORY

While young people have run away in almost every culture in all parts of the world for centuries, the phenomenon of runaway and homeless youth in the United States today is clearly a social issue of vastly different proportions. As the United States moved away from an agrarian to an industrial-based economy in the first half of this century, the role of youth in the family changed dramatically. Young people provided a ready source of manual labor to help keep the farm or business operating at a sufficient level to support a large and, typically, extended family. As the United States became more industrialized, jobs increasingly were reserved for adults. The perceived value of teenagers in the family underwent a major shift.

Accompanying and following this shift were other social and economic changes of great magnitude that impacted such areas as: the role of women in the work force, civil rights, the use of technology, globalization of the economy, the availability of illicit drugs, and the use of mass media. These social, technological, and economic changes have created stresses on families quite different in intensity and nature from those earlier in the century.

In response to these rapid changes and new pressures on families, programs to address the needs of runaway and homeless youth began to take hold in communities across the country in the late 1960s and early 1970s. Chambers of commerce, Junior Leagues, community planning councils, United Ways, and other organizations interested in the welfare of adolescents and their families assisted in the formation of community-based, youth-serving agencies in San Francisco, Columbus, Charlotte, San Diego, Boston, Bismarck, Iowa City, Royal Oak, Miami, Redmond, Austin, New York and hundreds of other cities and towns.

These organizations were designed as alternatives to traditional service programs and served as safety nets to prevent runaways from becoming enmeshed in law enforcement and criminal justice systems that in the long run were more destructive than helpful. In the beginning, these services took the form of crash pads, hot lines and drop-in centers. The hope was to keep youth out of adult jails and detention centers and off the streets. Later, after federal funding was available, the programs became more stable and more focused on effective intervention strategies.

What was not evident in the 1960s and 1970s, nor in earlier reports about runaways, were the reasons youth fled their homes. Family conflict, physical and sexual abuse, and alcohol and other drug abuse were and remain the key causal factors for runaway behavior and for young people to become homeless. What has become apparent over a number of years in working with homeless youth who cannot, nor want to go back home is that physical and sexual abuse are major causal factors for their condition. This awareness has led practitioners and researchers to begin to look more closely at runaways for similar family dynamics. Consistently, whether in federal reports to Congress or in independent studies, family conflict, alcohol and drug abuse, school problems, and physical and sexual abuse are cited as reasons young people leave home.

At their best, community-based programs of the 1990s work closely with young people and their families to assist them in learning the skills they need to communicate and live together whenever possible. At times, efforts needed to reunite families require intensive intervention in order to help family members learn new, more productive ways of relating to each other and ways of managing their lives. If a youth cannot go back home, the staff help youth learn basic life skills, finish school, become employable and find a job, develop leadership skills, and learn positive values about family life and keeping oneself healthy. The programs have become masters at coordination and collaboration to meet the array of developmental, educational, legal, health, vocational, social, and psychological needs of these vulnerable but resilient young people.

DEFINITIONS

The following definitions describe the situations of young people who leave or are without a home.[1]

- *Runaway* refers to a youth under the age of 18 who is away from home at least one night without the permission of a parent or guardian.

- *Homeless youth* lack parental, foster home, or institutional care. These youth have left home often with the knowledge of their parents or legal guardians. Some young people from other countries can also find themselves homeless and face language, cultural, and legal barriers. These young people are sometimes referred to as "undocumented," "unaccompanied," or "on their own."
- *Throwaway youth* are young people left to fend for themselves because parents/guardians have thrown them out of the home without concern for their welfare.
- *Street youth* are often long-term runaway, homeless, or throwaway youth who literally live day-to-day on the streets. Some sleep in parks, others in abandoned buildings, or in some other type of makeshift shelter.
- *System youth* have been at one time or are still in custody of the state due to child abuse, neglect, or other serious family problems. Some are placed in a series of foster homes and may eventually leave the system, that is, run away, of their own volition for many of the same reasons they originally left their homes.

INCIDENCE

Determining the incidence of runaway and homeless youth is a difficult task. The major reasons include: there is no common agreement about what constitutes runaway behavior; both runaway and homeless youth are away from home for reasons of family conflict, abuse, alcohol and other drug abuse problems in the home, and other reasons that may contribute both to their own and their caretakers' reluctance to fully acknowledge or remember the runaway episodes; both groups of youth are typically transient; and both runaway and homeless youth generally distrust adults and service systems and hence often choose to avoid them.

The most recent national study, "Youth with Runaway, Throwaway, and Homeless Experiences: Prevalence, Drug Use, and Other At-Risk Behaviors," conducted by Research Triangle Institute, indicates that an estimated 15 percent or 2.8 million youth living in households in the United States reported a runaway experience (defined as youth who stayed out overnight without permission in the last 12 months).[2] Half a million of the household youth reported a runaway experience *and* having spent a night in a shelter, public place, abandoned building with someone they did not know, or in a subway. The estimates from this study carry particularly strong weight because young people themselves were asked about their experiences in a household survey. Previous studies typically sought parents' responses or required parental permission for youth to be interviewed, a factor that creates biases in the data gathered.

The National Incidence Study of Missing, Abducted, Runaway and Thrownaways (NISMART),[3] estimated the number of runaways and "thrownaways" to be between 162,700 and 577,800. Other estimates of incidence of runaway and throwaway episodes have ranged from 519,000 to 635,000[4] to over 2 million.[5]

Reports from the field to the National Network for Youth, a membership organization that includes programs working with youth who have run away or are homeless, tend to support the higher incidence numbers. The disturbing fact is that outreach workers report more young people living on the streets, and shelter staff report younger youth coming for shelter. While data validate the scope of the phenomenon, debating the actual number of youth who have run away or are homeless can deflect attention from the hard reality of the dire circumstances in which so many young people live.

DEMOGRAPHICS

The ages of runaway and homeless youth generally range from 12 to 21, although examples can be found of young people who are both older and younger than the ends of the range. Government reports typically indicate that the majority of youth who run away are between 14 and 17 years of age and those who live on the streets are between 16 to 21.[6] The former range is partially influenced by services provided at the federally funded runaway and homeless youth basic centers, which are restricted to serving youth under age 18.

Female youth served by shelters are typically about 60% of the total and males 40%.[7] The percentages are almost reversed by gender for youth on the streets.[8] The Research Triangle Institute (RTI) household survey indicated that the split in males and females with runaway experiences was 51% and 49%, respectively. Regarding race/ethnicity, RTI found 31.7% of youth in the shelter survey were white, 40.7% were black, 19.7% Hispanic, and 7.9% other. Data collected from street youth indicated that 45.9% were white, 27.4% black, 17.7% Hispanic, and 9% other. Among youths in the household survey, 61% were white, 16% black, 18% Hispanic, and 5% "other."[9]

REASONS YOUTH LEAVE HOME

In most cases, running away is a means of escaping numerous problems that exist in the "home environment," be it the natural family, extended family, foster home, or group home. The Government Accounting Office report[10] on homeless and runaway youth found that 75% of runaway youth "cited the relationship with a parent figure or other adult in the home as the primary problem"; 18% of runaway youth reported parental neglect; 29%, parents too strict; 16%, drug or alcohol abuse by parent or others; and 8%, domestic violence. The RTI study noted that 71.9% of youth under 18 spent a night away from home because of an argument with someone in their household.[11]

Runaway youth often flee family situations that they themselves cannot solve. For those who access runaway and homeless youth basic centers, their stay in a shelter may be just a few days before the family is reunited through counseling. Others run from sexual, physical and/or emotional abuse, violence, and severe conflict. If these young people access a runaway and homeless youth basic center, they may stay in a shelter until a safe living situation is found. If they do not receive basic center services, they may stay with friends or live with exploitative adults. Others find refuge on the streets.

Many runaway and homeless youths who have also had contact with juvenile courts or the public child welfare agencies frequently experience being the unwitting victim of these systems. It is typical for youth who have been abused to act out their anger by being rude and hostile to adults, particularly those in authority. After all, "trusted" adults have abused them, so they have no cause to take older people's expressions of goodwill at face value. The common response to this is to lock the youth up or punish the "unruly" behavior rather than determining why the young person is so angry.[12]

RISK FACTORS

Adolescents typically are seen as one of the healthiest groups of Americans and have one of the lowest overall death rates of all groups of citizens in the United States.[13] However, in several areas, adolescent health has deteriorated over the past three decades. Often referred to as the "new morbidity," these changes have occurred in areas such as alcohol and other drug use, HIV, school dropout rates, teen pregnancy, violent behavior, suicide, and depression. Unlike other groups, adolescents are more likely than younger or older Americans to die of injuries—including accidental injuries, suicide, and homicide.[14] Youth who have run away or are homeless have greater than average physical and mental health challenges.

According to the General Accounting Office (GAO), in a report based on 44,274 records of runaway and homeless youth served from October 1985 through June 1988 in federally funded runaway and homeless youth basic centers, 26% of the homeless and 29% of the runaway youth reported physical and/or sexual abuse.[15] Similar data, cited in 1987 by Yates, Mackenzie, Pennbridge and Cohen,[16] showed one-quarter of homeless youth reporting sexual abuse as compared with 8% of non-homeless youth. In the same study, homeless youth were about four times more likely to have experienced physical abuse than their non-homeless counterparts. The 1991 National Association of Social Workers (NASW) study showed more than 60% of runaway and homeless youth were physically or sexually abused by their parents and 25% experienced violence by other family members.[17]

Numerous studies have documented higher rates of substance use among runaway and homeless youth (particularly youth having multiple runaway experiences) than among those youth who have never run away.[18] The 1991 study by the National Association of Social Workers[19] also estimated that one-fifth of the runaway and homeless youth surveyed were alcoholics, indicating a higher than average rate for chemical dependency. These studies were confirmed by RTI's work: "In the household component [of the survey], lifetime substance use among youth with runaway and homeless experience is high when compared to those without such experience. Substance use appears higher among street youth than shelter youth."[20]

Higher levels of use of substances raises the risk for youth who have run away or are homeless for higher sexual activity, more sexual partners, more unprotected sexual behaviors, increased sexual contact with injection drug users, and increased use of injected drugs themselves.[21] Sex in exchange for basic survival needs is much more frequent among these youths than in the non-runaway population.[22] HIV seropositivity rates among runaway and homeless youth range from 2 to 10 times higher than the rates for other young people.[23]

Indications of learning disabilities or attention deficit disorder were manifested in 85% of homeless youth receiving emergency shelter or drop-in services. Additionally, two-thirds of homeless youth have one or more psychological disorders. Rates for these disorders follow: conduct disorder, 48%; major depression, 19%; mania, 21%; post-traumatic stress disorder, 13%; schizophrenia, 10%; and any one or more diagnosis, 66%.[24] Anger is the primary emotion felt by these youth, for they see themselves violated by "the world."[25]

The majority of runaway and homeless youth lead transient lives. Hence, school attendance and academic performance issues are frequent with this population. Also, when in traditional school environments, health and mental health problems experienced as a result of their living conditions are typically viewed as discipline problems that require punitive actions, thus exacerbating the youth's difficulties.[26]

Not surprisingly, the problems referred to above are frequently viewed by the youth themselves as insurmountable. Flight is the only option that appears to be available to them to change the family, school, peer group, or their own behavior. The immediate stressors are temporarily relieved. In cases of abuse, this flight can be part of a struggle for survival. However, flight to unsafe environments only replaces old dangers with new ones.

THE OLD SYSTEM OF HANDLING STATUS OFFENDERS

Prior to the early 1970s, status offenders—including runaway and homeless youths—could be locked in secure detention. In 1971, one-third of the 600,000 children in secure detention pending hearings were status offenders. Of the 85,000 committed to correctional institutions at that time, 23% of the boys and 70% of the girls were adjudicated status offenders.[27] On the basis of this research, the National Council on Crime and Delinquency (NCCD) adopted a policy urging the removal of status offenders from the jurisdiction of the juvenile court. Joining the council with similar declarations were the National Association of Counties, the American Legion, National Alliance for Safer Cities, and the National Council of Jewish Women—to name a few. NCCD did not rule out the intervention of the law enforcement for very young runaways.

Judge David Bazelon of the United States District Court of Appeals for the District of Columbia, commenting on this population at the time, said, "The situation is truly ironic. The argument for retaining beyond control and truancy jurisdiction is that juvenile courts have to act in such cases because 'if we don't act, no one else will.' I submit that precisely the opposite is the case: because you act, no one else does."[28]

Research also demonstrated that the status offender was frequently female, non-white, and from large, poor, and single parent or broken families.[29] The detention of status offenders, some voices noted, consumed much of the available resources that could be used to strengthen the status offender's family or provide opportunities for growth (since over 90% of correctional budgets were for the detention, rather than for treatment costs.[30] The fact that status offenders spent more time than delinquents in correctional institutions underlined the resource-wastage effort.[31] The Children's Defense Fund at the time noted that over 80% of the status offenders in custody posed no threat to the community or to themselves.

The debate on removing status offenders from the juvenile justice system was by no means one-sided. Whereas the Juvenile Justice Standards Project, sponsored by the Institute of Judicial Administration and the American Bar Association (both non-governmental entities, without vested interests in the then-current system) endorsed the removal, the Task Force to Develop Standards and Goals for Juvenile Justice and Delinquency Prevention (a governmental group comprised of practitioners or professionals) hesitated and urged that the courts retain some measure of jurisdiction over the population. This group, however, urged a movement to a family-based approach rather than a return to considering the youths as offenders.[32]

A jurist at the time summed up the joint commission's perspective with the following rendition of an old prayer:

> God grant unto juvenile court judges the competence to intervene effectively into the lives of juveniles who are a serious hazard to our society, the forbearance to refrain from coercive interference in interpersonal, family conflicts which are private, and the wisdom to discern the difference.[33]

A study in 1972 noted that 24 states and the District of Columbia had a variety of special categories for status offenders, including runaway and homeless youth (CHINS—Children In Need of Supervision—(Persons) PINS, (Youth) YINS, (Families) FINS, (Minors) MINS, etc.). Other states had mixed categories, while 19 classified them as delinquents.[34] In some instances, there were different classifications based on gender. Studies of the effects of the special categories indicated they resulted in more youths, rather than fewer, referred to juvenile courts. While detention periods were successfully reduced, no studies produced evidence of changes in the youths. Community service programs outside the legal system showed results superior to those in the legal system, both in terms of long and short-term goals (although the studies were noted to be limited).[35] States such as Florida, New York, and California found that even such status-offender specific codes did not keep such youths out of correctional facilities.

Some have argued that status offenses, including running away, are but the first step on the road to delinquency and then to criminality. However, at least one study did not show that escalation; rather, most youths with criminal histories began committing criminal offenses.[36]

The first two states to separate status offenders from delinquents were New York and California. In 1970, the California Legislature's Interim Committee on Criminal Procedure reported as follows on the effectiveness of status offender category (Section 601 of the Welfare and Institution Code):

> Some youngsters who go through the courts under Section 601 turn out to be fine, mature adults. Others don't. But, for every truant, runaway, promiscuous girl, or unruly teenager who gets into the courts, there are thousands of minors with identical backgrounds, identical problems, and identical experiences who never get caught, never see the inside of the courtroom, and never receive any kind of "help." Some of these youngsters also turn out to be fine, mature adults. And some of them don't. But the proportion of those who avoid the courts and still turn out well is probably as great as or greater than their less fortunate counterparts who are given the benefit of court supervision and control. No one can prove that truants who become wards of the court end up better educated than those who do not. No one can show that promiscuous teenagers who are institutionalized have fewer illegitimate children than those who are not. Finally, no one can prove that unruly, disobedient minors who come under court supervision end up in prison less often than those who do not.[37]

RUNAWAY AND HOMELESS YOUTH MAJOR GRANT PROGRAMS

In 1974, then-Senator Birch Bayh (D–IN) introduced the Juvenile Justice and Delinquency Prevention Act. The act was passed by Congress and signed into law by President Carter (P.L. 93-415). The act provided incentives and consequences to ensure that juvenile offenders were removed from adult jails, that status offenders were not treated in the juvenile (or adult) correctional systems, that resources were provided for runaways and homeless youths, and that delinquency prevention activities were funded.

Congressional interest in issues surrounding youth leaving home initially surfaced in 1974 with the establishment of the Runaway Youth Act (RYA). This program became Title III of the Juvenile Justice and Delinquency Prevention Act to address the problems of runaway youth and their families. By passing this legislation, Congress responded to public concern about increasing numbers of youth under the age of majority who, after leaving home, were at risk of physical and sexual exploitation. Congress amended the RYA in 1977 to extend the program to homeless youth (hence, RHYA). Since that time, the RHYA program has been reauthorized for four-year time periods. The last such action was in 1992.

The RHYA legislation was an important departure from traditional means of reacting to troubled youth who were status offenders. RHYA acts as an alternative to juvenile justice and law enforcement systems by offering grants to community-based agencies that serve youth in crisis. Services offered through this grant program include short-term shelter services with an array of components. These basic centers, the core service delivery model for the RHYA, provide a range of services designed to accomplish two goals:

1. Reunification of families whenever possible, and
2. Alternative placement of the youth when reunification is not appropriate. The services provided include outreach, counseling, aftercare, and referral to health care, educational, and other needed services.

The basic centers are guided in their development and operation by fourteen program standards, which set forth key areas, such as 24-hour access, a two-week time limit on a stay in a shelter, youth participation in program design and implementation, and coordination of services with critical referral sources.

In addition to the basic center grants, the RHYA provides for transitional living programs designed to meet the specific needs of homeless young people ages 16 through 21. The Transitional Living Program (TLP) was incorporated into the RHYA during the 1988 reauthorization to address the need for longer-term care. First funded in 1990, these RHYA programs provide services to homeless youth aged 16 through 21 "for whom it is not possible to live in a safe environment with a relative, and who has no other safe alternative living arrangement." The programs provide shelter and an array of comprehensive social services for up to 18 months with the overall goal to increase young people's independent living skills and ability to be self-sufficient.

Approximately 86 TLP projects are currently funded across the United States. Grantees are predominantly private, non-profit agencies, but also include a few public agencies. Projects funded under the TLP are intended to:

- provide shelter through group homes, supervised apartments, host family homes, or similar facilities;
- provide services that increase independence for all participants, for example, information and counseling in basic life skills, interpersonal skill building, educational and vocational advancement, and mental and physical health care;
- provide on-site supervision, directly or indirectly, at each facility that is not a family home;
- provide an adequate staff-to-client ratio to ensure that each youth receives adequate services and supervision;
- develop an individualized, written transitional living plan that includes referrals and coordination of services and law enforcement, educational, vocational, training, legal, welfare and health care services; and
- develop outreach programs to identify and recruit eligible youth.

Congress also passed the Drug Abuse Education and Prevention Program for Runaway and Homeless Youth as part of the Omnibus Anti-Drug Abuse Act of 1988. The purpose of this program is to fund demonstration and other direct service delivery projects that target runaway and homeless youth. The intent of the program is to supplement existing basic centers by providing additional funds to better address the needs of runaway and homeless youth in this area. This funding helps agencies provide such program components as longer-term aftercare services, peer counseling, family and individual counseling, assessments, education and training, and improved coordination of local services—all necessary to prevent alcohol and other drug abuse.

THE PRESENT SYSTEM

There is no "system" per se for dealing with runaway and homeless youth; rather, what exists is a collection of shelter and service models that respond to local conditions and funding availability. However, the incentives of the Runaway and Homeless Youth Act and the influence of the research has led to some common themes. They include:

- A voluntary admissions policy. Youths are generally free to self-select among the limited housing and treatment options. Most programs also utilize some criteria to assess appropriateness of admission.
- Non-secure shelters. Coercive, restricted or locked facilities for runaway and homeless youths are few in number.
- A perception of the population as victims or dysfunctional. It is generally agreed in the provider community that the youths are not so much opposed to authority but have participated in or been victims of dysfunctional families. As a result of this perspective, services often use positive role models, professional staff, and a range of services.
- A low priority among law enforcement. Whereas most programs have agreements, formal or informal, with law enforcement to refer these youths, in fact most referrals are from other sources.
- The importance of community resources. Given the demographic information presented, the solutions to the presenting situation often involves multiple needs and, therefore, multiple resources. Sheltering the youths is but the first step in a process to deal with the identified problems. In some instances, age and availability issues preclude a return home and have led to the transitional living program as part of the act and to the development of independent living programs.
- Professionally trained staff. Many shelters and programs begin with all-volunteer staffing; however, it is common that staffing moves to the use of professional therapists, case managers, child care staff or houseparents over time due to problems trying to meet the extensive family, mental health, substance abuse and other needs with little training.
- Continual resource issues. Most of the shelters and services are provided by the private, non-profit sector. As such, they are traditionally underfunded and much time is spent in the pursuit

of resources. Since usually no one funding source claims responsibility for the population, each is able to fund the service as they are moved.

In addition to shelters partially funded by the federal government (about 370 in 1995), other governmental entities are also involved in supporting, in part or in full, shelters and services for runaway and homeless youths. Some states, like California, have adopted policies to guide their funding efforts. In other cases, the funding simply is in the budgets and narratives of the various bureaucracies.

A comprehensive review of the shelters supported by the private sector (donations and grants from businesses, churches, individuals and foundations) has not yet been compiled; nonetheless, those shelters and services provided directly or indirectly through that support are substantial in number and may be more than those partially funded through the federal government. As youths have showed up in food bank lines and at the doors of adult shelters, many of those organizations have expanded their service/client range.

Not to be overlooked is the range of options pursued by youths who are unaware or distrustful of "system" resources and simply choose to live on their own, with friends or with adults who may or may not have their best interests at heart.

It is commonly acknowledged that the system of shelters, whether those with funding from the United States Department of Health and Human Services, or from state, regional or local governments, or by private donations and the use of volunteers (it is frequent that shelters/services have all funding sources listed above), serve only a small percentage of runaway and homeless youth, perhaps only one in fifteen.

Compounding the issues of appropriate provision of shelters and services is the fact that many youths seeking help are those who have voluntarily or involuntarily left group or foster home care. The youths, with histories of abuse/abandonment/neglect, often compounded by justice, mental health, developmental and/or substance abuse problems, sometimes are not helped by the short-term nature of the shelters and services for runaway and homeless youths without foster or group care backgrounds. State officials in charge of administering the group and/or foster home systems, however, are particularly ready to use the shelters for their youths in the absence of other alternatives. Because of the funding profiles of many of the agencies providing shelter and services, the state child welfare officials find themselves with a comparative gold mine: shelter and services with someone else picking up the tab.

A special category of runaway and homeless youths are pregnant and parenting teens. The reasons for youth homelessness have been well documented; in addition, teens are often kicked out of the family home after becoming pregnant. Of street youth involved in prostitution and survival sex, over half become pregnant.[38]

Pregnant and parenting teens do not fit into existing family or youth shelter systems. Their age bars them from participation in most adult family programs; their familial status bars them from most youth programs. They have different service needs from other homeless youths because they have familial responsibilities. In addition to comprehensive case management, teen parents need assistance to develop strong parenting skills. They need access to affordable child care so that they may attend school or work training programs. They need to be assisted to participate in early infant and toddler medical care, as well as their own health care and family planning. Their counseling needs are different from those of other teens because they have dual responsibilities. The high incidence of sexual abuse in this population mandates special efforts to deal with the self-esteem and developmental problems that not only interfere with their ability to make decisions for themselves but for their children.

CHANGES IN THE WIND

In the last decade, there has been a mounting public concern with crime and violence, particularly youth violence. At the same time, cynicism about the effectiveness of social services has also risen. Many have linked the two and have clearly expressed their preference for sanctions rather than services. Underlying factors, such as poverty and abuse, are diminished in this scenario. Globalization of industry, the ascendancy of the service sector (together with lower wages), the changing landscape of companies in light of downsizing and mergers, and the changing of the guard in political life—all are factors that ratchet up the pressure in individual homes and families and affect how our children are treated. And yet, in the search for some way out of the thicket, the tendency is to seek out simple and quick solutions.

To a large extent, the runaway and homeless youth population has been ill-served by these perceptual trends. Even though the research has clearly shown that delinquent and status offender populations are different, they are sometimes linked in the public eye.

Legislatures across America have been enacting "get tough" laws, with the result that each week brings an additional 1,700 new jail cells, in a country that already leads the world in incarceration rates (both adults and juveniles). Not only have resources been diminishing, but many of them are being applied to secure facilities.

Status offenders have not been immune to these trends. In Washington State, the "Becca Bill," named after a youthful homicide victim while she was a runaway, provides for up to five days of secure detention for runaways in locked facilities. The bill, now law, contained a section providing for 180 days of detention for "chronic" runaways (defined as three or more runaways) which was vetoed by Governor Mike Lowry. The success of the Becca Bill was seen as largely due to a well-orchestrated lobby of a federation of parents of runaway children. A "harboring" provision of the legislation requires shelters to report their knowledge of the runaway to the parents, police, or Department of Social and Health Services, within eight hours. It is unclear whether outreach services personnel are required to report such youth to authorities. In any event, youth advocates are predicting a chilling effect on the willingness of runaways and homeless youth to avail themselves of services.

On a very practical level, the action of Washington State with the "Becca Bill" may jeopardize the $1.5 million formula grant to the state under the Juvenile Justice and Delinquency Prevention Act, which is tied to the provision of non-secure shelters.

In many states, such efforts are dubbed as part of the "parents' rights" movement. Representative Steve Largent (R–OK) has introduced a Parents Rights Act in Congress, which would assert the right of parents to control their children. The view of status offenders as victims would presumably be lessened should this bill be enacted. The present trend toward the elimination of program-specific grants in favor of block grants from the federal government to the states (with fewer mandates and consequences) will certainly empower states to craft solutions that are more amenable to local pressure groups; in this environment, it is to be expected that more states will emulate the Washington State example (and many have already expressed such interest).

Advocates for status offenders, including those serving runaways and homeless youth, have stressed that the effects of secure detention on runaways, as demonstrated in the previously cited research, will overwhelm the provision of services to deal with the serious family and personal issues and will, in fact, make outcomes worse. The research has demonstrated that such youth do not come out of juvenile jails ready to learn, with newfound attachment to their parents and to their communities.

Lost is the name of the sage who opined that "The only thing we learn from history is that we don't learn from history."

ENDNOTES

1. National Network of Runaway and Youth Services, *To Whom Do They Belong?: Runaway, Homeless and Other Youth in High-Risk Situations in the 1990's.* Washington, D.C.: 1991.
2. Greene, J., et al., *Youth with Runaway, Throwaway, and Homeless Experiences: Prevalence, Drug Use, and Other At-Risk Behaviors.* Washington, D.C.: U.S. Department of Health and Human Services, Administration for Children, Youth and Families, Family and Youth Services Bureau, 1995.
3. Finklehor, D., et al., *National Incidence Study of Missing, Abducted, Runaway and Thrownaways.* Washington, D.C.: U.S. Department of Justice, Office of Juvenile Justice and Delinquency Prevention, 1990.
4. Opinion Research Corporation, *National Statistical Survey on Runaway Youth.* Washington, D.C.: Department of Health, Education and Welfare, Office of Human Development Services, 1976.
5. U.S. Department of Health and Human Services, Inspector General's Office, 1983.
6. U.S. General Accounting Office (GAO), *Homelessness: Homeless and Runaway Youth Receiving Services at Federally Funded Shelters,* GAO/HRD 90-45, 1989. Also see: U.S. Department of Health and Human Services, Administration for Children, Youth and Families, *Annual Reports to Congress* (on runaway and homeless youth programs), 1988, 1989, 1990, 1991, 1992.
7. Greene, J., et al., op. cit., 1995.
8. Ibid.
9. Ibid.
10. General Accounting Office, op. cit., 1989.
11. Greene, J., et al., op. cit., 1995.
12. Hughes, D., "Running Away: A 50/50 Chance to Survive?" *USA Today,* 1989, pp. 64–66.
13. Office of Technology Assistance (OTA), "The Adolescent Health Report," Volume 1, Washington, D.C., 1991.
14. Ibid.
15. General Accounting Office, op. cit., 1989.
16. Yates, G. et al., Risk Profile Comparison of Runaway and Non-Runaway Youth, *American Journal of Public Health, 78,* 1988, pp. 820–823.
17. National Association of Social Workers, *A Summary of Findings from a National*

Survey of Programs for Runaway and Homeless Youth and Programs for Older Youth in Foster Care. Silver Spring, MD: Author, 1991.

18. Windle, M., Substance use and abuse among adolescent runaways: A four-year follow-up study. *Journal of Youth and Adolescence, 18,* 1989, pp. 331–343.

19. National Association of Social Workers, op. cit., 1991.

20. Greene, J. et al., op. cit., 1995.

21. Rotheram-Borus, M.J. et al., "Preventing HIV Among Runaways: Victims and Victimization." In Ralph DiClemente and John L. Preston (Eds.), *Preventing AIDS: Theories and Methods of Behavioral Interventions,* New York, NY: Plenum Press, 1994.

22. Yates, G. et al., op. cit., 1988.

23. DiClemente, R.J. et al., Determinants of Condom Use Among Junior High School Students in a Minority Inner City School District. *Pediatrics, 89,* 1992, pp. 197–202.

24. See: Cauce, A.M. et al., "The Mental Health of Runaway and Throwaway Adolescents," Summary Report, Seattle, WA: Youth Care, 1994; and Morgan, C.J., "Learning Problems in Homeless Adolescents—Preliminary Results," Seattle, WA: YouthCare, 1993.

25. Rotheram-Borus, M.J., et al., op. cit., 1994.

26. National Association of Social Workers, op. cit., 1991.

27. National Criminal Justice Information and Statistics Service, Law Enforcement Assistance Administration, *Children in Custody—A Report of the Juvenile Detention and Correctional Facility Census of 1971.* Washington, D.C.: U.S. Government Printing Office, 1974.

28. David L. Bazelon, "Beyond Control of the Juvenile Court," *Juvenile Court Journal,* Summer, 1970, p. 44.

29. "Ungovernability: The Unjustifiable Jurisdiction," *Yale Law Journal,* June, 1974, pp. 1383–409.

30. K. Burkhart, "The Child and the Law—Helping the Status Offender," Public Affairs Committee, Pamphlet No. 530, 1975.

31. Gerald R. Wheeler, *National Analysis of Institutional Length of Stay: The Myth of the Indeterminate Sentence.* Columbus, Ohio: Youth Commission, 1974, p. 18.

32. *Families With Service Needs: Jurisdiction and Scope of Authority,* National Advisory Committee on Juvenile Justice Standards and Goals, Task Force on Juvenile Justice and Delinquency Prevention. Washington, D.C., U.S. Government Printing Office, 1977, pp. 311–314.

33. From an article by Orman Ketcham, L.L.B., "Why Jurisdiction Over Status Offenders Should be Eliminated from Juvenile Court," *Boston University Law Review, 57(4):*645–662, July 1977.

34. Mark Levin and Rosemary Sarri, *Juvenile Delinquency: A Comparative Analysis of Legal Codes in the United States,* Ann Arbor, Michigan: University of Michigan, Nation Assessment of Juvenile Corrections, 1974.

35. Rosemary Sarri, "Status Offenders: Their Fate in the Juvenile Justice System," *Status Offenders and The Juvenile Justice System: An Anthology,* National Council on Crime and Delinquency, Hackensack, N.J., 1978, p. 74.

36. Stevens H. Clarke, L.L.B., "Status Offenders *Are* Different: A Comparison of Offender Careers by Type of First Known Offense," *Journal of Research in Crime and Delinquency, 12(1):*51–60.
37. California, Legislature, Assembly Interim Committee on Criminal Procedure, *Report: Juvenile Court Processes,* Sacramento, CA, 1970, p. 7.
38. Deisher, R.W., Farrow, J.A., Hope, K.R., Litchfield, C., "The Pregnant Adolescent Prostitute," *American Journal of Disabled Children, 143:*1162–1165, 1989.

Chapter 11

HOMELESS IN TRANSIT FACILITIES: "WHERE DO WE GO FROM NOWHERE"?

RITA SCHWARTZ

A POLICY FOR PUBLIC SPACE

In the summer of 1995, a new housing facility opened on West 42nd Street, across from the Port Authority Bus Terminal near Times Square, in New York City. It provides permanent housing for 360 formerly homeless people, some who are chronically mentally ill, some in treatment and transition, and others now working. It is managed by the Manhattan Bowery Corporation (Project Renewal), a citywide social service provider, under contract with the New York City Department of Homeless Services. Project Renewal is also under contract with the Port Authority to provide social services at both the Bus Terminal and the World Trade Center. The Partnership for the Homeless provides case management services as a support to the population served at the terminal.

At the opening, after the tour and celebratory speeches, two men who now have homes in the building, talked about their lives—early child abuse, family alcoholism, economic failures, drug use, lost childhoods through deaths and deprivation. They described living on the streets in several cities, including Boston and Los Angeles, in boxes, subways, terminals, tunnels, parks and sleeping on the pavement.

Each one, through odd circumstances, found his own way into the Port Authority Bus Terminal. There they met, as one man put it, "guardian angels" who counseled, supported rehabilitation efforts and guided them from the bus terminal into long-term treatment programs, job training, jobs, and now, homes of their own. They gave credit for this new lease on life to *Operation Alternative,* a program designed by the Port Authority in conjunction with the bus terminal police and social service agencies to serve the homeless in and around this major multi-modal transportation facility. For those from the Port Authority who were present, it was a validation that time and money were well spent.

THE HOMELESS AT TRANSPORTATION CENTERS

A yearlong study, sponsored by the port authority and conducted in 1989, investigated homeless persons living in transportation facilities in 30 cities nationwide. This report, entitled "The Homeless: the Impact on the Transportation Industry," determined that the population of homeless who gravitate to transportation facilities are typically single individuals with serious physical and emotional difficulties, permanent transient couples and elderly women. They often have little or no income, have histories of institutionalization because of mental illness or prison terms, have difficulties maintaining relationships, and often have been victims of domestic violence or abuse. Typically this is a group with little or no self-esteem and for whom providing the basics of life (food, warmth, shelter, keeping clean and maintaining personal care) creates problems of a magnitude most of us cannot imagine.[1]

A transportation center serves the needs of this marginal population. These facilities are often open twenty-four hours a day, warm in winter and cool in summer, with police protection and bathrooms for washing up and laundry, offer the possibility for panhandling, free food and some "action." Why move from this kind of "caring community" with these many opportunities to an alternative such as a soup kitchen, large shelter or street, where life is hard. Better alternatives must be made available to entice a homeless person from the transit system.

Every day, thousands of travelers and commuters use the port authority's transportation facilities. Before the implementation of *Operation Alternative,* an additional 1,000 people used these facilities as homes. As the numbers of homeless persons increased, many more took up residence in the bus terminal and other buildings. These people were particularly resistant to offers of assistance, with a range of problems, including mental illness, substance abuse, physical abuse, loss of jobs and family structures, prison records and chronic homelessness. The amenities built in for the comfort of the traveling public were also amenities the homeless could enjoy: toilets, food, climate control and safety. Passenger discomfort grew, store owners complained and the agency was faced with a situation that appeared "out of control." To make these facilities user-friendly and satisfy customers, the agency had to make some serious decisions.

Operation Alternative is an innovative program, instituted originally at the Port Authority (PA) of New York and New Jersey's midtown Manhattan Bus Terminal, and is the largest and busiest of its kind in the country. Begun in early 1992 and now expanded to other PA operated terminals, *Operation Alternative* offers persons in need alternatives to staying in the terminals by making options available through on-site social service providers. It is based on several years of experience with various service models and combines three important elements: involvement of police, public relations, and social services.

In order to balance the needs of the traveling public, the vendors, and the rights of the homeless, *Operation Alternative* was initiated at the bus terminal and became the model for other port authority operated facilities, including the World Trade Center, Newark International Airport, La Guardia and John F. Kennedy International airports, the George Washington Bridge Bus Station, the PATH transportation hub at Journal Square in New Jersey, and the PATH stations along Sixth Avenue in Manhattan—from Greenwich Village to Penn Station. Volunteers of America (New York) is responsible for social service programs at the New York airports, the Manhattan PATH trains and the George Washington Bridge Bus Station. The city of Newark Health and Human Services Division outreaches to the homeless at Newark airport, and Catholic Community Services assists in Jersey City. Project Renewal serves the World Trade Center.

DEVELOPMENT OF PUBLIC POLICY

Public spaces, particularly those open long hours, serve as a safe haven for those who use them as alternative shelters. These people often interfere with the primary function of the facility. Transportation terminals, libraries and parks offer the homeless safe space, few rules, bathrooms, places to rest, food and opportunity to panhandle. The rights of these individuals need to be protected, but so do the rights of those who want to use these facilities for the purposes for which they are designed.

Conflicts arise from the uses and misuses of public spaces. New York City and other cities abound in lawsuits over appropriate uses of train and bus stations. Transit agencies worry about how to keep free from littering, graffiti and crime; maintenance becomes increasingly costly as some are taken over by the homeless or those who prey on them.

TACKLING THE HOMELESS PROBLEM

Homeless persons in transportation terminals reflect complex ethical and social problems and raise a number of conflicts and policy questions for transportation agencies:

- Should transportation dollars be used to provide social services?
- Should revenues be used to subsidize reduced or free fare to enable homeless people to get to job or welfare interviews?
- Does diversion of transportation personnel diminish the transportation industry's ability to carry out its primary mission?
- Should the police be trained to do "social work"?
- What are the legal and ethical issues around homeless people vs. tenants, patrons and the traveling public?
- Who pays and what works?
- Are there long-term solutions?
- Whose "right" is more right?

Although hard-to-reach street homeless people are relatively few in number when compared to the general population, management and budget decisions for transportation facilities in many cities often are determined by this small group. Design, maintenance and staffing decisions are made based on the need to protect people and property. Facilities are managed defensively. Benches have swirled arms or are removed, fences have pointed edges, bathrooms are closed or not provided at all, areas are fenced off, hours of operation are adjusted and modifications made to lighting and sound systems.

THE PORT AUTHORITY DECISION

The port authority made a decision to invest in a humane set of options, integrated with a public safety component of rules and regulations, designed to regulate behavior of all people using the public spaces.

The port authority invests approximately three million dollars of its annual operating revenue to fund eight outreach teams in an effort to create a more attractive environment for customers while offering alternatives to homelessness in a humane and dignified manner.

Transportation facilities are not the place for people to live. They are designed for the hundreds of thousands of passengers served each day. Homeless people affect the primary mission—to move people and goods in an orderly, safe and efficient manner, with staff trained to perform these tasks. But a policy decision that committed PA resources and staff time was made in order to improve customer services. Although the PA believes that the primary responsibility for providing social and medical services lies with appropriate social/health/welfare agencies, those agencies' budgets could not assume the intensive outreach and referral programs which were realized as necessary to improve the quality of life in the systems.

It is increasingly clear that all public and private systems are in some way interrelated. If one strains and fails, those who cannot be served will appear at the doorstep of another; therefore, if mental health, drug rehabilitation, housing and job training programs are cut, those losses create an additional population of people without alternatives, who will find a transportation facility an attractive, safe place to live.

TACKLING THE HOMELESS PROBLEM

It was found that PA staff—from maintenance, to police to facility managers—were confused about their roles and responsibilities in dealing with the homeless. They did not know how to approach them, when to leave them alone, what the rules were and whether or not they were putting themselves in a compromising position. Can one easily tell the difference—from a distance—if someone who is lying on the floor is dead, diabetic, drunk, drugged or dangerous? No one wants to take risks. In most cases, staff avoided contact with those who were panhandling, sleeping or setting up housekeeping.

It is difficult to measure the cost of loss of morale, particularly within the police force, when officers are not clear about their roles. Individual officers reported both frustration at their inability to enforce the law effectively and their continued feelings of demoralization stemming from the seemingly never-changing status of homeless people. The possibility of disease or injury concerns police officers and can become a negotiation point for their unions. In cities and systems which have police forces without an "injured in the line of duty" clause in their contracts, officers are sometimes reluctant to confront potential hazards.

For those whose primary mission is to provide safe and secure transportation, the presence of homeless persons, whether dangerous or not, oftentimes gives a perception of an uncaring system that is not fulfilling its contract with the rider.

POLICE RESPONSE AND TRAINING

In almost every city across the country, police departments are the first line of contact with the homeless, and transit police have quickly learned techniques to manage this new population.

Homelessness is not a crime. Rather, it is a social condition. Henry DeGeneste, former Superintendent of Public Safety for the Port Authority, states " . . . police involvement in this problem is essential and unavoidable . . . police officers play a dynamic and critical role in the operation of facilities by aiding travelers, seeking to deter crime by patrol and community liaison functions and intervening in crisis situations. They are an essential point in handling the homeless."[2]

Port authority police receive training in working with social service agencies. The mentally ill homeless present the most frustrating challenge for police who maintain order in transportation centers, although more than 80 percent of those found in PA facilities present combinations of problems which also include substance abuse, respiratory ailments and AIDS. In port authority facilities as well as in the New York City transit system, the most common diagnosis for street people is M.I.C.A. (Mentally ill-chemical abuser). Police departments often need to provide additional training in health-related issues.

- Police need to make quick judgment calls regarding the needs of a street person; when to "hold" and whom to call for assistance.
- Additional counseling is needed for police to assist them in dealing with the emotional impact and frustration created by constant contact with multi-problemed people.

In New York City, several police agencies deal with the homeless at transportation facilities, including the port authority police, the New York City Police Department Transit Bureau, the Metropolitan Transit Authority Police, including Metro-North, and the Long Island Rail Road and Amtrak. Each of these police forces has now had some level of training and each has social service agencies attached to their operations. Civilians attached to these police forces or agencies have been assigned responsibility for liaison with social services.

Social service agencies have been selected for their specific skills in working with particular populations to develop programs in the transportation facilities. Skilled outreach workers, mental health and substance abuse counselors are scheduled long hours, all year round.

Consistent, competent staff are trained to communicate with service-resistant street people and to identify and make the connections to the appropriate service agency. A key element is the continued coordination/communication between the social service worker and the police officer.

This commitment has resulted in increased services for the homeless, more competent policing, improved physical conditions at facilities, better tenant relations, higher ridership and improved staff morale. Customer surveys for the last three years give consistently higher marks each year for the turnaround of transportation facilities.

POLICE GUIDELINES

In many cities police steadfastly refuse to move past their role as law enforcers and accept little or no responsibility for the welfare of the homeless in their facilities. It is the policy of the port authority to assist individuals who need social services as well as to maintain law and order.

> The port authority police follow a procedure known as an escalatory process: They inform and advise, warn and admonish, eject, summons and arrest. This approach, coupled with consistent offers for social services programs, makes up the basic concept of *Operation Alternative.*

PATROL GUIDELINES

Any persons, regardless of their intent, who enter or remain in or upon premises which are at the time open to the public do so with license and privilege unless they defy a lawful order not to remain, personally communicated to them by an authorized person. That license is revoked when an individual violates PA rules and regulations or other codes, ordinances or regulations of the state or city.

There are clearly posted rules and regulations at all facilities which are carefully followed by the police on duty, to regulate all persons' behavior. These are respectful of individual civil rights and mindful of the need to keep civil order.

If an individual is given a lawful order to leave the premises and that person refuses and defies the order, the person is in violation of the criminal trespass statute.

All police receive training in techniques in working with the homeless.

Because the PA is a multi-modal agency, police are often transferred from one facility to another. Their training and experience with the homeless is consistent for all facilities and allows for continuity. The police training has served as a model for Amtrak police, New York City police, and the Miami police. These police forces either through their academy or the hiring of consultant trainers have a curriculum developed for the particular needs of the police officer, public policy, customer relations and the homeless. The elements of the training include:

- managing street people in crisis
- understanding the homeless and reasons for their living in transportation terminals
- confrontation and conflict management strategies, including negotiation of conflicts and defusing situations
- understanding alternatives to homelessness
- development of resource guide and discussions with the social service partners
- definition of civil rights/legal implications
- community policing
- juveniles

At the port authority, public affairs staff meet with tenants, store owners and civilian workers such as staff, toll takers and airline personnel to train them to understand the role of social services and how to best make use of the program.

The training component developed by the staff of Project Renewal and the Partnership for the Port Authority World Trade Center and Bus Terminal include sessions on:

- communication skills
- interviewing techniques
- the chemically dependent client
- reaching the homeless mentally ill
- cultural sensitivity
- development of strong resources
- dealing with staff burnout

THE RESULTS

There has been positive change. People have alternatives. No longer do they have to sleep on the platforms on PATH. They are continuously offered assistance, both by police and outreach workers. Linkages are made to other service providers. People's lives are improving. The number of homeless taking up residence in all of facilities is lower.

Police morale is up and crime continues to drop. The police, knowing that social services are strongly in place, can trust social services to do their job, allowing the police officer to pay more attention to those who are involved in more serious crimes.

While the agency continues to face continuing budget pressures, a policy commitment has been made to keep the funding in place and continue the programs for the homeless. It is a good business decision— good for tenants, the traveling public, employees and the reputation of an agency willing to be a good citizen.

OTHER TRANSIT SYSTEMS

The city of New York Police Department (NYPD), equally concerned about "quality of life" has developed several approaches to assist police officers' working with the homeless. Police Commissioner William Bratton's policy strategy number 5 has a strong policy statement and operational procedures regarding the protection of public spaces.[3] This strategy addresses public disorder and techniques for dealing with dangerous mentally ill street people, noise, misuse of public space, graffiti and squeegee window cleaners. The commissioner refocused resources in order to develop quality of life task forces.

The NYPD, in 1994, established a 24-person Homeless Outreach Team. Headed by a lieutenant and several sergeants, this carefully selected unit underwent several weeks of special training at the police academy in conjunction with the New York City Department of Homeless Services to learn street outreach, develop the confidence of chronic street people, reach into street encampments and gain the trust of the homeless so that they can refer them to social services in the network. This unit wears a casual/partial uniform and uses vans to travel through the city searching out needy individuals and responding to other police officers. They have successfully developed linkages with the social service/health agencies in the city.

The transportation authority has a 24-hour, seven-day-a-week operation. Its main objective is to provide assistance to the homeless in the terminals and on the NYC subway system in obtaining social services.

In 1994, the team transported 5,103 homeless persons for assistance.

The Metropolitan Transit Authority (MTA) Outreach Team works in cooperation with a staff of civilian social workers and conducts joint outreach efforts on the subways. They patrol tracks and inspect tunnels and through these efforts have reduced the number of accidents and deaths on the system.[4]

The social service component, Connections, has developed a major public information campaign, with car cards on every subway and bus advising the traveling public of their efforts to: Help the Homeless/MTA Connections. This literature asks the ridership to refrain from giving food or money to the homeless on the system and to report anyone in need to a transit worker or outreach worker.

Public relations and publicity campaigns help the traveling public understand the role of the police and social services and advise them of the appropriate long-term ways to help the homeless. The port authority distributes cards to the traveling public asking: **"Do you help when you give to panhandlers?"**

The materials describe the work the social service providers offer people in the terminal. Community groups in cities including New York, Portland, Oregon, and Seattle, Washington have developed transportation vouchers for the public to give to the homeless as well as public information campaigns that urge support of social service agencies rather than individuals.

Public-private ventures for public information and education assume joint responsibility for operation and cost for these campaigns. The involvement of the business community in developing vouchers and printed materials to advise and educate the traveling public has had a wide-reaching effect on panhandling and other quality of life matters.

U.S. DEPARTMENT OF TRANSPORTATION PROJECT

Other systems in other cities are still struggling with this problem of responsibility. Some cities, long known for their liberal policies, are turning their downtown areas into "mean streets." Seattle, Santa Monica, and San Francisco, for example, have enacted a range of policies and laws to chase the homeless from the streets and public transit systems. The public is getting tired of the homeless and wants something done.

In 1991 the U.S. Department of Transportation (DOT), under the aegis of the Federal Interagency Council on the Homeless (HUD), funded a demonstration project in three cities—New York City's Staten Island ferry terminals (both sides of the harbor), Baltimore (downtown transportation hub) and San Francisco (at the Transbay Terminal). The purpose of the three projects was to assist transportation facilities impacted by homeless persons. This was a unique grant. For a federal agency which appears to have nothing to do with homelessness, funding a social service program as a way to serve and evaluate its basic operations was unusual. DOT recognized that homelessness affects all government agencies. This funding required a coordination of services with several agencies, including the Department of Labor, the Department of Agriculture, Mental Health, and the Veterans Administration. DOT's funding allowed the projects selected to expand staffing, space and scope of work and evaluate the impact on these transportation hubs.

The federal funding has ended, with the following results. New York City and Baltimore found the project to work successfully in enticing homeless people from the terminals and into programs. The grants were awarded to agencies that established clear links to the MTA in NYC and the MTA in Baltimore. Connections were established with other providers and the heavy flow of people into the terminals has diminished. Both cities have continued the projects and are using local resources for funding. Both have demonstrated that they have been able to improve both the quality of services to the homeless and reduce the number of homeless people residing in targeted transit settings and surrounding street locations.

San Francisco has terminated its program. Travelers Aid, the agency operating the program, worked successfully with the most hardened street population, which sometimes numbered 400 people a day. However, San Francisco's linkages did not exist and the question of responsibility for this population was debated by CalTrans and the mayor's office. With the city's budget crises, the level of demand far exceeded the level of supply. Many homeless people were rousted from the Transbay Terminal and moved further from the city center. Quality of life crimes were prevalent around the terminal, and the pressure to "do something" from the travelers and vendors forced the closing of the terminal. In August 1993, CalTrans closed the terminal at night.

The entire demonstration project closed late in 1994. The demonstration grant points to some particularly useful information. The project mandated a high level of local interagency cooperation, believing that it could act as a catalyst for high level of service integration, which could improve the delivery of services to the homeless in the localities.

- It demonstrated that linkages must be available for useful referrals.
- Police "ownership" and solid training is essential.
- Local political commitment is critical to program implementation and support.
- Interagency cooperation may have to be mandated.
- Data collection must be maintained in order to develop comparative follow-up materials.
- Public information and education programs require continued feedback from consumers.

URBAN SPACE

In major cities, with limited public space, agreements and arrangements must be made for sharing this resource. The Citizens' Committee for New York conducted a conference in spring of 1995: *Common Ground— Your Space, My Space, Our Space.* They developed a document entitled *New York City's Bill of Rights and Responsibilities,* which states:

> New Yorkers need publicly accessible, well-maintained public spaces that welcome people from all backgrounds. But at the same time, New Yorkers need to agree about their rights and responsibilities in maintaining these public spaces. Civic *and* civil rights and responsibilities in public spaces mean that all people have the right to public spaces. The spaces need to be safe and secure, they should be clean and inviting. And importantly, people have a responsibility to act in public spaces in ways that are respectful of others, that do not interfere with access to, or enjoyment by others and that in no way interfere with the First Amendment rights guaranteed to all."[5]

Although the citizens' committee focus is primarily on park land and public areas, the goals for public transit space are quite the same. People using public transit space need the same reassurances as they would have in any other public area. Civil rights and civil order need to be maintained.

SUMMARY

Given the length of time it may take to engage a mentally ill chemical abuser whose life is in chaos, the transportation industry continues to ask whether or not it is cost effective to spend funds which could be used for other purposes and to involve staff in a business which essentially is not the one for which those who work in transportation services have been trained.

Services for the homeless should be considered as a thoughtful public policy. A public servant should look for ways to assist persons who truly need help in finding appropriate alternatives. Until long-term solutions for the homeless are found in our society, we are mindful that this is more than a temporary emergency. It is a situation to be faced for the foreseeable future. Developing appropriate responses at transportation and public space terminals becomes part of business planning. Attractive, secure environments available for the users of transit and other public facilities is the goal for excellence in customer service. Sadly, the burden of the homeless is one transportation agencies will be forced to address for years to come. We would be shortsighted if we did not devote our resources and energy to becoming part of the solution.

ENDNOTES

1. Schwartz, Rita, *The Homeless: The Impact on the Transportation Industry.* The Port Authority of NY and NJ, 1989, pp. 13–16.
2. Henry De Geneste, *Policing Transportation Facilities.* Port Authority of New York and New Jersey, 1994, p. 125.
3. Commissioner William Bratton, *Reclaiming the Public Spaces of New York,* Policy Strategy No. 5, New York City Police Department, 1994.
4. New York City Transit Authority Police Department, *Homeless Outreach Unit,* Training Document of Department, 1994.
5. Tony Hiss, Citizens Committee of New York, *Common Ground Rights and Responsibilities,* The Commonwealth Foundation, 1995.

Chapter 12

HOMELESSNESS AND THE POLICE
IN PHOENIX, ARIZONA

MARY ORTON AND TERRY MCDONALD

TWO INCIDENTS

"Hey! You can't take that in there!" The uniformed police officer gestured at the homeless man carrying a wooden pallet into the sanctioned homeless campground. The man, who had struggled with the pallet for several blocks and who was already 50 feet inside the fence, dropped the pallet and glared at the officer. The officer was enforcing a rule of the nonprofit operator of the campground who had asked that no pallets be allowed in after the quarterly cleanup. The shelter administrator standing by began to worry that the day's first serious confrontation was about to begin.

It was a hot summer afternoon in the mid-1980s in Phoenix. The police department, by stationing several officers at the entrance to the campground, was providing a much needed and appreciated service for Central Arizona Shelter Services (CASS), the shelter operator in Phoenix. CASS operated a large indoor shelter in addition to this campground, but the several hundred homeless men and women who lived in the campground were sometimes too much to handle for the small community-based organization. During situations such as this quarterly cleanup, when tempers were likely to flare, the police department provided an atmosphere of security and calm.

But this particular officer was not used to working in the downtown area or among homeless people. Unlike the members of the regular walking beat assigned to the neighborhood, he did not know the names of the regulars in the area and was not acquainted with the jocular, familiar way the walking beat officers address homeless people, engendering mutual respect and acceptance.

"I ain't taking it back out," said the homeless man, preparing to walk away from the pallet he had dropped. "It's too damned heavy."

"Oh, yes, you are," said the officer, starting to walk toward the man.

"Wait, I'll help you carry it," said the shelter administrator. The man gaped at her, walking toward him in her business suit and heels. "Well, if the lady asks me to, I guess I will," he said. He picked up the pallet and carried it out.

This incident is in sharp contrast to another that happened not long afterwards. When a group of homeless people set up camp on a city easement across the street from the CASS shelter, the officers knew all the people involved, which made all the difference.

The CASS director had called the police department to ask for help when the group began congregating. She had learned from experience, as had all the homeless service providers and businesses in the area, that large numbers of people camping in one place can mean trouble. Not only do fights break out, but it is disconcerting and threatening to the customers and employees of the agencies and businesses on the street.

As the police arrived, so did several television news crews, alerted by one of the campers. Knowing they had a potentially huge audience, hand-painted signs appeared and some of the homeless people became loud and belligerent. The officers who responded had been on this beat for years. They moved quietly among the crowd, talking to people, calling them by name, engaging them in conversation. While a shelter staff member talked to the television crews, explaining that the situation had become more volatile precisely because they were present, the police were gradually persuading the homeless people to disperse. Most had already been asked to leave the CASS shelter due to significant violations of rules, so they had nowhere to go. The police set a deadline for dispersal, which passed, and still some homeless people were there. But slowly the crowd was getting smaller. When the final television truck left the scene, persuaded that they were part of the problem, so did the last camper.

If the officers who responded to the call had not known the people, this situation could have had a tragic ending. Many of the people involved were rough men accustomed to the hardships of the street. The officers had listened to the stories of each one of those men at some time in the past. Not only did they know them all by name, but the officers had been given their own street nicknames by the homeless people. These officers had a reputation for fairness and had acted with kindness and respect towards the people on the street. For example, if they found someone with a misdemeanor warrant, they might have let that person take care of personal business before booking her, perhaps waiting a day before making the arrest. All this helped to build the relationships that allowed them to avoid a negative encounter that could have reflected badly on the city and the department.

THE HOMELESS PROBLEM IN
THE UNITED STATES AND PHOENIX

Homelessness is not a new problem in the United States. Discussions of homelessness are found in minutes of town meetings as early as the seventeenth century. Townspeople would provide for persons who were "settled," but did not consider newcomers and transients to be their responsibility. Settlement rights were granted by being born into an accepted family or through the vote of town members. Local homeless people might receive a small support payment or be placed in a poorhouse. People who were considered likely to become a burden, such as widows, children, the disabled, or the elderly, were often encouraged to leave town. In the nineteenth and twentieth centuries, clear distinctions were made in most states' welfare legislation between the settled and transient poor, with benefits available mostly for the former. (This continued until 1969 when the Supreme Court declared it unconstitutional for states and local governments to restrict benefits according to length of residence.)

There was a dramatic increase in homelessness during the Great Depression. Although no definitive counts of homeless people were made, the Federal Emergency Relief Administration housed 125,000 people in transient camps in 1933. A 1934 survey of social agencies in 700 municipalities estimated that there were 200,000 homeless people in those towns and cities. The highest estimate, during the worst of the Depression, was 1.5 million homeless people.

During the 1950s and 1960s, homelessness declined with the post-war unemployment rate but did not disappear. Working men's districts, first seen in cities in the nineteenth century, still existed, though they were now becoming disreputable "skid rows." Historically, they had provided inexpensive housing, restaurants, and bars along with casual employment offices for traveling or newly arriving tradesmen and laborers. As business districts expanded and grew nearer to the skid rows, these poor areas in central cities came to be seen as eyesores. As automobiles and post-war housing programs pulled the rug from underneath downtowns, the working men's districts soon became home to only the deinstitutionalized mentally ill, the substance abuser, and the low-income elderly.

In the mid-1970s, many single-room-occupancy hotels (SROs), which provided inexpensive downtown housing mostly for single men, were razed to make way for parking lots, office buildings, and apartments for young professionals. Directly as a result, homelessness grew at an alarming rate. Homeless people became more visible to the public as they were no longer confined to their downtown rooms, and because of the decriminalization of status crimes like public inebriation and vagrancy. More and more families and women were also seen on the street, and the average age of homeless people began to drop.[1]

Homelessness in Phoenix

The homeless problem in Phoenix became visible during the winter of 1982–83, when several urban camps emerged accommodating dozens of homeless persons.[2] This followed the destruction in the summer of 1982 of Phoenix's skid row, called the Deuce.

The Deuce, named for Second Street, was razed as a result of a study by the Ad Hoc Committee on Solutions to Transient and Inebriate Problems in Central Phoenix, convened by Phoenix mayor Margaret Hance.[3] The technical committee assigned to this blue-ribbon committee recommended that a study be conducted of the people who were viewed as causing the problems, so that a response appropriate to the problem could be crafted. Unfortunately, the ad hoc committee members turned down this recommendation, asserting that they already knew the nature of the people.[4] Their report recommended that all services catering to the "transient and public inebriate" be moved out of the central city in order to allow for downtown redevelopment.

These services included not only bars, missions, and charity dining halls, but low-cost hotels, rooming houses, and boarding homes. In a passage reminiscent of the town meetings of seventeenth-century America, it also recommended that agencies providing services to the poor should target their services to residents and give only information and referrals to travelers. When the Deuce was demolished in mid-1982, at least 1,500 SRO hotel rooms were razed.[5] The urban camps that sprang up that winter were composed mainly of former residents of these hotels. The city had inadvertently made its homeless problem far worse than before. City leaders found themselves forced, within a few months, to support the creation of a shelter in the downtown area to mitigate the problem they had created.

On the basis of Census Bureau counts, in 1985 there were approximately 6,000 homeless persons in Maricopa County on any given night. More than 8,000 different homeless persons were served by the county and its social service contractors in 1989–90.[6] The city of Phoenix has estimated, based on the count of 6,000 for the county, a homeless population of 3,000 persons at any one time.[7]

Following is the distribution of homeless persons in central Phoenix in the early 1980s:

- 40% employable,
- 20% mentally ill,
- 20% substance abusers,
- 10% physically disabled,
- 5% elderly, and
- 5% persons who chose to be homeless.[8]

From January 1, 1990 through August 31, 1991, the following facts were gathered about homeless people served by county contractors:

- 74% were male, 26% were female.
- Children comprised 18% of the group, while 50% were 18 to 34 years old and 32% were 35 or older.
- 55% were white, 21% Hispanic, 15% black, 8% American Indian, and .5% Asian.
- 59% of the households had been homeless for 4 weeks or less; 22% had been homeless for 1 to 6 months; 4%, 6 to 12 months; and 15%, more than a year.[9]

If a community wishes to reduce its homeless problem, it is vital to know and understand these facts. The most appropriate response to homelessness may very well be a mass response such as a large shelter, but it must find ways to address individually each homeless person's problems.

The Housing Connection

Anyone searching for causes or solutions to homelessness must address the issue of housing affordability. Census data from 1990 show a startling 84 percent of poor households in the Phoenix metropolitan area lived in housing that is not affordable. (Affordable housing costs no more than 30% of gross income for rent and utilities.) A full 67% of poor households paid more than 50% of their income on housing. In order to house adequately all poor households in the area, 46,400 new low-cost housing units were needed.

Only 23% of poor renters in the Phoenix area received government housing assistance, one of the six lowest rates of metropolitan areas in the country. Typically, Aid to Families with Dependent Children (AFDC) payments are more available than housing assistance, but payments in Arizona are less than is necessary to afford housing. In 1992, the maximum AFDC payment in Arizona was $334 for a family of three. The fair market rent for a two-bedroom apartment in Phoenix was $544 in 1990, $210 more than the entire AFDC grant.

The shortage of affordable housing in Phoenix has grown significantly since the mid-1970s. From 1975 to 1989, the shortage grew fourfold, so that in 1989 there were more than three low-income renters for every low-cost rental unit. This ratio was one of the six highest in the country.[10]

In 1989, the Community Council (a community planning group) produced a report on affordable housing that focused on a different group of renters and homeowners: those making 45% to 60% of the median income of the county. For a family of three, the income for this group was less than $19,109. The committee found that 64,147 of these households were at risk of becoming homeless because they paid more than 30% of their income for rent and utilities. The report noted that the vacancy rate in rental housing was 10%, but that high rate was not having the effect of lowering rents. The committee examined the effect of cutting housing construction and rehabilitation costs as a way of reducing costs to the consumer, but found that these cuts would have little effect in making housing affordable. The committee concluded that additional housing subsidies were needed to prevent more households from becoming homeless.[11] Today, however, the outlook for even continuing existing housing subsidies is bleak.

RESPONSE TO HOMELESSNESS IN PHOENIX

The St. Vincent de Paul Society and the Salvation Army were the first agencies to respond to the large numbers of homeless persons that appeared in "tent cities" in downtown Phoenix in the winter of 1982–83. The Phoenix Consortium for the Homeless (later renamed the Phoenix

Consortium to End Homelessness) recommended to the city that the following three-tiered system of services be developed for homeless people:

> *Tier I:* a short-term, emergency shelter in downtown Phoenix;
> *Tier II:* a transitional, medium-term residential facility in the urban area; and
> *Tier III:* long-term residential facilities, including SROs in urban areas and a rural facility for the chronic alcoholic.

It further recommended that the Tier I emergency shelter serve as a broker to bring homeless people together with the services they needed to get off the street. In January 1983, St. Vincent de Paul opened such a shelter on Madison Street near downtown Phoenix, and a few months later the Salvation Army opened an "overflow" shelter for the remainder of the tent city population. This was done with the approval and support of the city of Phoenix, and the Phoenix Police Department was involved in the planning and helped with the implementation.

In early 1984, the city began a search for a new shelter operator, as St. Vincent de Paul and the Salvation Army had decided they could no longer operate their shelters past mid-1984. A request for proposals that would have given $100,000 in city funds to a new shelter operator generated no responses. The city funded the Community Council to form a blue-ribbon committee to recommend a resolution to the dilemma. The committee suggested that a new organization be created and that the city contract with it to operate the shelter. CASS was created as a result of this recommendation. The Phoenix City Council chose a site on Madison Street near downtown Phoenix for a permanent homeless shelter a few blocks from the original St. Vincent de Paul shelter.

Although CASS was never a part of the city of Phoenix, the fact that it was created in response to a city need has provided the opportunity for close cooperation and collaboration between the city and CASS throughout the years. For example, because there are so many homeless people living on the streets near CASS, the city provides weekly street sweeping to keep the area clean. The Policy Advisory Group that was instituted by CASS in its first year of operation included the Phoenix police chief as well as representatives of other agencies that would be affected with every change in CASS policy. As documented more fully below, the city provides more police protection in this area than in most neighborhoods of Phoenix.

CASS's mission has never been simply to shelter the homeless. Rather it has been to help homeless people find their way permanently off the street. This approach, and CASS's determination to work closely with the city on the problem of homelessness, has made it easy for the city (and other governmental entities) to support CASS, both financially and with city services.

MADISON STREET

The city decision to site the CASS shelter on Madison Street was due primarily to the presence there of many homeless people, attracted by existing services and opportunities. A free lunch was (and is) provided daily by St. Vincent de Paul, and a city-run campground for homeless people (now closed) was already in operation there. CASS was given the use of government-owned buildings for the new indoor shelter that would house 400 single men and women. This eventually grew to accommodate families, who were later moved to an apartment complex 10 miles north of downtown.

Within its shelter, CASS has grown to provide:

- a case management system, to help its homeless guests get back on their feet with referrals and advocacy on a one-to-one basis;
- a jobs program, to teach the homeless how to look for work and to give concrete assistance in job placement; and
- a developmental child care center for preschool children.

Meanwhile, because there were so many homeless people in the area, other agencies began to open offices on Madison Street. Today, along a six-block stretch of Madison Street, there exists:

- CASS, with 400 beds for single men and women;
- St. Vincent de Paul, which provides a daily lunch for anyone who is hungry;
- Andre House, which provides breakfast, dinner, showers, lockers, and a jobs program;
- a county health clinic for homeless and formerly homeless people;
- a county medical outreach team for homeless people not in shelter;
- a contract post office and general delivery site for homeless people; and
- an adult education program run by the Downtown Neighborhood Learning Center.

Mixed in with these agencies are several businesses that have existed on this street for decades, and which find their ability to survive hampered by the sheer number of homeless people in the neighborhood. Clustering services for homeless people in the same area has distinct advantages, including making services very accessible to the people. Most homeless people have no transportation apart from their shoes, and even when given bus tickets most people find the public transportation system in Phoenix woefully inadequate. Clustering services also promotes collaboration among service providers and makes each service dollar go further. Some in the police department prefer this centralized approach because it is easier to manage the problem. However, the concentration clearly hurts the surrounding neighborhood. The homeless people on the street include some who have no interest in the shelter, some who have been banned from the shelter, and some who have been turned away for lack of space. The Phoenix Police Department, by default, becomes the primary agency serving these people's needs.

POLICE PRESENCE ON MADISON STREET*

The City's Responsibility

From the first, the city recognized that siting CASS on Madison Street brought with it some responsibility to the existing residential and commercial neighbors, and so established a walking beat of police officers in the neighborhood. The walking beat was not unique in the city; all the housing projects and the downtown core area also have walking beat teams. In 1992, the walking beat was changed to a bicycle beat. The police are admired and respected by homeless service providers and business owners alike for doing an exemplary job in the neighborhood.

Some of the officers serving the area today have been there for 10 years, while others are new to the beat. Despite the difficulties of working with homeless people, police personnel vie for the homeless beat assignment. It is never boring, there is always a lot of activity, and some officers prefer working with homeless adults more than the juveniles

---

*For the details of this section, and for their dedication and high-quality police work in a difficult setting, we are indebted to the following police officers who serve this area and who spent an afternoon with us telling us about the beat: Bernard Delaney, Kathi Kuester, Al Galindo, Gilbert Hernandez, Cary Immel, Steve Mack, and Ramiro Silva.

they encounter in other neighborhoods. (There are few children on the street in this area. The homeless families with children do not tend to stay after mealtimes.) In addition, it is a satisfying job, particularly when they are able to help someone in need.

Stories abound of people who eventually found their way off the street, often with the help of one or more of the police officers who work on Madison Street: the couple who found jobs within a few weeks and were independent within two months, and whose children were given bicycles that Christmas by one of the officers they met on Madison; the alcoholic who found a listening ear in the officer who booked him, and who later said that the officer's kindness was an influence on him as he attempted (and succeeded) to go straight; the young man who left the shelter and returned some months later with a good job, driving a decent car.

However, there are different kinds of people on the street. Some are newly homeless and need to be told what and where the resources are so they can help themselves. Some are mentally ill or elderly and need to be protected. Some are hard-core street people who prey on the vulnerable. Some are late-stage alcoholics who are slowly dying on the street.

And some are more than they seem. Each officer has a story of an improbable person living on the street: a former state legislator from the Northeast, a former colonel in the Air Force, a former college professor, a famous artist, a lawyer, a doctor. The story that moved them the most was the one of the former police officer who had trained both the Phoenix police chief and the head of the state highway patrol. (The officers who talked to him at first did not believe him, so they checked and found his story was true.)

Listening is Important

Homeless people are very different, one from the other, just as people living in homes are different. They have in common the fact that many of their basic needs are not filled. One fundamental human need almost always goes unmet: they have no one to talk to, and no one wants to listen to their stories. As representatives of those in authority, the police officers often find themselves listening. One man flags down the team every day to talk to them about his wife and kids in California. Mentally ill people can have long, sometimes unintelligible stories that need to be told. By listening, police officers learn about the people they are there to serve. They also develop goodwill for the times they will have to return for enforcement activity.

One experienced officer explained that he listens without trying to remember the stories and without allowing them to affect him much. The stories are often heart-wrenching, but he cannot give in to the emotion without impairing his ability to do his job. He says he can acknowledge the homeless person needs to talk and will feel better if someone is listening, without getting emotionally involved. If the person is mentally ill, he lets her talk as long as he has time, and then simply says, "Good-bye, I have to go now." If he finds someone who needs help, he refers him to an agency that can help.

This officer says that there was only one time when he could not shield himself from the pain. It was close to Christmas. One of his fellow officers had dressed up as Santa Claus and was walking toward the shelter. In front of the shelter stood a couple with their two sons: a fourteen-year-old and six-year-old. The father said to the boys, "Look! There's Santa Claus!" There was absolutely no expression on the older boy's face. The officer said it was as if he had no hope, no dreams. He had never seen that look before, and although this incident happened years ago, he can still see the boy's face.

A Dilemma for the Police

Most people on Madison Street make a distinction between homeless people staying in the CASS shelter and those on the street in the area. Those living at CASS have accepted the CASS philosophy that they must be actively searching for a way off the street if they are going to stay in the shelter. Those who are able to work must be looking for work; even the mentally ill and physically disabled must be doing something for themselves or eventually they will be asked to leave. (The case management system provides the face-to-face contact that allows the shelter staff to be flexible with the individual's length of stay, to accommodate the abilities and disabilities of each person.) Thus, the homeless people at CASS are often viewed as those who are striving to regain their self-sufficiency.

The people on the street, by contrast, are often viewed as those who are not interested in ending their homelessness, and who are problems for the neighbors and anyone who comes into contact with them. Although the police are often called by the shelter staff to assist with problems at the shelter, they more often are working with the homeless people who are living on the street.

The people the police see day after day are those who have given up and are reconciled to street living. These people, mostly men, can mean trouble for the area and for the police. However, rarely do the homeless people ask for the badge number and supervisor's name of the bicycle beat officers. The officers feel that the homeless people take aggressive enforcement of the law as a sign of respect. Often, the police are enforcing the trespassing laws and have to tell homeless people to move on. It is tough for the officers when there is no place for the people to go, and the officers are likely to get some complaints. "Where do you expect us to go?" "I didn't get my check today, and now you're making me move." During the day, the police can suggest the city parks in the area, but at night there is no place to send them. The shelters are usually full and the parks are closed. The answer to the question "Where should I go?" must be answered by the policymakers in the community, not by the cop on the beat.

Working With Agencies

The officers who work Madison recognize that it is vital for them to know the agencies that serve homeless people. The police often serve as the first encounter for someone newly in need, and they make the first referral to the agency that is most appropriate for that person. Familiarity with the agencies helps them in other ways, too.

Long lines form three times each day on Madison Street when breakfast, lunch, and dinner are served. The police have learned that if they have the time to patrol the lines, they can avoid having to answer a call when a disturbance has broken out. If they are not there, the weaker people tend to get pushed to the back of the line. Also, they can sometimes find someone they are looking for in the line. They have found that being out in the weather improves their standing with the homeless people, and it helps them to get to know the people as they stand there and talk to them. This knowledge is helpful on a daily basis to the police personnel.

One bike team noticed a family that had joined the line for lunch over the course of several days. The size of the family originally caught their attention: two parents and four children under the age of five. Because the family members were clean and neat, they assumed that they were one of the many housed families that eat lunch at St. Vincent de Paul to make their income stretch to the end of the month and to prevent their homelessness. However, they soon saw the family living in a car near Madison Street.

They found that the family had been asked to leave several shelters because the father was not willing to follow shelter rules. The team was worried about children that young living on the street. The state welfare department's overtaxed Child Protective Services would not intervene because the children were getting fed and were not in obvious danger.

One of the officers talked to a detective who advised him how he could book the parents, forcing the children off the street and into the system. He then had a talk with the mother and told her that he wanted those kids off the street, and if she did not do it, he would. Within a few weeks, the father had a full-time job, and his employer was withholding some money from each paycheck to help the family save for the move-in costs of an apartment. This intervention satisfied the officers involved, as they knew they had made a substantive difference in the lives of those children.

Tools They Can Use

The officers who patrol the Madison Street area have developed a number of tools to help them in their work. Some are described below.

- *Authority to arrest trespassers.* It is sometimes difficult for a property owner to be present at a trespassing incident in order to ask officers to make an arrest. The Authority to Arrest Trespassers is a form signed by the property owner that allows the police to make an arrest in the absence of the owner. The police give one or two warnings before they book a suspect, and they share among all the officers in the area a list of the people who have been warned.
- *Bicycles.* The bikes make it easier to come quickly upon people and hear what they are saying without them hearing the officers. In an area where small-time drug dealing is a problem, this is a valuable advantage. It is also easier to chase someone on a bike than it is on foot.
- *Good relationships with other city agencies.* The police who work on Madison Street have a good relationship with the Sanitation Department. They have found that a discarded couch or a mattress on the street can encourage people to live there. With a phone call, the Sanitation Department supervisor will come by that day with her

truck and take the item away. Phoenix also has a strong neighborhood maintenance and zoning enforcement division, which will board up an abandoned building and bill the owner. After a call from the bicycle beat, they will have a crew out within a week to secure a building, with the police standing by to provide assistance.

- *Neighborhood associations.* The police work closely with neighbors and the neighborhood association. The neighbors often lend office space to the police or let them use a room for a stakeout if the view is good. Neighbors videotape illegal activity to assist officers with an arrest.

Sometimes it is useful to have a citizen call the department when there is a problem, instead of using internal channels. When budget cuts meant a severe reduction in police services on Madison Street, the CASS director and the head of the neighborhood association went together to the city council to ask that the personnel be restored. The council members were impressed to see the two groups working together, particularly since the neighbors had tried to close the shelter a few years before. The council agreed to reverse their decision and restore police service to the previous level.

- *Service providers.* It is important for police officers to understand any neighborhood in which they work. On Madison Street, homeless service providers are a significant part of the neighborhood. The officers on the street take the time to get acquainted with agency staff who are likely to call on them for assistance. These efforts ensure that a relationship has developed that allows people to call each other when there are problems.

Although there is no formal Memorandum of Understanding between the Department and CASS, a close working relationship has developed over the years. The sergeant in charge of the day shift attends the CASS board meetings. The CASS executive director has attended the Citizen's Police Academy and serves on the Department's Disciplinary Review Board and Use of Force Board. Walking beat supervisors often attend the weekly shelter supervisors' meeting in order to address specific problem areas and ensure good communication. The CASS director can, and does, call the police chief or one of his deputies when there is a large policy issue to be addressed. This mutually respectful relationship has proven invaluable to the city, the department, and CASS over the years.

CONCLUSION

Working with homeless people is a difficult job for a police officer. The problem never seems to be solved and the police are pulled among several forces, all of which want different outcomes for the situation. The property owners want the problem to go away, the service providers want the opportunity to help, the city council wants no riots or headlines, the homeless people want help or just to be left alone. The officers are expected to protect the residents, the business owners, the property, and the vulnerable homeless people, while jailing the bad guys. Walking this tightrope can be stressful.

It helps the officers on the street to understand the people they are dealing with and to know them as individuals. Each is different, and each is there for a different reason. None is beyond hope.

It may help police officers to understand the systemic problems that underlie the homelessness. It is easy but false to blame the homeless problem on the inability of a few people to control their drinking. Although these problems make homelessness more difficult to solve, the economic reality that has put housing out of reach for many of our community's workers continues to be the main issue that needs to be addressed.

Policymakers can help by providing some real alternatives for the people on the street. Having a shelter where homeless people can get assistance makes a considerable positive difference for everyone involved. However, as James Rouse, chairman of the National Housing Task Force, recently testified to Congress: "Behind the homeless on the street are millions of Americans who are right on the edge, and could be on the street tomorrow if they lost their jobs or had a medical emergency."[12] Making sure housing is affordable for the working people in the community is vital and is the best chance of significantly reducing homelessness.

ENDNOTES

1. P.H. Rossi (1989), *Down and out in America: The origins of homelessness*, Chicago: University of Chicago Press.
2. Phoenix South Community Mental Health Center (1983), *The homeless of Phoenix: Who are they and what should be done*, Phoenix, AZ: Phoenix South Community Health Center.
3. Ad Hoc Committee on Solutions to Transient and Inebriate Problems in Central Phoenix (1981), *Recommendations for the Care and Housing of Transients and*

Public Inebriates Displaced by Central City Redevelopment Activities, submitted to the Mayor and City Council, Phoenix, AZ.

4. William Jamieson (May, 1987), conversation with the author.

5. Maricopa Association of Governments Homeless Funding Coordination Task Force (1987), *Funding coordination for services to the homeless in Maricopa County,* Phoenix, AZ: Maricopa Association of Governments.

6. Maricopa Association of Governments Homeless Task Force (1991), *A regional partnership to end homelessness in the Valley of the Sun: Status report,* Phoenix, AZ: Maricopa Association of Governments.

7. State Homeless Coordination Office (1992), *Current status of homelessness in Arizona and efforts to prevent or alleviate homelessness,* Phoenix, AZ: Arizona Department of Economic Security.

8. Phoenix South Community Mental Health Center, *op cit.*

9. State Homeless Coordination Office, *op cit.*

10. P.A. Leonard and E.B. Lazere (1992), *A place to call home: the low income housing crisis in 44 major metropolitan areas,* Washington, D.C.: Center on Budget and Policy Priorities.

11. Community Council Affordable Housing Committee (1989), *Can your children find affordable housing? Executive summary of the affordable housing committee report,* Phoenix, AZ: Community Council, Inc.

12. In *Time* Magazine, April 11, 1988, as quoted by G. Barak and R.M. Bohm (1989), The crimes of the homeless or the crime of homelessness? On the dialectics of criminalization, decriminalization, and victimization, *Contemporary Crises* 13: 278–288.

Chapter 13

BALTIMORE'S PROJECT CONNECT

GORDON SCOTT BONHAM

The city of Baltimore demonstrated a homeless outreach project from 1992 through 1994. It was one of three projects for homeless people living in transit facilities funded by the Federal Interagency Council on the Homeless. Baltimore's transit "facility without a roof" was a six-block-by-six-block square which included the intercity bus terminal, two subway stations, major local bus transfer stops, and several stops on the light rail (which opened during the project). Homeless Outreach Team (HOT) workers convinced two-thirds of the homeless people they encountered to accept case management services, and placed in permanent housing one-fourth of those accepting case management. Analysis shows they may have convinced almost all to accept case management if they could have had up to five outreach encounters with each homeless person. They may also have placed three-fourths in permanent housing if enough interactions had occurred to allow them to identify nine or more needs of each homeless person and to spend at least $200 of the program fund pool. Successful placement in housing was primarily a function of program characteristics and the interactions of the program with homeless people, and not due to measurable characteristics of homeless people themselves. The HOT project involved city and transit police as part of a coordinating team, as a source of referrals to the HOT team, and as a source of information to the evaluation.[1]

BALTIMORE'S HOMELESS

Baltimore's HOT program began in an atmosphere of awareness and concern about the homeless population. Almost all business owners or managers who responded to a pre-program survey reported seeing evidence of the homeless population at least once a week. Most reported having to ask homeless people to leave their places of business, an

197

average of twice a day. Three-fourths (75%) said the presence of homeless people affected their ability to conduct business, and that Baltimore's homeless problem was getting worse. In separate surveys, half of both transit riders and transportation workers (57% and 52%) agreed that the number of homeless people had increased since the year before. Almost all transit riders reported seeing homeless people while waiting at transit stops or while they were walking to and from the transit stops (84% and 90%, respectively). Almost all (83%) of transportation workers had asked homeless people to leave the vehicles or facilities.

The recession in Maryland contributed to an increase in people with marginal resources. Additionally, Maryland reduced general public assistance just prior to the start of the HOT program. At least 900 general public assistance recipients in 1991 were known to be homeless since their welfare checks were delivered to shelters or to the Baltimore Department of Social Services.

Number

Identifying homeless people is difficult. Being without a home is not by itself a visible characteristic. Therefore, people can be identified as homeless only from what they say about themselves or from visible cues they give which others associate with homelessness. Some homeless people do not want to be identified as homeless and give few cues that they are homeless. Some people who have homes identify themselves as homeless as they panhandle for money or exhibit other behavior commonly associated with homelessness. In addition, homelessness is not a single state but ranges from doubling up with friends or relatives on a periodic basis to living 24 hours a day for long periods of time in public places or places not meant for human habitation. The number homeless on any given night is very different from the number who are homeless at some time during a year.[2] National estimates range from 228,621[3] to 735,000[4] homeless on a given night. Estimates have been offered as high as three million people who are homeless at some point over the course of a year.[5]

Shelter statistics for Baltimore during the decade before and during the HOT program show no discernable trend. Between 18,158 and 23,775 shelter beds were provided during each year of the HOT evaluation.[6]

One-fifth of the transit riders surveyed at the beginning of the HOT evaluation said they encountered five or more homeless people on the average each time they walked to or from the bus or subway stop. Almost all (96%) of the downtown businesses and residents responding to a separate survey said they encountered an average of 20 homeless people each week on the way to and from their businesses or residences.

While downtown transit riders and business owners/managers may define homeless people largely as visible panhandlers, drunks, or bag people in busy places during the day, police often identify them as people sleeping in public areas during a time when few other people are on the street. Police did not observe large numbers of street-dwelling homeless people during a February weekend at the beginning of the homeless outreach program. They observed 34 people during a three-night period, with 15 of these observed on Friday night (see Table 1). Two years later on a comparable February weekend, however, they observed 10 times that number. It is doubtful that the actual number of unsheltered homeless people living on the street increased this much in two years, as no other data show similar magnitudes of change. Although several police officers reported seeing fewer homeless people on the street during the 1992 survey weekend than they generally saw, it is probable that different counting procedures were inadvertently used, indicating the difficulty of identifying and counting homeless people.

Table 1
**NUMBER OF HOMELESS PERSONS OBSERVED BY POLICE,
ACCORDING TO 1994 POST BOUNDARIES**

Post	Description	1992	1994	1994/1992
111	East downtown	3	42	14
112	Charles Center, Inner Harbor	13	158	12
113	Howard St., Lexington Market (HOT target area)	12	39	3
114	Saratoga St. to Centre St.	6	39	6
121–3, 144–5	Remaining area west and north of HOT target area	0	67	n.a.
Total		34	345	10

Location

Determining where homeless people spend most of their time is as difficult as counting them. Homeless people are generally depicted as living in the centers of large cities. Certainly the U.S. population as a whole is concentrated in cities, and the poor are concentrated in the deteriorated areas of these cities. Homelessness, an extreme form of poverty, is likely to be concentrated in a similar way. Whether cause or effect, resources used by homeless people tend to be concentrated around city centers. Social density is high, providing opportunities for panhandling, and shelters, soup kitchens, and social services are located in low rent areas that can be reached on foot. Thus, the homeless people in Baltimore were most frequently identified in the areas surrounding the central business district.

The HOT target area was a six-block-by-six-block square adjacent to Baltimore's business district, three blocks north of Orioles' Park at Camden Yards, and seven blocks northwest of the Inner Harbor and National Aquarium. This is a major transit transfer area, as it is the only area in the city where the subway, light rail, and bus systems intersect. It also contains the intercity bus terminal. The area is relatively safe, provides places to sit, provides out-of-the-way places to sleep after stations close, and has substantial pedestrian traffic from which to panhandle food and money. Health Care for the Homeless, PATH/Travelers's Aid Society, the public library, an historic food market, a commercial pedestrian mall, and an office plaza are located within the HOT target area. Adjacent to the target area are a major soup kitchen, the Social Security building, and the University of Maryland Hospital, all of which provide services to homeless people. A nearby federal office building has also been found by homeless people to provide both above ground and underground privacy and protection from harsh weather.

The 1992 police count of homeless people suggested that the area targeted by HOT was appropriate for reaching street-dwelling homeless people. In 1992, about two-fifths (38%) of the recorded observations of homeless people were in the target area of the HOT program (Police Post 113). About the same proportion was in the central downtown area immediately east of it (Police Post 112). In 1994, however, only one-tenth (11%) of the homeless people observed by the police were living (sleeping) in the HOT target area. Almost half of the observations were in the central downtown area and the tourist area surrounding the Inner Harbor, areas immediately east and south of the HOT target area. The police did not record any observations of homeless people living in the Post 121–123 and 144–145 areas north and northwest of the target area in 1992. Almost one-fifth of the observations in 1994 were in these areas. Some of the differences between 1992 and 1994 could be due to boundary changes or to police including the area around the Inner Harbor in their 1992 counts. It is more likely that the differences in location are due to differences in the counting procedures.

The Mayor's Office of Homeless Services estimated in its proposal for the HOT program that Baltimore had 2,000–4,000 homeless people, and that 400 of them lived on the street in the target area. The Baltimore HOT program actually encountered 633 different homeless individuals in the target area during the 31 months of evaluation (February 1992 through August 1994).

Characteristics

A study of Baltimore's homeless population in missions, shelters and jails in 1986–87 found that one-third of the men were white, one-fifth were residents of Baltimore for less than six months, one-third were veterans, one-third were high school graduates, and one-fifth were working. Psychiatric evaluations found two-fifths of them had major mental illness and three-fourths had substance use disorders. Physical examinations uncovered an average of eight problems per person.[7]

The homeless people encountered by the HOT program were predominantly male, African American, and 25 to 44 years of age. Two-thirds had never been married. About half had substance abuse problems and a fifth had mental health problems. One-third had been incarcerated at some time in the past. Only one-third had any family support in the Baltimore area, even though half had been Baltimore residents for 10 or more years. Two-fifths had been homeless for two or more years. Few had jobs or sources of regular income, and most reported disabilities that would keep them from working. One-fifth were veterans. Half had visited Health Care for the Homeless, and one-third had been hospitalized during the previous six months.

Not everyone saw the same characteristics in the people they thought of as homeless. Business owners/managers reported a higher frequency of drug or alcohol problems, and a higher rate of mental/emotional illness, than recorded by the HOTeam. Different data collection methods might account for some differences, but it is very likely that the people the businesses observed and described as homeless were not the same people that the HOTeam encountered and identified as homeless.

Table 2
PERCENT ACCEPTING CASE MANAGEMENT BY CHARACTERISTICS
OF THE PERSON AND PROGRAM

Characteristic	Number	Percent Accepting
All People Encountered	551	60%
No Physical Health Condition		
February 1992–July 1992		
No Enticements		
HOT Workers #1,3,4	120	29%
HOT Workers #2,5	33	67%
Enticements	25	80%
August 1992–August 1994		
No Enticements or under $5	271	62%
Enticements $5 or more	39	90%
Physical Health Condition	63	81%

RESPONSES TO THE HOMELESS

Homeless people do not exist in a vacuum. People and institutions respond to them in various ways. Prior to 1992 when the HOT program began, the transit area community of Baltimore did not have a coordinated plan for interacting with homeless people. Transit riders, transportation workers, and businesses each responded in their own way.

Transit Riders

Transit riders were generally bothered by the presence of homeless people. One-fifth (20%) reported being bothered greatly by the presence of homeless people on transit vehicles and at transit stops, with an additional one-fourth (22%) bothered some and one-third (30%) bothered a little. Only one-fourth (28%) said they were not bothered at all by homeless people. This one-fourth is also the same as the proportion of riders who ignored homeless people they encountered. Nearly two-fifths (37%) of transit riders related giving money to homeless people they encountered on transit vehicles, at transit stops, and on the street.

Transportation Workers

Four-fifths (83%) of transportation workers reported that riders complained about the presence of homeless people on the vehicles, at the transit stops, or at stations. Four-fifths (83%) of the workers had asked a homeless person to leave the transportation facility, and three-fifths (56%) had escorted a homeless person from the facility. Half (56%) of the transportation workers said they had requested help from an outside social service agency for a homeless person, and one-fifth (22%) reported transporting a homeless person to a service. Yet transportation workers were involved with initiating only four outreach encounters between the HOT program and homeless people.

Business

The downtown business area of Baltimore had declined with the suburbanization of housing, shopping and offices. Lexington Mall and the Howard Street corridor were attempts to stop the declining use of the downtown area by improving public access and increasing service and retail opportunities. However, the merchants in the area complained that the number of homeless people and panhandlers in retail sales areas affected their ability to remain viable. Business owners/managers reported in the pre-program survey that they had to ask homeless people to leave their places of business an average of 10 times per week. Four-fifths said their customers and employees complained about homeless people who were in or around their businesses. Three-fourths had asked homeless people to leave the premises. The greater the amount of interaction business owners/managers had with homeless people, the more strongly they agreed that homeless people affected their ability to conduct business. However, half (49%) had seen their employees give homeless people food, money, vouchers, etc., and two-thirds (62%) had seen their customers give food or money to homeless people. Businesses helped initiate only 12 of the contacts between the HOT program and homeless people during the 30 months of the evaluation (less than 1 percent of all encounters).

Legal

Police respond to a wide variety of citizen and business complaints but are constrained by definitions of legal and illegal behavior. Homelessness is not illegal; most citizens feel sorry for homeless people, and most would not wish to punish them for not having a home. Panhandling, however, is different. While many people give money to panhandlers, they don't necessarily like it. The Baltimore City Council sought to make aggressive panhandling illegal under the pressure of business. It passed an ordinance during the HOT program (December 1993) to prohibit panhandlers from intimidating people on the streets by blocking their paths, using obscene or abusive language, or asking for money repeatedly after being refused. The ordinance outlawed panhandling of any sort at bus, subway, or light rail stops, or in the vehicles themselves. It also banned people from asking for money in exchange for washing car windows. The law was never implemented. It was ruled unconstitutional because it unfairly differentiated homeless people and beggars from others who aggressively solicited money.

The response of police to homeless people did not frequently involve social service programs like HOT. Police could have been involved in a maximum of 3 percent of HOT program encounters with homeless people. (HOT workers did not specifically identify police as a source or referral of encounter initiation as they did transportation workers and businesses.)

Homeless Services

Baltimore had a number of agencies which provided services to homeless people even before the HOT program. The Homeless and Environmental Services Unit of the Baltimore Department of Social Services (DDS) provided shelter and intensive case management services for three months to individual adults and families who sought their services for housing stabilization. During the first six months of 1991, DDS assisted more than 3,300 cases: 337 homeless families, 1,076 homeless adults, and 1,509 families and individuals facing homelessness.

Health Care for the Homeless began in Baltimore City in 1985 as a demonstration project. It provided health care services to 3,178 homeless persons in 1990 involving 17,851 separate encounters. It is located in the HOT target area.

A number of other agencies also served Baltimore's homeless. Many are represented on the Homeless Relief Advisory Board, which advises the city government on homeless issues.

Mayor's Office of Homeless Services

The city of Baltimore has a special unit in the mayor's office to address issues on homelessness. One of the functions of the Mayor's Office of Homeless Services is to prepare and implement a winter plan. The plan involves additional overnight accommodations using church sanctuaries, daytime accommodations, bus transportation to overnight shelters, street services, homelessness prevention, severe cold weather emergency services, and communication mechanisms. During the three years of the HOT program evaluation, the Mayor's Office of Homeless Services began several programs with outside funding. A Shelter Plus Care program provided 556 units of permanent housing for individuals disabled by mental illness, AIDS, and related illnesses. Homeless veterans benefitted from reintegration training funds, rental subsidies, and a homeless facility.

Table 3
PERCENT OF CASE MANAGEMENT CLIENTS PLACED
IN PERMANENT HOUSING

Characteristic	Number	Percent Accepting
All Clients	394	27%
9+ service needs recorded		
$200+ spent from HOT fund pool	50	74%
<$200 spent from HOT fund pool	62	37%
3–8 service needs recorded		
$50+ spent from HOT fund pool	48	48%
<$50 spent from HOT fund pool		
1+ years in Baltimore City		
Homeless <6 months	34	35%
Homeless 6+ months	83	12%
<1 year in Baltimore City	33	0%
1–2 service needs recorded	84	4%

Homeless Outreach Team

The HOT program evolved from a previous cooperative outreach effort involving representatives from the Social Security Administration, Health Care for the Homeless, and the Baltimore Department of Social Services. This group conducted street outreach one day a week in an area much larger than that on which the HOT program focused.

The Mayor's Office of Homeless Services was the applicant for and managed the HOT program. The Baltimore Department for Social Services housed the HOTeam of four case managers and a supervisor. The HOTeam itself was the heart of the project. It began work in February 1992. Workers reached out to street-dwelling homeless persons in the target area and provided case management services to those responding to the outreach. HOTeam case management identified client needs and linked them with existing social services.

Supporting the HOTeam was the Project Team, consisting of representatives from a number of organizations and agencies which interacted with homeless people. The Project Team met about every two months to share information and coordinate responses and services to homeless persons. The Baltimore City Police Department was among the 12 agencies represented.

PROBLEMS ASSOCIATED WITH HOMELESSNESS

Homeless people are frequently considered to cause "problems," even though transit riders frequently identified the "problem" as a society that does not do enough for homeless people. Some problems may be long-standing—1 HOT client in 7 (14%) reported childhood problems of homelessness, foster care placement, reform school, or running away from home.

Criminality

Although homelessness is not illegal, a substantial portion of homeless people have been involved with the criminal justice system. One-tenth (9%) of the homeless people accepting case management were on parole from prison. Another two-tenths (21%) had been incarcerated in prison but were not now on parole. One-tenth (14%) had some other type of criminal history, generally being on probation without imprisonment.

This may be no higher, however, than other people living in the central parts of cities but is substantially less than found in an earlier study when four-fifths had been arrested as an adult.[8]

Panhandling

Almost all transit riders have been approached for money, food, or cigarettes by people saying they were homeless. The frequency of panhandling did not change during the first two years of HOT. Over half (53% in 1992 and 55% in 1994) of the riders reported being approached by a homeless person either the day before or the day of the survey. A third (27% in 1992 and 29% in 1994) reported being approached 2–7 days before receiving the survey. Most of the rest said they were last approached eight or more days before the survey; only a few (3% in 1992 and 2% in 1994) had never been approached for money, food, or cigarettes. One-third (37%) of transit riders in 1992 and one-fourth (28%) in 1994 reported giving money to the homeless that approach them. What bothered transit riders in 1994 most about homeless people was their panhandling: two-fifths (39%) said they were most bothered by panhandling. In 1992, two-fifths (41%) of the transit riders were most bothered that not enough was being done for homeless people.

People were less likely to panhandle from transportation workers. About half of the transportation workers said they were not asked for anything by homeless individuals they encountered. Two-fifths (39%) in 1992 and one-fifth in 1994 reported that they were asked for money whenever they encounter homeless people. In both years, only 6 percent of the workers reported that they gave money to panhandlers.

Aggressive panhandling appears to be the underlying reason business owners/managers believe homeless people harm their businesses. A path analysis of their survey responses (using stepwise regression procedures) shows business owners/managers are more likely to agree that homeless people harmed their businesses when (1) they perceived that homeless people make their patrons, customers, or clients feel uncomfortable, and when (2) they personally have had more interactions with homeless people (see Fig. 1). Behind both of these factors is their linkage with panhandling. The more strongly business managers agree that "homeless are generally aggressive panhandlers," the more strongly they agree that "homeless people make our patrons or clients uncomfortable" and the more frequently they report interactions with homeless people. Owners/

managers' descriptions about the physical health, mental health, or substance abuse of homeless people have no independent effect on their reports that homeless people harm their businesses. It is the panhandling, not the mental illness or substance abuse, that they see affecting their business.

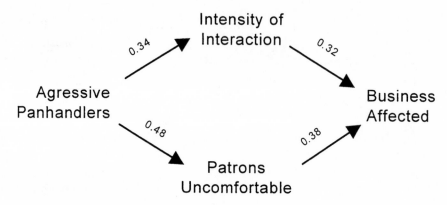

Figure 1. Factors affecting business attitudes toward homeless people.

Occupying Space

Officials of the metropolitan transit and intercity bus lines did not have any problems with homeless people, at least when "problems" are defined as formal customer or employee complaints. All of the surveys included as part of the evaluation, however, suggest a widespread presence and perceived problems with homeless people. Although the Mass Transit Administration (MTA) and Greyhound supported the Baltimore grant application, they told federal officials during the initial site visit that they did not have any problems with homeless people. This assertion was made again to the principal evaluator when arrangements were being made to review cost data and to interview employees. "Problems" appear to be officially defined as formal customer or employee complaints, i.e., public relations problems.

Half (50%) of the transportation workers surveyed in both years reported that they have no specific responsibilities to the homeless population. A small percentage in both years (5%–6%) reported that they had a responsibility to protect the homeless. A change occurred in worker reports over the two-year period of the HOT program. Workers placed greater emphasis at the end of the program on making transit pleasant and upholding the law, and less emphasis on finding shelter for the homeless persons. In 1992 over half (56%) of the workers reported asking social agencies for assistance, and one-fourth (22%) reported taking homeless people to the services they requested. In 1994 only one-tenth (11%) of the workers reported asking social agencies for assistance, and only one worker (6%) reported taking homeless people to the services they requested. In both years, about half the workers said they were most likely to respond to homeless people by asking them to leave the area.

Nuisance

Bottles, urine and other trash are often associated with homeless people. Business owners/managers reported seeing evidence of homeless people an average of 21 times a week. Transit riders did not have major concerns with garbage, dirtiness, or other problems that might be attributed to the homeless. Transportation workers were hesitant to assign litter problems to homeless people, but the intercity bus company did have problems with people leaving belongings in unlocked lockers.

The HOTeam frequently suspected abuse of substances by homeless people they encountered, and this generally increased over the course of the program. About one-fourth of the homeless people encountered at the start of the program and two-thirds of those at the end of the program were suspected to be abusing substances, even though there was substantial monthly variability around this trend line. Part of this increase could be associated with the Maryland cut in funds for substance abuse treatment in July 1992.

Needs of the Homeless

HOT workers identified an average of 7.2 different types of services needed by case management clients. One-tenth needed one service, but one client needed 81 services. Half of the clients needed five or fewer services.

Nearly four-fifths (78%) of the homeless people who accepted program services were assessed by case managers as needing case management services. Three-fifths (57%) had a need for permanent housing assessed. About two-fifths needed each of the following services: medical attention, food, transportation, and benefits. One-third had a need for temporary housing. Some clients may have needed additional or different services, but did not get to a point where their case manager could identify the need, either because other needs were more pressing, the homeless person did not mention the need to the case manager, or the homeless person did not remain in case management long enough for the case manager to identify the need.

PROGRAM SUCCESS

Outreach Success

The first function of the HOTeam was outreach to homeless people in the target area. HOT workers spent about one-fourth of their outreach time walking about the target area, searching for homeless people to approach, and an additional one-third of their time approaching and encountering people who appeared to be homeless. HOT workers recorded 1,300 encounters with homeless people in 30 months of the evaluation, but these were concentrated in the first part of the program.

HOT workers successfully convinced two-thirds of the homeless people they encountered to accept case management services. Most were recruited during or following the first outreach encounter. Most of those who did not accept case management during the first outreach encounter were never seen again by the HOTeam. When those initially rejecting case management were seen again, they were almost as likely to accept case management after the second encounter as were all homeless people after the first encounter. Statistical techniques suggest that almost all (98%) of the homeless people would have been recruited into case management if HOT workers could have encountered them at least five times. Those who accepted case management had about the same characteristics as those who did not. The only difference was in physical health. One-sixth (16%) of case management clients were suspected of having a physical health condition at the time they were first encountered by the HOT workers, in contrast to 1 in 10 of those who never became case management clients.

Success in Case Management

Once homeless people agreed to participate in case management, the HOTeam worked with them to identify and obtain the services they needed in the process of getting off the street. HOT workers identified 320 different providers to meet the needs of case management clients; only a small proportion of these (23) identified as a source of service more than 15 times.

Service Needs Met

The HOTeam recorded that 17 percent of individual service needs of their homeless clients were met with "excellent" success, and an additional 40 percent met with success. One-fourth (25%) of the service needs were not met at all. The success with which needs were met varied greatly by the type of service. Providers fully meet almost all (94%) of the needs of homeless clients for food. By contrast, providers fully met only one-fourth (28%) of the client needs for drug or alcohol treatment and one-third (35%) of the needs for permanent shelter. Failure of a need to be successfully met can be due to a number of reasons. One group of these is client failures—the failure of the homeless person to go to the provider or the refusal to do what the provider requires. Another group of reasons can be classified as service system failures—there is no provider who can give the service or there is no provider who can provide the service without reimbursement for costs. Lack of success in meeting needs was twice as likely due to the clients' failures as to service system failure.

HOT workers initially saw the Baltimore social service system as fairly responsive. Their evaluations dropped to a low one year into the program, but then steadily increased to a new peak at the end of the program. Overall, few (7%) clients were successful or very successful when the system had little or no success in meeting the clients' needs for services. When the HOTeam felt the social service system was very successful in meeting clients' needs, they evaluated half (48%) of these clients as very successful in the program and another fifth (22%) as fairly successful.

HOT case management services required actions on an average of eight different days per client. The HOT program had a pool of funds which HOT workers could use as either enticements to develop a case management relationship or to meet client needs that other social services did not meet.

Permanent Housing Success

The major goal of the HOT program was to get homeless people off the street and into permanent housing. Permanent housing required actions by HOT case managers on an average of 5½ different days to pursue each service need. The majority (59%) of the program's fund pool was spent in meeting three housing needs: household furnishings, permanent housing, and temporary shelter. By the time the evaluation ended, the HOT program had placed in permanent housing one-sixth (111) of all the homeless people they had encountered, or one-fourth (27%) of those who had accepted case management. HOT workers evaluated the majority of these placements as successful.

Factors Contributing to Success

Successful recruitment into case management was affected more by characteristics of the HOT program than by characteristics of the homeless people. Only homeless people with a physical health condition at the first encounter were not affected by program characteristics. Four-fifths of this small number accepted case management regardless of when they were encountered by the program, or how they were approached. For the majority, however, recruitment was highly successful (90%) when the homeless people were first encountered after the first six months (after the program had become established) and the HOTeam spent five dollars or more on outreach enticements. Less than one-third (29%) of the homeless people were successfully recruited during the first six months of the program when they were encountered by certain HOTeam workers and given no enticements. Some of the workers apparently did not have the experience or expertise to be a successful recruiter without assistance. However, they could become as successful as the other workers—for example, when they were assisted by enticements from the fund pool, or after they benefited from others' program experience through formal or informal training.

As with outreach, placement in permanent housing was primarily due to characteristics of the program, and the interaction of the program with homeless people, rather than to measurable characteristics of homeless people themselves. The most important factor was the number of needs for services which the HOT workers identified during interactions with homeless clients. Next most important was the amount of program funds spent on behalf of the clients. Three-fourths (74%) of the clients were placed in permanent housing when HOT workers identified nine or more service needs and spent $200 from the fund pool in meeting those needs. One-third to one-half (35%–48%) of clients were placed in permanent housing if HOT workers identified and recorded three or more needs and spent $50–$199 on them. Practically none (4%) of the clients were placed in permanent housing when the HOT worker interacted with the homeless person only enough to identify one or two needs.

Client characteristics showed a relationship with permanent housing only among clients with some degree of interaction with the HOTeam, but with little spent for them from project funds. When HOT workers identified 3–8 service needs and spent less than $50 on the client, then homeless people who had lived in Baltimore a year or more and had been homeless less than six months were more likely to achieve permanent housing than those who had lived in downtown Baltimore for less than a year or had been homeless for six months or more. Under some other models of program-related factors, it was slightly helpful in getting permanent housing if the homeless person was female, had some source of income or benefits, or had never needed Health Care for the Homeless. In general, however, measurable characteristics of homeless people had minor direct relationships to permanent housing placement.

The effectiveness of a program such as HOT is not dependent upon characteristics of the homeless people over which workers have no influence. Rather, the effectiveness depends upon maintaining involvement of the homeless people in the program, carefully determining and documenting their needs, and having resources that can help meet gaps in the existing social service system.

Visibility of Success

The general weight of the evidence suggests that the HOT program was effective in helping many homeless people find alternatives to living in the transit center of Baltimore. However, a case management program able to help people who had not been helped by existing social services required a lot of interaction with homeless people in order to successfully move them into permanent housing. The HOT program could be only a small step to an overall solution to the problem of homelessness in society, a problem which is seen as growing. Homelessness by itself is not visible. While notice by transit riders, transportation workers, and business owners/managers of a reduction in the number of homeless people might suggest the HOT program was successful, the lack of this notice does not mean the program was unsuccessful. It does say that a HOT program by itself will not solve all the problems of homelessness, nor rid an area of all the problems attributed to homeless people.

A program like HOT can make a difference. With enough contact, it can convince most homeless people to accept case management services. When it has substantial interactions with clients, identifies and records all their needs, and makes sufficient program funds available to case managers, it can place most clients in permanent housing. Measurable characteristics of homeless people are not important in these circumstances. It makes little difference whether the homeless are men or women, black or white, young or old, recent or long-term homeless, educated, veterans, mentally ill, substance abusers, physically disabled, or anything else. It is only when a program like HOT is starting up, has little sustained interaction with homeless people, and spends little of its own funds to entice them or meet gaps in available services that some of these characteristics are associated with success in achieving permanent housing.

ACKNOWLEDGMENTS

This report is part of a larger evaluation conducted under contract to the City of Baltimore, Mayor's Office of Homeless Services (Account #4276-303-209-00-000). The research demonstration project was carried out under a grant from the U.S. Department of Transportation, Federal Transit Administration (Project #MD-08-0033) to Baltimore City, Joanne Selinske, Project Officer.

Gordon Scott Bonham, Ph.D., Director, Center for Suburban and Regional Studies, Towson State University, was Principal Evaluator for the HOT program. The research and analysis are those of the author, and do not necessarily represent the opinions or policies of Towson State University, the City of Baltimore, or the U.S. Department of Transportation.

ENDNOTES

1. Bonham, G.S., & Hart, J.A.: *Outreach to Homeless People in Baltimore's Transit Center.* Report No. 6. Towson, MD: Towson State University Center for Suburban and Regional Studies, 1995.
2. Culhane, D.P., Dejowski, E.F., Ibanex, J., Needham, E., & Macchia, I.: *Public Shelter Admission Rates in Philadelphia and New York City.* Washington, D.C., Fannie Mae Office of Housing Research, 1993.

3. U.S. Department of Commerce. *Census Bureau Releases 1990 Decennial Counts for Persons Enumerated in Emergency Shelters and Observed on the Streets.* Washington, D.C., 1991.

4. Committee for Food and Shelter. *Characteristics and Housing Needs of the Homeless: Final Report.* Washington, D.C., 1987.

5. National Coalition for the Homeless. *Fatally Flawed: The Census Bureau's Count of Homeless People.* Washington, D.C., 1991.

6. Maryland Department of Human Resources, as reported in Bonham, G.S. & Hart, J.A. *Outreach to Homeless People in Baltimore's Transit Center.* Report No. 6. Towson, MD: Towson State University Center for Suburban and Regional Studies, 1995.

7. Breakey, W.R., Fischer, P.J., Kramer, M., Nestadt, G., Romanoski, A., Ross, A., Royal, R.M., & Stine, O.C.: Health and mental health problems of homeless men and women in Baltimore. *JAMA, 262:*1352–7, 1989.

8. Bonham, G.S., & Hart, J.A.: *Outreach to Homeless People in Baltimore's Transit Center.* Report No. 6. Towson, MD: Towson State University Center for Suburban and Regional Studies, 1995.

Chapter 14

DEALING WITH HOMELESS POPULATIONS: THE PORTLAND MODEL OF PUBLIC-PRIVATE PARTNERSHIPS

The Association for Portland Progress (APP) is a nonprofit downtown business association; its mission is the beneficial growth and development of the Portland, Oregon's central city. Established in 1979 as an advocacy group, the association has supported the development of the downtown Transit Mall, the Light Rail system, Waterfront Park, downtown housing in all income ranges, and Pioneer Place (a Rouse Company retail and office project). These and many other public and private improvements have kept downtown Portland the vital centerpiece of the city and earned it recognition as one of the best downtown areas in the United States.

Since the late 1980s, the association has provided, in addition to advocacy, a variety of services and programs focused on the betterment of downtown Portland. Those services include management of publicly owned short-term parking garages, sidewalk cleaning, and security services for the public spaces in downtown.

APP involvement in the delivery of these services occurred out of a sense of necessity brought on by a variety of circumstances. Since the 1960s, developments in jurisprudence, rooted in the civil rights movement, have led to the striking down, on constitutional grounds, of laws against vagrancy, loitering and public begging. Many of those laws were applied in perniciously discriminatory ways, and the demise of those practices cannot be mourned by any fair-minded individual. However, the application of those cases has had negative effects on the use and management of public spaces. In the words of one commentator:

> These cases, which helped end American apartheid, were then used to trump many legitimate community interests and to elevate all kinds of individual desires into assertions of rights. They are now used to ... assert a right to sleep

216

and eat in the public space of one's choosing, and to beg in any way one pleases.[1]

In addition, the evolution of mental health treatment towards a community-based outpatient paradigm has led to the deinstitutionalization of thousands of people suffering from chronic mental illness. Failure by state and federal governments to adequately fund these community programs has resulted in thousands of people falling through the cracks.[2] As a result of these factors, downtowns across the U.S. have experienced increased populations of "street people" or transients inhabiting their public spaces, and the larger community has fewer of the tools, be they vagrancy laws or mental institutions, traditionally used to regulate the behavior of these individuals.

As an organization, APP believes a vital "heart" (downtown) is crucial to the health of a city and region. In the 1980s, public resources to clean and maintain public spaces and to police those spaces were not keeping up with the demand created by these trends. Competition, in the form of suburban office parks and regional shopping malls, threatened downtown's business base, which in turn posed a threat to a significant part of Portland's tax base. It became clear that if government could not devote more resources to supporting downtown, the private sector would be required to. Having the private sector take the lead in supporting the downtown area would be good business for APP's members and good for the city as a whole.

Thus, it was somewhat indirectly that APP got involved in the issue of homelessness. APP's interest in homelessness stems from the fact that the downtown is where a relatively high concentration of poor people live. In addition, downtown has a significant stock of low-income housing and is the focus of many of the programs and services designed to serve this population due to its central location and the availability of mass transit.

Downtown also is that part of the city that everyone regards as their own, where even the majority of the private property is designed for substantial use by the general public. Parks, plazas and public buildings provide many venues for people who have nowhere else to go. The challenge has been to create an environment where all interested users of the downtown area can coexist. There are several factors that contribute to this challenge—a concentration of the needy in this area and shrinking budgets and resources to support them, and judicial precedents to allow ready access by indigent persons to public places. Needless to say, these factors do not in general enhance downtown's image as a business location. Thus, it has been part of APP's agenda to mitigate the impact of these trends on downtown in order to achieve its mission.

To better understand APP's role in Portland's approach to the issue of homelessness, it is necessary briefly to look at the broader context in which that role evolved. Portland is a city of about one-half million residents. Both Oregon as a state and Portland as a city were particularly hard hit by the recession of the early 1980s. Like many large and mid-sized cities, homelessness became an issue of local importance during that time. It proved to be a divisive problem. One camp saw homeless people as victims of an uncaring economic system or society, while the other saw them as lazy individuals looking for a free ride. The fact that the region was slow to recover from the recession put a second, perhaps related issue on the top of people's agenda: the issue of economic development.

In the mayoral election of 1984, J. E. "Bud" Clark ran on a platform that spoke to both addressing the problem of homelessness and promoting economic development. Both issues had powerful constituencies. Supporting economic development was the business community wanting to get Oregon on track with the economic expansion being experienced by much of the rest of the country. Supporters addressing homelessness were advocates who tapped into Oregon's and Portland's long-held progressive beliefs on social justice. Those two issues butted heads directly in the north end of Portland's downtown, its historic skid road. Old Town, as the area is called, has a high concentration of low-income housing and social services for the indigent. The city's downtown revitalization efforts were spreading north from the retail/office core into Old Town. Conflicts resulted between those interested in seeing the area prosper economically, and the advocates for the indigent—those at risk of being displaced.

On the neighborhood level, Old Town business people objected to finding "transients" sleeping in doorways when they arrived at work in the morning. Even more objectionable was arriving to find their doorway had been used as a latrine overnight. Public inebriation (to the point of passing out), drinking in public, disorderly conduct, aggressive panhandling and loitering were other behaviors that the community found objectionable. Calling the police to address those behaviors, many of which were no longer criminal in nature, was proving frustrating to all concerned.

Mayor Clark saw that those supporting both agendas shared one fundamental goal—they wanted to get the poor off the streets and out of doorways and parks. He sought to harness the support of both constituencies through his twelve-point plan for "Breaking the Cycle of Homelessness," published in 1986. The plan clearly and comprehensively addressed the issue of homelessness. It also tapped broader community support by emphasizing the personal responsibility of the needy to get help and the idea that everyone must conform to community standards of behavior. To quote from the plan, the entire package was designed to:

1. Reach out to homeless people who need help in becoming part of the mainstream of community life;
2. Be firm with those who do not adhere to community standards for behavior; and
3. Create an environment in which business can flourish and major economic development agendas can be pursued.[3]

Thus, the plan advocated balance: help for the homeless balanced by expectations that they would behave in ways that did not negatively impact the business environment. The plan advocated the development of a continuum of services, from emergency services such as mass shelters and soup kitchens, to transitional housing with case management, to permanent housing. In addition to this continuum of housing alternatives, the plan envisioned drug and alcohol treatment services and employment efforts which would enable homeless individuals to make permanent changes in their lives. It was first in the area of creating employment, followed by a role in enforcing community behavioral standards that APP has been involved in the issues.

EMPLOYMENT

One of the fundamental tenets of the twelve-point plan is that individuals need the opportunity to work, to become self supporting if they are to truly leave the ranks of the homeless. It is not merely a matter of finding these people a job. Many homeless individuals have not worked regularly in years. They do not have even minimal job skills—such as the self-discipline to get up and get to work on time every day—that most other people have. Employing them presents unique challenges that most employers want to avoid.

At the time of the promulgation of the twelve-point plan, one of the nagging problems suffered by the north end of downtown was the profusion of litter on the streets generated by the many individuals loitering there. Mayor Clark and APP formed a partnership to address that problem and to create a pilot employment effort for homeless individuals seeking to change their lives. The city gave APP a grant for $60,000 to provide sidewalk cleaning services to the north end of downtown. APP agreed to hire formerly homeless, recovering substance abusers to fill the half dozen jobs funded by the grant. APP agreed to provide the supervision and training necessary for this cleaning crew.

In 1988, APP formed its first "Downtown Clean & Safe" special services district.[4] As a result, APP expanded the sidewalk cleaning program from 20 square blocks in the north end of downtown to the whole Downtown Clean & Safe" district—208 square blocks encompassing the entire central business district. The budget was expanded from $60,000 to almost $300,000. The Clean & Safe "cleaning crew" now employs a dozen individuals. They start at minimum wage; their task is literally to sweep up cigarette butts and other litter on every block within the Clean & Safe district. At the time they are hired, they are equipped with a reflective vest, lobby dustpan and garbage can on wheels. In addition to salary, they receive basic benefits: health insurance, vacation and sick leave.

In order to enhance their chances of success on the job, crew members must meet certain basic rules: report to work everyday, on time, clean and sober. Failure to comply with the rules will lead to discipline, including possible dismissal. Each crew member is referred to APP by a downtown agency serving the homeless. The APP supervisor has a working relationship with their case manager. If the supervisor suspects the employee is relapsing, he passes the information on to the case manager who addresses the issue with the employee.

Through the partnership with the social service agencies, APP has learned to develop a series of simple attainable goals that teach the discipline these individuals need, raise their self-esteem and foster the work habits that they will need to be successful in the "real" world. For example, when an employee has successfully worked for APP for six months, he is issued a pair of high-quality work boots to complete his work uniform. "Getting your boots" is a sign of success in the cleaning crew.

Crew members who succeed have career options. The two "crew chiefs," each of whom supervises six cleaners, are both former crew members.

Through hard work and the demonstration of their ability to be responsible for others, they have the higher status and pay of these positions.

APP has enhanced employment opportunities for the crew by blending the program into other activities of the association. APP manages seven publicly owned, short-term retail parking structures. As part of its management function, APP provides janitorial services to these parking garages. Successful members of the sidewalk cleaning crew can be "promoted" to a janitorial position in one of these parking structures. As such they are paid more and have responsibility for the day-to-day cleaning and maintenance of the structure. Besides the added responsibility, these jobs have the benefit of being under cover, which in Portland's rainy winters is truly a significant advantage.

Finally, APP has created a heavy-duty cleaning crew as part of Downtown Clean & Safe. This team washes sidewalks and the downtown transit malls and removes graffiti from public and private property within the district. They also operate vehicles and other motorized equipment. These are APP's highest-paying maintenance jobs and the end of our "career path" for the maintenance workers and sidewalk cleaning crew.

The cleaning program encompasses over 20 jobs, 75 percent of which are filled by formerly homeless individuals. In the ten years since the program started with city money, APP has "graduated" dozens of individuals into "real" private sector jobs.

ADVOCACY AND SERVICES

In addition to directly providing jobs and training opportunities, APP has taken on an advocacy role. Many homeless individuals are substance abusers, and some are chronically mentally ill. Both of these conditions are legally defined as "disabilities," entitling individuals to the assistance of the Oregon Vocational Rehabilitation Division (VRD). APP learned that VRD served only a very small number of people from the north downtown area (roughly 10 per year). The reasons were many and complex. VRD had no office in the area, so potential clients had to travel across the Willamette River into northeast Portland to apply for services. VRD had a fairly slow process for qualifying individuals for services (3–4 weeks), and given the transient nature of these individual's life-styles, VRD often could not find them to inform them they had qualified for these services. North downtown case managers were also unfamiliar with the assessment, training and employment opportunities

VRD possessed so they made inconsistent attempts to qualify their clients.

Through APP's intervention, many of these barriers have been overcome. By hosting joint meetings of the VRD and service provider staffs, the barriers in the system were identified and many have been removed. VRD staff began visiting the shelters and service provider sites to take applications for benefits; VRD shortened the time it took to qualify clients for benefits; and all participants developed personal relationships and an understanding of each other's offerings. As a result, in the first year after this process was initiated the number of north downtown referrals being qualified by VRD increased to 10–15 *per month*.

ORDER MAINTENANCE AND COMMUNITY POLICING

As previously stated, the impact of the transient population on downtown was a serious issue from the perspective of the downtown business community. People sleeping in doorways, becoming inebriated in parks, or aggressively panhandling on downtown streets were seen as threats to the economic vitality of the central business district.

That perspective was confirmed by surveys of downtown Portland users. When asked about the impediments to coming downtown, respondents said they felt "unsafe" there. When queried more closely about why they did not feel safe, they identified panhandlers, street drinkers and chronically mentally ill individuals as the reason for their anxiety (though few people reported being seriously threatened by these individuals).

None of these behaviors is treated as serious crimes in Oregon. While it is illegal to drink in public in Oregon, the justice system no longer incarcerates offenders. Police officers observing someone drinking in public will only confiscate the alcohol. A person incapacitated from drinking will be taken to the Hooper Detox Sobering Station where he or she will be "dried out" and then released back to the streets. Panhandling is generally regarded as constitutionally protected free speech. The only limitations on it are that the person asking for money cannot harass those he asks or block their passage along the sidewalk in the process of making his request.

Requests for additional police resources by both the downtown business and residential community were unsuccessful. In the bigger picture, downtown's street disorder could not equal gang violence when competing for the police bureau's scarce resources. It is difficult to argue with such decisions.

In response to this situation, APP formed Downtown Clean & Safe, the special services district that also funds the sidewalk cleaning program. In fall 1988, Downtown Clean & Safe deployed two dozen "Portland guides," supported by a half dozen "patrol officers." The "guides" are quasi-uniformed, unarmed, radio-equipped individuals with a dual mission: they are goodwill ambassadors for downtown and "eyes and ears" for the police. In the first capacity, they provide directions, information and assistance to the users of downtown; in the second, they are trained to observe and report suspicious or potentially illegal activity. They are all trained in CPR and first aid.

The patrol officers are uniformed, armed (they are all Bureau of Police Standards and Training qualified), and generally they are retired police officers. They bring an average of 20 years of police experience to their positions. They too are radio-equipped. The patrol officer's function is to support and supervise the guides, respond to calls for assistance from the guides, and to provide a more authoritarian presence out on the street than the guides do.

Both categories of personnel serve to create a law enforcement presence on the streets, making law-abiding citizens feel more comfortable, and discouraging those who would break the law or behave badly from doing so. APP's security personnel interface effectively with the police and private security providers around downtown. APP has created a downtown "security network" as a forum where private security providers, other public security forces (i.e., Federal Protective Services), and the Portland Police Bureau can share information about current problems, issues and trends.

The guides and officers are particularly effective with regard to discouraging street disorder. When they observe a "man down" (someone incapacitated by substance abuse), they contact the Central City Concern's Hooper Inebriate Emergency Response Service (CHIERS) outreach van, an arm of the Hooper Detox Center. CHIERS will transport the inebriate to the sobering station to "dry out." This removes the individual from the street where he might be victimized or suffer from exposure to the elements and allows other downtown users to go about their business without having to deal with this person's problem.

Panhandling is another behavior that the presence of guides and officers discourages. They politely encourage panhandlers to refrain from establishing themselves in one place for long periods of time, providing them with information about where the panhandler can find services they say they need. If the panhandler refuses, guides will actively discourage citizens from contributing to the panhandler. They do this by distributing information (in the form of a leaflet) encouraging citizens to support programs that serve the needy rather than giving change to panhandlers on the street. This leaflet is part of our "Real Change NOT Spare Change" education effort. Its premise is that many panhandlers use the money they receive to buy alcohol or drugs, substances that materially contribute to their need to beg for money. In short, people who give cash to panhandlers may be "enabling" them to live non-contributing lives.[5] The result of the guides distributing this information by standing on either side of a panhandler is that his contributions drop off and he chooses to move to a part of town where his requests are not balanced by contrary information.

Lastly, the presence of APP personnel helps insure that panhandlers behave appropriately. If a guide or officer witnesses someone aggressively panhandling, they can serve as the complaining witness so the police can cite the panhandler for the offense. The "victim" is typically a downtown user who has little or no interest in getting involved in a prosecution for aggressive panhandling. They only want to "get away" from this individual who is forcefully soliciting change from them. Citing panhandlers is rarely necessary—most have gotten the message that if they "work" downtown, their behavior needs to be appropriate.

While it is dangerous to assert cause-and-effect relationships when no empirical proof exists for such a linkage, Portland Police Bureau crime statistics indicate that crime has decreased in downtown Portland since the guides and officers were put out on the streets. Perhaps more significantly, Portland Police Bureau statistics indicate that street disorder problems have decreased in downtown since the program was implemented.

The relationship between APP and the Portland Police Bureau (PPB) has evolved into a strong partnership. PPB helped develop the training for the guides and the criteria for the officers. They have participated in the guide training academies, along with the Multnomah County District Attorney's office. Out on the street, Portland Progress has a good reputation with the rank and file officers. The Bureau of Emergency Communications recognizes Portland Progress as a downtown service provider when dispatching 911 calls received from the guides/officers.

Guides and officers provide assistance to PPB at their request between 150 and 200 times per year. After seven years, it is fair to say that the PPB regards the guides and officers as an important resource for addressing downtown problems.

One problem guides and officers have not been able to adequately address is how best to deal with the chronically mentally ill. While APP has provided limited training to our personnel from the downtown mental health service provider, this population presents challenges that only qualified mental health professionals can effectively address out on the street. Many of these people are too disoriented to respond appropriately to interactions with our personnel. Because many do not trust anyone who approaches them on the street, encouraging them to seek food and shelter at local agencies is fruitless. Alarmingly, their numbers continue to grow. Oregon has recently closed its state hospital, transferring those patients not qualified for release to local psychiatric wards. Many people have been discharged to community-based treatment programs. Some of them lose touch with the program and wind up out on the street. Because of their "trust issues," they do not seek help.

In 1993, faced with rising numbers of mentally ill homeless on Portland's streets, APP formed a partnership with Mental Health Services West (MHSW), the downtown mental health service provider, to create Project Respond. This mobile outreach effort is staffed by two qualified mental health professionals. They patrol the Central City, responding to calls for service from the police, businesses, and other social service providers. They provide on-site assessment of the subject's mental health status. They have the capability to hospitalize anyone who needs immediate care and treatment. Perhaps more importantly, they are able to build a relationship with the "client" and get them to accept the services they need. They have become an invaluable adjunct to the security patrols and the Portland Police in managing street disorder.

APP's role in the creation of Project Respond took several forms. It committed funds from the Clean & Safe district to help support the pilot program in 1993 (roughly $70,000 in the first year; over $100,000 in subsequent years). APP helped MHSW prepare their operations plan for the program. Particularly important was advising them of how best to craft the program in order to be marketable to the downtown business community to whom they would be going for additional resources. APP provided assistance on grant applications with letters of support and testimonials when MHSW pursued these other funding options.

MHSW has succeeded in gaining commitments for $1.2 million over a three-year period, including receiving major grants and corporate donations. In their words, APP's support was crucial for their credibility as they pursued those resources. From APP's perspective, the partnership has been fundamental in helping downtown address a serious problem.

CONCLUSION

For almost ten years, Portland has been making a good-faith effort to address the issues of homelessness in a comprehensive, humane way. The Association for Portland Progress has participated in that effort in ways that contribute both to the goal of addressing homelessness and to the advancement of APP's mission—maintaining the health of Portland's Central City. The problem of homelessness has not been solved in Portland, but there is broad consensus as to what needs to be done to address the problem. Resources remain the most significant limitation on the community's ability to achieve its goal. Creative partnerships, like Downtown Clean & Safe and Project Respond, have helped fill gaps while expanding the resource base.

ENDNOTES

1. Robert Tier, "Maintaining Safety and Civility in Public Spaces: A Constitutional Approach to Aggressive Begging," *Louisiana Law Review,* Vol. 54, p. 287, 1993.
2. See, for example, Alice Baum and David Burnes, A Nation in Denial, The Truth About Homelessness, Boulder, Colorado: Westview Press, 1993.
3. Susan Stone, "Breaking the Cycle of Homelessness: The Portland Model," A Publication of the Office of the Mayor of the City of Portland, Oregon, Revised September 1988, p. 21.
4. This special service district has been copied in dozens of cities around this country and Canada. Known as Business Improvement Districts (BID), Business Improvement Zones (BIZ), Business Improvement Areas (BIA), and/or Economic Improvement Districts (EID), they raise funds from the businesses and/or property owners within their boundaries. The funds, generated as taxes, assessments or fees, are usually levied by local governments which then, under an agreement with the payers, turn the funds over to an APP-like organization to deliver services to the district that have been identified by the payers as desirable for the district. The most common service profile includes some kind of enhanced security, cleaning and marketing/promotion services for the district.

5. This view is not original to APP. Several downtown social service agencies have partnered with the association over the years to spread this message. Their clients, a number of whom have worked for APP in the cleaning program, have confirmed, anecdotally, that many panhandlers use the money they receive for alcohol and/or drugs.

INDEX

A

Abused women (*see also* Domestic violence), 6, 78
Acupuncture, 92
African American, 7, 10, 25, 26, 153, 154, 185, 214
Agnos, Art, 100, 101
Aid to Families with Dependent Children (AFDC), 186
AIDS/HIV, 10, 28, 67, 139, 155, 173, 205
Alliance for the Mentally Ill (AMI), 147
American Civil Liberties Union, 111
American Journal of Public Health, 5, 11, 16
American Psychiatric Association, 144
Amtrak, 34, 173, 175
Andre House, 188
Anti-poverty Coalition, 111
Archer, Dennis, 13
Association for Portland Progress (APP), 138, 139, 140, 142, 216, 217, 218, 220, 221, 222, 223, 224, 225, 226
ATM, 35, 96, 102
Attention Deficit Disorder (ADD), 156

B

Baltimore (MD), 15, 32, 35, 178, 197–215
Battered Women's Shelter, 118, 119, 120, 124, 127
Bayh, Birch, 158
Bazelon, David, 156
Becca Bill, 164
Berkeley (CA), 34, 87, 88, 89, 90, 91, 92, 93, 94, 96
Berkeley-Oakland Support Services (BOSS), 92
Beyond Shelter, 100, 101, 114
Boston (MA), 168

Bratton, William, 176
British Common Law, 23
Broward County (FL), 68
Brown, Willie, 99, 105, 113, 114
Bus therapy, 60
Business Alliance, 14, 15

C

California v. Greenwood, 49
Carter, Jimmy, 159
Case Management, 92, 134, 135, 142, 143, 145, 148, 161, 163, 168, 188, 191, 197, 204, 205, 206, 209, 210, 211, 212, 213, 214, 219, 220, 221
Catholic Community Services, 170
Center for Substance Abuse Prevention (CSAP), 15
Central Arizona Shelter Services (CASS), 181–196
Chamber of Commerce, 37
CHIERS Program, 138, 140, 223
Child Care, 126, 127, 128, 188
Child Protective Services (CPS), 193
Children's Defense Fund, 157
Cisneros, Henry, 6
Civil rights, 22, 56, 111, 114, 132, 150, 174, 175, 179, 216
Clark, J.E., 218, 219, 220
Cleveland (OH), 33
Coalition on Homelessness, 111, 112, 113
Colonial Era, 21
Community-based organizations, 15, 74, 90, 92, 151, 159, 181, 217, 225
Community health workers, 16
Community Partnership Initiative, 15
Community policing, 15, 175, 222, 223
Community Services Officer, 65
Computer-aided Dispatch (CAD), 70

Congress, 7, 77, 151, 158, 159, 160, 195
Connecticut v. Mooney, 42–56
Continuum of Care, 37, 114
Corniel, Marcelino, 3
Criminalize, 3, 12, 13, 21, 22, 26, 27, 30, 32,
    34, 38, 53, 96, 101, 105, 111, 114, 115
Crisis Intervention Team (CIT), 143, 144, 146
Crisis poverty, 6

D

Dallas (TX), 31, 32, 33
DeGeneste, Henry, 173
Deinstitutionalization of mental hospitals, 9,
    132, 133, 184, 217
Detoxification, 59, 91, 104, 138
Detroit (MI), 13
Domestic violence, 18, 63, 90, 118–130, 154,
    169
Downtown Clean & Safe, 220, 221, 223, 225,
    226
Drop-in program, 143, 156
Drug overdose, 11
Drug treatment program, 8, 11, 77

E

East Side Detail, 63, 64
Education, 16, 52, 122, 126, 127, 128, 142, 159,
    160, 177, 179, 188
Eighth Amendment, 32, 54, 113
Emergency shelter, 13, 14, 15, 26, 27, 29, 37,
    58, 60, 65, 66, 71, 75, 76, 77, 78, 81, 88,
    90, 94, 98, 99, 100, 101, 103, 104, 105, 112,
    114, 118, 119, 120, 121, 124, 126, 127, 142,
    143, 144, 148, 153, 154, 156, 159, 160, 162,
    169, 185, 187, 188, 191, 192, 193, 198, 200,
    201, 204, 205, 211, 212, 219, 222
Employment, 16, 92, 114, 122
Equal Protection Clause, 36
Eviction, 91, 98

F

Federal Emergency Relief Administration, 183
Federal Interagency Council on Homeless-
    ness, 177, 197
First Amendment, 35, 179
Food stamps, 15

Fourth Amendment, 42, 45, 46, 47, 48, 49, 50,
    51, 52, 53, 54, 55

G

Gilded Age, 21
Giuliani, Rudolph, 16
Golden Gate Park, 9
Great Depression, 3, 21, 26, 183
Greyhound, 208

H

Hance, Margaret, 184
Harris County (TX), 118, 119, 120, 121, 124,
    125
Hayes, Robert, 52
Health care, 52
Health Care for the Homeless, 200, 204, 206,
    213
HELP Program, 64, 65, 75, 76
Hepatitis, 10
Hispanic, 7, 10, 143, 153, 154, 185
Homeless Outreach Team (HOT), 176, 197,
    198, 199, 200, 201, 202, 203, 204, 205, 206,
    207, 208, 209, 210, 211, 212, 213, 214
Homeless Outreach Unit, 74, 75, 76
Homeless Relief Advisory Board, 205
Hooper Detox Station, 222, 223
Housing, 16, 22, 26, 37, 52, 65, 68, 88, 90, 92,
    94, 99, 100, 106, 110, 113, 115, 118, 119,
    124, 126, 128, 133, 134, 141, 143, 145, 148,
    161, 172, 183
Houston (TX), 118, 119, 120, 124, 125
Houston Area Women's Center (HAWC), 119,
    120, 121, 127
Hunger, 26

I

Immigration, 21, 126

J

Jail, 8, 16, 27, 36, 107, 108, 110, 151, 159, 164,
    210
Joliet (IL), 64
Jordan, Frank, 98, 99, 100, 101, 102, 103, 104,
    105, 111, 112, 114

Journal of the American Medical Association, 10

Joyce v. City and County of San Francisco, 106, 113

Juvenile facility, 8

Juvenile Justice and Delinquency Prevention Act, 158, 159, 164

K

Kelly v. Florida, 50

Kozol, Jonathan, 7

L

Lamb American Psychiatric Association Report, 9

Largent, Steve, 164

Lawyers Committee for Civil Rights, 111

Los Angeles (CA), 63, 64, 168

Lowry, Mike, 164

M

Malnutrition, 11

Manhattan Bowery Corporation, 168

Maricopa County (AZ), 185

Matrix Program, 26, 98–117

Measure "O", 93, 94, 96, 97

Mental health, 9, 59, 77, 78, 80, 81, 82, 88, 102, 104, 105, 115, 132, 135, 136, 137, 139, 140, 141, 142, 143, 146, 147, 148, 155, 156, 160, 161, 162, 172, 173, 201, 208, 217, 225

Mental Health Services West, 132, 139, 141, 225, 226

Mental hospital, 8, 132, 133

Mental illness, 8, 9, 11, 63, 66, 69, 74, 75, 76, 82, 89, 92, 99, 104, 131, 132, 133, 134, 135, 136, 138, 139, 140, 141, 142, 143, 144, 146, 147, 148, 168, 169, 173, 175, 176, 179, 184, 185, 190, 191, 201, 205, 208, 214, 217, 221, 222, 225

Metropolitan Transit Authority, 74, 177, 178

Miami (FL), 32, 33, 54, 175

Miami Meal Tax, 37

Milwaukee (WI), 35

Mobile Crisis Team, 89

Modified Payments Program, 103

Montgomery County (MD), 65

Multi-agency Service Center, 92

Multi-service Centers, 100

N

Nashville (TN), 37

Nation in Denial, 8

National Academy of Sciences, 8

National Alliance to End Homelessness, 124

National Association of Social Workers, 155

National Coalition for the Homeless, 52

National Council on Crime and Delinquency (NCCD), 156

National Crime Victim's Survey, 121

National Housing Task Force, 195

National Law Center on Homelessness and Poverty, 12, 23

National Mental Health Association, 133

National Network for Youth, 153

Native Americans, 21

New Haven (CT), 43

New York City, 15, 16, 34, 73, 168, 170, 173, 175, 177, 178, 179

New York City Department of Homeless Services, 168, 176

New York City Transit Police, 73, 74, 75

NISMART, 153

O

Omnibus Anti-drug Abuse Act, 160

Operation Alternative, 168, 169, 170, 174

Operation Last Stop, 76

Operation Weed and Seed, 14, 15

Orange County (CA), 12

Outreach, 15, 16, 37, 38, 65, 73, 74, 75, 76, 88, 89, 92, 94, 101, 103, 105, 106, 107, 114, 115, 127, 132, 135, 139, 140, 141, 142, 143, 144, 145, 147, 148, 153, 159, 160, 164, 170, 171, 172, 173, 176, 177, 188, 197, 203, 206, 210, 212, 223, 225

P

Panhandling, 12, 23, 33, 34, 35, 36, 38, 59, 60, 62, 64, 87, 88, 89, 90, 91, 93, 95, 101, 102, 169, 170, 172, 177, 198, 199, 200, 203, 204, 207, 208, 218, 222, 223, 224

Parents Rights Act, 164

Partnership for the Homeless, 168
Partnerships, 14, 15, 216–226
People v. Davenport, 53
Phoenix (AZ), 181, 183, 184, 185, 186, 187, 194
Police-community relations, 6
Police Executive Research Forum, 17, 61, 64, 72
Poorhouse, 183
Port Authority of New York and New Jersey, 168, 169, 171, 172, 173, 174, 175
Portland (OR), 132, 137, 138, 140, 142, 146, 177, 216–227
Portland Guides, 223, 224, 225
Post-traumatic Stress Disorder, 6, 156
Pottinger v. City of Miami, 54, 113
Poverty, 30, 35, 96, 163
Problem-oriented Policing (POP), 68, 83
Project Connect, 197–215
Project Renewal, 168, 170, 175
Project Respond, 131–149, 225, 226
Prostitution, 25, 122, 163
Psychiatric Emergency Operation Team (PEOT), 137, 138
Psychiatric symptoms, 8, 9, 10, 11
Public health, 9

R

Rachael and Her Children, 7
Racism, 26
Religious Witness, 111, 112
Rental subsidies, 205
Respiratory illness, 11
Robert Wood Johnson Foundation, 61
Rosenheck, Robert, 5
Rouse, James, 195
Runaway Youth Act, 159, 160, 161

S

Salvation Army, 104, 112, 186, 187
San Francisco (CA), 9, 13, 14, 15, 16, 26, 32, 33, 36, 98, 99, 100, 106, 107, 111, 113, 177, 178
Santa Ana (CA), 12, 13, 32, 35
Santa Monica (CA), 60, 64, 177
Seattle (WA), 34, 35, 68, 177
Second World War, 22
Section 8 Housing, 124

Selective enforcement, 29
Sexual abuse, 6, 122, 150, 154, 155, 163
Sexually transmitted disease, 10
Shelter Plus Care, 205
Sidewalk Cleaning Program, 220, 221
Single Room Occupancy Hotels (SROs), 99, 103, 106, 107, 142, 184, 187
Skid Row, 24, 63, 64, 183, 184, 218
Social Security Administration, 206
Social Workers, 25, 58, 59, 75, 82, 99, 101, 103, 108, 126, 132, 171, 177
Special Combined Action Team (SCAT), 65
St. Vincent de Paul Society, 186, 187, 188, 192
Stanford University, 8
Station Enhancement Program (SEP), 74, 76
Status Offenders, 156, 157, 158, 159, 164
Statute of Laborers, 23
Stewart B. McKinney Homeless Assistance Act, 6
Substance abuse, 7, 8, 16, 63, 66, 68, 71, 81, 82, 90, 103, 105, 115, 155, 161, 162, 169, 173, 184, 185, 201, 208, 209, 211, 214, 221, 223
Suicide, 11, 68, 140, 155
Survival sex, 10, 163

T

Teen pregnancy, 155, 163
Tenderloin Housing Clinic, 103
Throwaway youth, 152, 153
Transbay Terminal, 16, 178
Transportation centers, 169, 171
Transit facilities, 168–180
Transitional Living Program, 159, 160
Travelers Aid, 178
Tuberculosis, 10, 67

U

Underclass, 22
Urban Institute, 5
U.S. Census, 5, 185
U.S. Conference of Mayors, 7, 8, 10, 13, 101
U.S. Department of Housing and Urban Development (HUD), 5, 6, 15, 128, 143
U.S. Department of Justice, 13, 14
U.S. Department of Transportation, 15, 177, 178
U.S. Supreme Court, 12, 13, 24, 30, 31, 52

United States v. Gooch, 54
United States v. Oliver, 49
United States v. Taborda, 45

V

Vagrancy, 23, 24, 30, 31, 34, 36, 37, 184, 216
Veterans, 7, 201, 205, 214
Vocational Rehabilitation Division (of
    Oregon), 221, 222

Volunteers of America, 170
Vouchers, 38, 104, 124, 141, 177, 203

W

Washington, D.C., 35
Winkleby, Marilyn, 8
World Trade Center, 168, 170, 175